TILAK AND GANDHI
PERSPECTIVES ON RELIGION AND POLITICS

TILAK AND GANDHI

PERSPECTIVES ON RELIGION AND POLITICS

Jyoti Sharma

GYAN PUBLISHING HOUSE

New Delhi - 110002

TILAK AND GANDHI
Perspectives on Religion and Politics
(Political Science, History)

ISBN : 81-212-0571-9

Published in 2001 in India by
Gyan Publishing House
5, Ansari Road
New Delhi 110 002
Phones : 3282060, 3261060 Fax : 3285914
E-mail : gyanbook@del2.vsnl.net.in
Visit Our Web Site At http:\\www.gyanbooks.com

Laser Typesetting: Grow Computers, Delhi
Printed at: Mehra Offset Press, New Delhi

To

My Parents

and

Children

CONTENTS

Foreword ix

Preface xi

1. Religion and Politics 1

2. Tilak: Religion and Modernisation 35

3. Gandhi: Morality and Secularism 133

4. Lokmanya and Mahatma 201

5. Interaction between Religion and Secularism 227

Appendix I 245

Appendix II 297

Bibliography 319

Index 327

FOREWORD

As we have already moved into the orbits of the 21st Century, one feels that, with the absence of the ethical and cultural dimensions of the state craft, the ongoing march of the process of globalisation has perhaps created a climate of inequity, intellectual acquiescence, and a psyche of restlessness. In his report on "Our Creative Diversity" in 1995, former Secretary General of the united Nations and President of the World Commission on Culture and Development Perez de Cuellar had highlighted this aspect when he said that the economic approach was perhaps not the best way to solve the development crisis of the economies, the cultural issues of the systems have also to be addressed. With the perceptible emergence of politics as a self-perpetuating power doctrine, the very basic objective of the state to assist in the self-actualising process to fulfil the inner requirements of an individual for its continuous moral growth has been negatived. The State has failed to initiate the process of creative political participation of its citizenry in the systemic structural interaction. "The supreme test of all political institutions and industrial arrangements, said philosopher John Dewey, "shall be the contribution they make to the all-round growth of every member of society.

Since 1990s, with process of globalisation engulfing the very life-being of the developing economies of the Third World, there has been a growing academic interest in the study of ethical and political dimensions of the state governance.

As one looks at the literature on politics and religion these days, it seems, there has been a growing interest in the study of Gandhi and Tilak in India. On the issue of religion and politics, Gandhi said that "those who say that religion has nothing to do with politics do not know what religion means." Throughout the pages of "Kesari", Tilak tried to synthesize the concept of social action propounded by the Vedantic philosophy with the modern dimensions of social justice, democratic ethics and human compassion. It went far beyond the Kantian ethics of the 'Critique of Practical Reasoon' and T.H. Green's 'Prolegomena to Ethics.'

In her work on "Tilak and Gandhi : Perspectives on Religion and Politics", Jyoti Sharma seeks "to examine and explain the curious and important nexus between religion and politics in the light of the political philosophies of Tilak and Gandhi." The work is divided into five chapters on various aspects of religion, modernisation and secularism. The author demonstrates an impressive understanding of the subject, and this undoubtedly makes her work demanding and desirable. I agree with the author that "The resurgence movement was a kind of national democratic awakening of the Indian people. It believed in the traditional, organic and associative outlook as against the individualistic, critical, rationalistic and materialistic trends of modern western civilization. While referring to the concept of secularism, the author rightly concludes that "the temple or dome of secularism rests on the pillars of equity (i.e. justice), tolerance and goodwill."

The work provides a well-researched and authoritative guidance to the concepts of religion and politics by Tilak and Gandhi.

K.K. Panda

19.01.2001
University of Delhi

PREFACE

Religion has perhaps been the most powerful single factor in the development of the Indian culture and civilisation. Arnold Toynbee's characterisation of India's cultural evolution as one display of a "manifest tendency towards an outlook that is predominantly religious" looks apt. Religion, as *dharma*, has predominantly shaped the distinctive values of our culture and way of life, that has been a fusion of many different strands—the Dravidian, the Aryan, the Buddhist, the Islamic and the Western. India has been unique in its capacity to assimilate within its culture, elements from many different sources.

Religion as the dominant mode of political thinking has been an integral part of the totality of culture. The political philosophy of India has arisen out of social experience over the ages. It has evolved in time—that specifies rise, continuation, decline, or transition of different social situations. With changes in social relations, philosophical perspectives have been undergoing change. Thus, *dharma* as a dynamic concept has subserved both religion and politics. The sacred and the temporal have been the basic functioning units of our cultural ethos, developing into a new brand of secularism which is religious in the affirmative. The relation between theology and politics has also been defined and specified within the *Dharmasastra* and *Arthasastra* schools of thought. It was a matter not of controversy but of complementarity.

From the early times, the promotion of *dharma* (law, duty, morality and religion) was regarded as the foremost aim of the state. The king, the political head, was expected to encourage piety and virtue and to aid religious institutions. The government was not based on religious dogma, and considerable impartiality could be evidenced in the treatment accorded to the various sects. Nevertheless, ethical norms drawn from religious sources were practiced and preached. The conception of *dharma* in relation to the state indicated that the latter operated within the framework of the former.

In promoting *dharma,* the Hindu kings built temples, granted them large endowments, and exercised strict supervision over their affairs. The state was tolerant of all creeds and frequently aided them all. The religiously tolerant Hindu state which patronized all sects impartially, provided one of the historical bases of secularism. However, the traditional Hindu state cannot be equated with either a theocratic or a modern secular state, as the essential basis of a modern state is the institutional separation of state and religion. In this respect, the Hindu state was decidedly not secular, for one of its chief functions was the active promotion and patronage of religion. It may be termed symbolic of *sarvadharma samabhava,* i.e., *dharma-sapeksha,* but not of *dharma-nirpeksha.*

However, a clear-cut distinction was made in ancient Indian polity between the functions of the priest and the king. The Vedic king discharged no priestly functions; he performed no sacrifices on behalf of the nation, as was done in ancient Egypt and Greece. A conception of the two powers—the temporal and the spiritual—existed from earliest times in India and was supported by a divinely ordained social order.

The struggle between the church and the state, which occupies such a prominent place in early medieval European history, had a rather pale counterpart in ancient India. In the *Gautama Dharmasutra* (500 B.C.), it has been stated that the king's authority could not touch the priests, since his prosperity depended on their support. Other texts warned that the gods would spurn the king's oblations if he failed to employ a qualified *Brahman* priest. By bowing three times before the *Brahman* at his coronation, the king accepted his own subordinate position, and his success depended on continued recognition of this fact. Bitter curses were pronounced against rulers who confiscated and violated these injunctures.

The early theory of the two powers clearly distinguished between temporal and spiritual authority. But, undoubtedly, this theory was itself based on religious assumptions and expounded in religious texts. It was derived from the idea of the divinely created social order in which each *varna,* not caste, had its particular function to perform in the furtherance of *dharma*. The supremacy of *dharma* was the central conception in early Hindu political thought.

This view stands in stark contradiction to Machiavelli's dictum of complete separation of religion (church) and the state. In Machiavelli's view, to say that moral goodness will result in political goodness is political idiocy. Yet, the great divorce between religion and politics, as projected by Machiavelli, on closer analysis reveals that the Western conception refers to religion as organised religious groups and as religious beliefs and practices which may or may not be associated with such groups. The underlying assumption of this concept of separation of state and religion is simply that religion and state function in two basically different areas of human activity, each with its own objectives and methods. It is not the function of the state to promote, regulate, direct or otherwise interfere in religion. Similarly, political power is outside the scope of religion's legitimate aims. On the contrary, the Indian culture embodies religion not as an imposition but as a way of life. The relation between religion and politics, in the Indian context, has always been an issue of everlasting consequences. The relation has continued, both with optimism and pessimism. Nevertheless, tension was not entirely absent between religion and politics, for the latter often took a ruthless turn, and thereby stimulated transcendental speculation in Indian religious life.

The advent of the Muslims in the medieval ages marked a watershed in history of India. The society established by Prophet Mohammed (Pbuh) in the seventh century A.D. comprised an integrated religio-political community. It gave no recognition either in theory or in practice to the distinction between spiritual and temporal. Religious devotion and political allegiance were merged, for Prophet Mohammed (Pbuh) was both the Messenger of God and the divinely appointed Ruler and Commander.

The rapid territorial expansion of Islam saw an important period of Muslim rule in India—the Delhi Sultanate (1211-1526) and Mughal Empire (1526-1757). The religious policies of the Muslim rulers ranged from the tolerance and syncretism of Akbar to the bigotry and fanaticism of Aurangzeb. During the period of the Delhi Sultanate, heretical Shia's sects such as the Ismaili and Qarmatians were subjected to severe persecution by the orthodox Sunni government, and many Muslims belonging to these sects were imprisoned and executed. The public worship of Hindu idols was generally forbidden, and Hindus were not allowed to build new temples or repair old ones. The sentences of criminals and prisoners of war were readily remitted and the individuals were granted daily allowances upon embracing Islam. The conversion of Muslims to Hinduism, on the other hand, constituted the crime of apostasy and was punishable by death. The *jizya*, a special tax levied on all non-Muslims, was both a heavy financial burden and a badge of inferiority worn by the non-Muslims.

The nexus between religion and politics continued. However, a qualitative and quantitative change was clearly visible. It was only Akbar who followed a policy of broad religious tolerance and equality of treatment for all his subjects. The components of the institutional separation of religion and the state would probably have appeared as strange to Akbar as to a sixteenth-century Hindu monarch in South India. But on the whole, the marginal impact of Sufism brought in a semblance of secular belief in the Islamic community.

The religious policy of the British Government in India was complex, for it was the result of an attempt to combine three conflicting roles. One, religious policy was dictated by the commercial-imperial objectives of the British Government, second, by its status as an Indian ruler, and third, by its official profession of Christianity. During much of the first half of the nineteenth century, all these three roles were being carried out simultaneously. Debate on questions of religious policy was frequently inconclusive, for there were three basic assumptions to choose from, each leading to a different conclusion on many issues.

The cry of "religion in danger" was one significant factor in the situation leading up to the mutiny of 1857. The Indian nationalist movement received considerable initial impetus from the reformist Hindu sects of the latter half of the nineteenth century. Leaders of the Hindu renaissance, such as, Swami Dayanand Saraswati and Swami Vivekananda abandoned the earlier defensiveness, and in different ways confidently proclaimed the superiority of Hinduism and culture over the Christian West. It was also an opportunity to reintroduce the masses to their glorious past. The new concept of an Indian Nationality was founded on the only common bond of a territorial unity of India. The Hindus for once, found nothing revolting even in that assumption to their deepest religious or cultural or racial sentiments. The Indian National Congress, however, received no direct inspiration from this source at the time of its founding in 1885. The leading members of the Congress were western-educated Indians who subscribed to the ideals of British liberalism.

The British, too, while they favoured the Indian movement as an antidote to any possible revival of Hindu nationalism, took good care to see the Muslim solidarity intact as Muslims did not suffer in any way be catching the contagion of this new Indian nationalist cult. For the British knew that if the Muslims also joined that cult as whole-heartedly as the Hindus did, then there would really be a united Indian nation—a contingency likely to prove perhaps more dangerous to British supremacy in India than a Hindu revival could single-handedly prove to be.

Thus, the policy of dividing Indians on communal lines (the notion of religion serving as the basis for the new political process based on popular participation) and giving support to the communalists became, from the end of the nineteenth century onwards, an important instrument of colonial policy in the effort to thwart the rising national movement. Virtually, since the founding of the Indian National Congress, parallel with its growth through different stages, and as an accompaniment to the process of constitutional reforms, the official policy of active promotion of communalism was developed. Communalism was presented by the colonial administrators as the problem of the defence of minorities. And the defence of minorities became a major part of the theory of imperialist legitimisation as its other components—welfare of the colonised, civilising mission, white man's burden, etc.—got increasingly discredited. The imperialist statesmen, officials and ideologues at that stage said that Britain had to continue to rule India because it alone could protect the minorities from domination, exploitation and suppression by the majority. The aim of the British policy of divide and rule was to check the politicization of the Indians, to curb their consolidation and unification and to disrupt the process of the Indian nation-in-the-making.

The late nineteenth and early twentieth centuries witnessed a mighty struggle for control of the Congress. The two factions, the Moderates and the Extremists, held radically different views as to the proper ends and means of the nationalist movement. The Moderates, represented by such leaders as M.G. Ranade and G.K. Gokhale, continued the liberal tradition. The Extremists, led by such leaders as Bal Gangadhar Tilak and Aurobindo Ghose, combined the Western ideas of patriotism and nationalism with the religious symbolism of Hinduism. Nationalism identified with religion, became an absolute; India became the Mother, the goddess to whom fervent and undivided devotion must be given. Besides, the partition of Bengal in 1905 created a Muslim-majority area, which widened the breach between the two communities, and gave further stimulus to Extremist activities. Nationalism was not a mere political programme, but a religion that had come from God.

In 1920, when the Congress came under the leadership of Mohandas Karamchand Gandhi, Nationalism, once again, instilled its deep roots in religious faith. Gandhi asserted that "those who say that religion has nothing to do with politics do not know what religion means." His exhortations with regard to the restoration of moral values in political practice might appear utopian in the present context when politics has gone downhill. But for him, it was a practical proposition. Gandhi's power as a politician was based upon the Hindu reverence for a saint, for the ascetic who renounces personal comfort in order to attain a higher end of social service. Gandhi used religious terminology to explain the objectives of the nationalist movement. In the future, he believed, India would become Ram-rajya, the kingdom of Lord Rama, a golden age of peace and prosperity. Gandhi's religious faith, however, was utterly different from that of the Extremists. He declared that his Hinduism included all that he knew to be best in Islam, Christianity, Buddhism and Zoroastrianism. And above all, Gandhi strove for Hindu-Muslim unity, convinced that ultimately both religions were true and valid and were complimentary to each other.

In this context, the present work *Tilak and Gandhi: Perspectives on Religion and Politics* seeks to examine and explain the curious and important nexus between religion and politics in the light of the political philosophies of Tilak and Gandhi. The choice of both the leaders Lokmanya and Mahatma from a constellation of famous personalities draws on an undisputable fact of their popularity and immense capacity for mobilization than anyone else in the pre-independence era. It was Tilak and then Gandhi who stirred the masses, and brought in a new awareness that pushed the society forward.

Tilak spoke the idiom of the masses of the majority, explaining the significance of political action in Hindu philosophical terms, as a sacred *dharma* ordained by God to fight the alien ruler. Lord Krishna's message and exhortation to the disspirited Arjuna to take to arms and fight and overcome the foe was eternalised and reinterpreted in the context of the Indian political situation to kindle the militancy that was believed to have been lying dormant in the Indian (Hindu) and to wake him up from the stupor. Using such mass belief systems and political myths, the extremist leadership communicated by the use of popular religious symbols, their message to the masses more successfully than the liberal tradition had done. No wonder Tilak was dubbed as the 'father of Indian unrest' and he owned it proudly, while he unsuccessfully sued the libellous journalist, Sir Valentine Chirol, for damages.

During the entire Gandhian era, the political leadership, by the use of religious Hindu idiom, exhibited moral courage, integrity, and faith in means as well as in ends. A blending of mass agitational methods, inspiring courage to face force, but not use counter-force, together with a willingness to play the game of constitutionalism whenever that was required, gave the Gandhian era a peculiar strength that created a suitable niche for both the agitator and the polished debator in the wide spectrum of the national freedom movement.

Religion and politics have been juxtaposed in a queer fashion even in the post-independence era. There has been a psychological metamorphosis in the religious claims to politics and the perennial debate on secularism has acquired strong political overtones. The question is: What is the relation between religion and politics and what are its implications to the nation-building process and economic development? What indeed are the constraints of a secular polity? This work is an attempt to answer these questions after tracing the genesis of the concept of the relationship between religion and politics within the broad contours of

Tilak's and Gandhi's political philosophies and their impact on the masses.

Thanks are due to the staff of Nehru Memorial Museum and Library, Gandhi National Museum and Library, Indian Council of World Affairs Library and the Central Reference Library, University of Delhi for their prompt help in consulting the volumes housed there. I am also grateful to my friends and colleagues for offering constructive criticism.

To my in-laws, I extend my special thanks for offering unfailing help and cooperation which went a long way towards the completion of this work. I am also indebted to my parents and to my brother for their encouragement and understanding. Forebearance and patience shown by my children, Chirag and Jashnadeep, during the preparation of the manuscript is affectionately acknowledged. Last but not least, no word or language is ever sufficient to express my heartfelt veneration and affection to my husband for his perpetual inspiration and moral support without which this work would have not seen the light of the day.

New Delhi **Jyoti Trehan Sharma**

20th Sept. 2000

CHAPTER 1

RELIGION AND POLITICS

The variety of religious response has perhaps been the greatest in South Asia. Hinduism, Buddhism, Jainism and Sikhism had their births here. Christianity, Islam, Zoroastrianism and Judaism came from without and developed their own indigenous forms in the land. Each of these has developed its own great tradition—those rites and beliefs declared orthodox by the leaders, shared widely by its followers, codified in its scriptures, debated in its literature and institutionalised in its great shrines and organisations. Each also has its folk traditions—the parochial beliefs and practices of the populace that combine elements of the great tradition with local religious customs. The great religions have always primarily dealt with the questions of ultimate meaning and order, and their mythologies have always tried to explain the origin, purpose and destiny of the universe, of the society and of the individual. Their value systems provide charters for human organisation and behaviour, while their rituals—frequently associated with the life cycles of gods and humans as also with the cycles of the seasons—recreate cosmic and social order.

"It is inevitable that religion and politics should affect each other. Even a religion so other-worldly that its adherents turn away from politics is still affecting political interests, for its adherents are politically neutralised; they are leaving a clear field for those who are actually pursuing political goals."[1] The words exert an appreciable influence to exhibit the relationship between religion and politics that plays a vital role in the society in its own multi-dimensional way and seeks to accumulate power in order to establish an effective control over the society. The mode and the technique of the control and the field of action may largely be divided in a civilised society, but the fact remains that a large number of individual or group social actions receive their sanction not only from political power but that they also have religious legitimacy.

The relationship between religion and politics has been a fundamental issue of all ages, and has attracted the attention of thinkers—both Oriental and Occidental; past and present. In the contemporary situation, the subject needs no justification when the world at large is hankering after peace. In the modern times, under the garb of civilizing mission, many things are done, which will make a moralist shudder in despair. Modern diplomacy is generally actuated by bewildering urgency, expediency, and very often, selfish motives, and in spite of its high-sounding intentions, it aims at realising self-interest at the cost of others, disregarding the dictates of morality.

Man's quest to satisfy his various kinds of needs has resulted in the emergence of a variety of institutional arrangements. There has been the institution of the Church as organised religion on the one hand, and politics in the form of interplay of organised interests, on the other. In certain societies, this division may not be very clear. Instead, there may be an overlap and religion may not be used as a medium for the satisfaction of intellectual and aesthetic needs only, but also of the material ones. Similarly, in some situations, politics may not be used to cater only to the material needs of a society but some intellectual, aesthetic and spiritual needs as well. However, the degree of complementary and the degree of contrariety between religion and politics or between the sacred and the temporal has always differed from time to time and from one society to another.

Every religion is a product of human evolution and has been conditioned by social environment. Since man has developed from a state even lower than savagery and was once intellectually a mere animal, it is reasonable to attribute to him in that state no more religious consciousness than is possessed by an animal. What then are the factors and means whereby humanity has encased itself in this shell of religion, which almost everywhere has been raised as a protective growth about the social body?

The simplest answer to this question has been that man is not a mere animal but differs from the beast in having an immortal soul and a religious instinct. Assuming that there are no races which can be shown to be utterly devoid of religion, this element of human thought, because it is universal, one must consider as essential; hence, being essential, belief in a soul and in spiritual life is part of human nature. Based on this natural conviction, religion is the product of man's religious instinct.[2]

It is inevitable, however, that this study embraces man in the past as well as in the present, and the psychological processes of the pre-historical man cannot be known. A modicum of safety lies in the recognition of danger and, historically speaking, it is justifiable in treating low forms of religion like low forms of art as comparatively primitive. The truth is that many habits and habitual attitudes start as a recognition on someone's part of forces which it is in his interest to obey, and this is imitated by those who merely find it convenient to follow suit. Orthodoxy maintained in ancient India, that there was one inspired religion, namely Hinduism, and all other religions were decadent forms of it, while in the sixth century B.C. heterodox Hindus said that all religions were invented by the priests for their own profit.[3] Hinduism, as perhaps other religious systems also, has proliferated supernatural and transcendental reasons for habits which could not call upon a remembered origin. Taboos thus acquire the same outward authority and justification that religious observances have.[4]

Religion is the first characteristic in the Indian make-up which plays a large part in both confinement and persistence. It is a universal and significant social phenomenon, no doubt, but the widespread ignorance and inarticulateness that surrounds it brings the researcher to the problem of defining it. Much of the discussion of amateurs is noted chiefly for being futile and endless rather than for its being enlightening. Many an argument about religion has undoubtedly ended with hard feeling, if not with blows. However, the difficulty of any problem is hardly a valid reason for giving it up. Religion and religious conceptions, beyond being systems of belief and patterns of worship, constitute a central component, as Max Weber pointed out, in the construction of the basic symbolic and institutional premises of societies and civilizations.[5]

It would be safe to begin with the oft-quoted statement of Matthew Arnold, because many persons assume that religion and morality are very similar, if not identical. Arnold wrote that "the true meaning of religion is not simple morality, but morality touched by emotion."[6] Such a reduction of religion to morality would rule out much that universally has been considered the proper subject matter of religion. For theologian Friedrich Schleiermacher, "To take everything individual as a part of the whole, everything limited as representative of the infinite, -that is religion."[7] Perhaps Schleiermacher states his meaning more simply, when he says later that the essence of religion is to be found in the feeling of utter dependence upon the infinite reality, that is, upon God. It appears arbitrary, however, to limit religion to the feeling of dependence.

Another approach to religion that emphasizes the intellect rather than the emotions, is that of the Danish philosopher of religion, Harold Höffding: "That which expresses the innermost tendency of all religions is the axiom of the conservation of values."[8] The key to the understanding of this definition is in the last three words. All religions, Höffding believes, have, as their characteristic function, the task of expressing, and conserving the more important values, such as truth, goodness and beauty.

A more radical suggestion has been advanced by a leading American philosopher and educator, John Dewey. He proposed that the noun "religion" be dropped, and the adjective "religious" be used, which he defines as follows: "Any activity pursued in behalf of an ideal and against obstacles and in spite of threats of personal loss because of conviction of its general and enduring value is religious in quality."[9] In Dewey, we have a person who believes in the ideal of equal educational opportunity for all citizens regardless of race or colour, and who intelligently and courageously labours to see this ideal practised in his community and nation. This is essentially religious.

James B. Pratt wrote: "Religion is the serious and social attitude of individuals or communities towards the power or powers which they conceive as having ultimate control over their interests and destinies."[10] Pratt's definition comprehends the important factors and seeks to be so general and meaningful that it will hold for any specific instance of religion. Religion is by its nature a crucial and all-important concern. It confronts everyone with the ultimate issues of life.

All these definitions of religion in the West seem to have a wide sense of ineffectiveness in the Indian context. If the content and quality of 'religion' in India differs from the religion as known in the West, it is perhaps also different in meaning and essence. Religion in India has to be understood as a continuous social process in which old and new residues, and their combinations entail the future of all the communities.

Religion, through the ages, has been a stabilising force, a positive motivational factor in society. Religion, woven into the material of Indian life, makes such elaborate and apparently changing patterns that observers vie with each other in eschewing generalizations while yearning for certainty. One is free to have any and every belief or no beliefs at all, without forfeiting one's religious denomination or affiliation. Religion is a value system. It is a philosophy of life, that has guided man's search for Meaning in the universe, for Reality behind appearance and for Purpose in life. Religion was made to evolve as a principle of integration of the apparent and the Real that made the universe lawful and ordered in accordance with its Purpose.

Religion in India emerged not as religion but as *Dharma*[11] and the entire population belonged to the broader characteristics of Hinduism. Dharma comes from the verbal root 'dhri' meaning to hold together, to maintain, to support' (the universe).[12] *Dharma* is the eternal pattern which regulates the movement of the heavenly bodies and orders the energy of the atom; it is the external and internal law of being; it is *Sanatana*, eternal, and that which is eternal is also universal. Without *Dharma*, the universe is crude, material chaos, purposeless and amoral; the relative world and the Real world are forever separated, the perfection-orientation of imperfection is forever lost.[13]

The classical Indian philosophy of the right ordering of man in society and in the state rests upon the foundation of this integrating principle. It is one of the four chief expressions of man's natural instincts, the other three being—*Kama* (natural desires), *Artha* (material prosperity) and *Moksha* (spiritual liberation). *Dharma* strives continually to harmonize the changing panorama of phenomena, not in a static order but in a just and 'continually-becoming' dynamic universe, the moral purposefulness of creation and the imperative of each individual living in harmony with *Dharma*, implies conscious decision-making and free choice. *Dharma* is the core concept of Hindu political theory profound in its implications and subject to varied theory and definitions. It is more than law, for it is what underlines and creates law in the universe. The conception of *Dharma* was a far-reaching one embracing the whole life of man. The writers on *Dharmasastra* meant by *Dharma* not a creed or religion but a mode of life or a code of conduct, which regulated a man's work and activities as a member of society and as an individual and was intended to bring about the gradual development of a man and to enable him reach to what was deemed to be the goal of human existence.[14]

The concept of *Dharma* also specifies different spheres of life as different systems of ethics. It is this segmentation which allows the Indian society to incorporate the new and the original, by containing them within small compart mentalized areas of behaviour.[15] Ethics supports the force of custom and deference to familial and social authority. The term actually denotes a whole series of duties: personal, social, moral and religious. Every situation calls for a specific code of behaviour, a specific *dharma;* indeed the conception of a common standard of behaviour, of an "absolute" ethic, is alien to the Hindu way of life. *Dharma* is essentially a logic of behaviour in a variety of settings; it forms the basis of customary virtue.[16]

The concept of *dharma* is more than a codification of duties and functions. It involves a kind of *Weltanschauung*, a world-view—the world-view of *anasakti* or non-attachment. In considering various duties and functions, the devout Hindu is enjoined to think of them objectively without any sense of attachment or interest. For the Supreme *Dharma* (and here it also can be translated as "religion") is the salvation of one's own soul. This being the highest virtue, it was to be valued above all social bonds and duties. In trying to reach that state, however, and so long as the ties of this world were not given up altogether, *Dharma* consists in a faithful pursuit of the duties endowed to one's role and station in life. Because the principal emphasis is "duties to" rather than "rights against", it was good to be satisfied with one's lot and not to crave that which did not belong to one. Hence the Hindu's emphasis on a limitation of wants and contentment with his lot, on tolerance rather than revenge, and on restraint other than exuberance.[17]

Being highly pluralistic in structure, the Hindu society has been able to retain primary loyalties and thus make for a high degree of personal security and cohesion. Added to this are the metaphysical norms and orientations of tolerance, non attachment, and contentment which help the society to absorb tensions and to blunt the edge of sufferings. There is among the Hindus a marked tolerance of deprivation, a low sensitivity to humiliation, and cynicism with regard to the use and abuse of power.[18]

It is beyond doubt that the Indian civilization had an ancient, well-developed and highly articulate philosophy of life. Integrated with the civilization's philosophy of life was a theory of politics, that is, a theory of the relation of the individual to the political community and a plan for the 'right ordering' of that community, an explanation of the purpose of common political life integrated with the explanation of the purpose of life itself. In other words, the value system of the civilization was integrated into the political system of the particular political community through the political philosophy.[19] It should not be forgotten that the political thought was an integral aspect of the Indian philosophy, and there was no artificial separation into political, social and religious affairs. As Dickinson wrote: "Until the art of politics is brought into touch with the spiritual life, it will remain what it has been, barren and fruitless, and until we connect the spiritual life with the political and political with the spiritual, both will remain paralysed."[20]

Historically speaking, in India, the pattern of interaction between religion and politics has had varied social consequences, no doubt. However, before making an attempt to analyse this equation, it would be most appropriate to begin with the meaning of politics, not only as an institutional arrangement but also as a process of mobilization.

Politics was considered the "master science", since, dealing with *Dharma*, it covered that vast range of human relationships that MacIver has so aptly termed "the firmament of law". In this respect, *Dharma* is the creator of the state and political science is more than a study of government.[21] In the current situation, there are two usages of the word 'politics' which differ considerably, more in their implications than in their superficial characteristics. With the convergence of modern political science and sociological theory, the once extreme claims by political theorists for autonomy, supremacy and especially universality of their subject have been somewhat moderated, so that politics is now often defined (i) merely as the area of formal government in its-widest sense, including all processes directly or indirectly associated with it;[22] (ii) in an alternative interpretation, used by some political scientists and many sociologists, as focusing on certain roles and processes which exist in any situation, collectively or otherwise—irrespective of whether these are concerned with government or not. The referent for the second definition is the notion of power. To this extent the potential or actual use of power implies the presence of the 'political' in many subsystems of society— economic, religious, etc. Not that there is any agreement about the meaning of power; this 'dispersed' definition of politics has merely diffused the reference from one subsystem throughout all of society.[23]

There is at present little agreement on the precise definition of the status of politics. The process of sociological 'shrinking' of the primary and all-embracing nature of politics, which began with Marx and Max Weber, has continued—in spite of occasional efforts at re-expansion—right up to its crystallization as just one of four equal social subsystems by Parsons. For many writers, the political system still retains some considerable primacy in society. The most usual locus of relevance is still the state, or what is general to a society—the inclusiveness of political society contrasted with the parochialisms of family, class, local community and sect' (Wolin). The most usual medium is power, in the last resort defined as 'legitimate, heavy sanctions', or 'physical force' (Weber), or more recently, in an economic analogy, as 'cash' contrasted with a nexus of prestige or influence in the form of 'credit' (Deutsch).[24]

Politics, in addition to being a series of social actions in a system, is also an academic discipline—while sociology is only such a discipline. Hence politician, or political activist, is a distinct role, while being a member of a society (the social equivalent) is not. However, considerable and continual stress has then to be laid on the multiple relationship between the observer, the participant and the process observed, One particular political process which is not only central to all political activities, but makes political change comprehensible as something other than a series of set pieces or tableaux is mobilization. At some stage of historical development, every society undergoes one or several processes of mobilization; when such mobilization is political, it creates or develops the growth and strength of the polity, and may well extend the range as well as increasing the saliency of the political system. It is also the major accelerating factor in both the extent and level of political acculturation.

There only three processes of systematic long-term social mobilization *en masse;* military, religious and political. Since all three fulfill broadly similar functions in creating a community, they have much in common. For one thing, they all relate to people tightly together in a distinct and often novel form, by evolving particular structures and by giving people common goals and reference groups. In doing so, mobilization processes either substitute new priorities for previous ones, or create conscious priorities on a general scale for the first time, where none existed previously.[25]

The question is how does political mobilization differ from other forms of mobilization? Considering the nature of mobilization in the context of the four basic components of the social hierarchy-roles, collectivities, norms and values—there is a simple progression that mobilizing people makes them either into a mob (if non-institutional but based on some general belief) or a collectivity by coercion (if institutional but not based on a general belief; press-gangs, enforced savings, etc.). Mobilizing people plus norms equals the minimum of political action. Mobilizing people plus values might be called a revolution or, if institutionally induced, a mobilized nation-at-arms.

But in real life, things are not often as simple as this. No doubt social or political action increases in scope and intensity as issues move from the lowest level of roles to antipathy or support for norms or even values. The mobilization of collectivities (or conversely their identification as social and political obstacles to mobilization) need not end with escalation to the next highest category on the scale: norm-oriented action.[26] Mobilization is not a structure in the strict sense; the assignment of a systematic function according to structure-functionalism has little meaning. Indeed it could well be viewed as a dysfunction in a strictly systematic context; some writers of considerable sophistication certainly suggest such an interpretation; for instance Huntington, who argues that mobilization and political institutionalization of process are, or may be, dichotomous.[27] It, is therefore, proposed to adopt a somewhat wider definition of the concept which includes notions of meaning and direction and which is based on process and action.

Political mobilization is a form of social mobilization which corresponds to a particular era and certain special needs. In a sense it is historically the last and latest of the forms of mobilization, following religious and military mobilization as potential alternatives or complemen-tarities. This aspect of substitution and complementarity is important, for although the propensity of a society to become mobilized may vary over time, the form such mobilization will take is perhaps governed by more general factors which are not entirely within the control of each society but correspond to some form of international culture, Political mobilization may, thus, be considered as differential commitment and support for collectivities based on cleavages.[28] Historically, the spur to political mobilization has usually been a means of getting existing, autonomous authority to change its norms, values or structures – in other words, based on the articulation of interests.

Beneath the new and adapted means of mobilization in developing countries, both ideological and structural, there lurks a concept of legitimacy, substantially different from that of the West. The latter postulates a notion of the state or nation and its legitimacy embodied in a historical tradition and based on a long period of national development and autonomy which has been internalized by the participants. In developing countries, there are the aspects of association and dissociation, which can only be understood as part of synthesis with more traditional styles of authority legitimation. In an essay, based on a long experience of India in particular and South-East Asia in general, Hugh Tinker has highlighted the drama-turgical basis of legitimacy in these countries.[29]

Essentially, the structure of legitimacy orientations in many traditional as well as developing societies is based on the ability of the ruler to provide a show, whose symbols and processes are held to be in keeping with the ascribed status of legitimate rule. It is also related to the fact as to how the political leaders or a politicized group within a specific religious tradition and its membership make use of "religious" beliefs, practices and institutions to provide cohesiveness to the realm and legitimacy to the holding of power.[30] Examples of this, of course, are abound in history. Some of the more famous ones include Constantine in the fourth century A.D., Asoka in the third century B.C., and

Han Wu-ti in the early Han dynasty of the second century B.C. Therefore, to identify the typology of Indian culture, it would be necessary to resuscitate the true religious culture in a modern society by way of integration of religion with politics for strengthening normative public behaviour. As the most important ingredient of political culture, Arnold Brecht proposed, "religion can, possibly, be a useful tool for national integration and unity consciousness by affirming virtues propagated by all religions.[31]

How should religion be related to the political order? There are basically three major views in this regard. The "separationists" quote, what must be one of the devil's favourite texts, "Render unto Caesar the things that are Caesar's and unto God the things that are God's," and religion ends, it appears to many, cultivating mystical experiences and practising a few mysterious rites connected with birth, marriage, and death. The "controllers" are equally emphatic, whether it be those who claim that religion, as in the form of the church, should control the state, or those who are sure that the best arrangement is for the state to tolerate religion and its institutional organization as a possibly useful but potentially dangerous voluntary association.

Many persons consider both these positions extreme and untenable. The third, or middle-of-the-road position, holds that whereas religion and political science deal with clearly distinguishable issues, each must take cognizance of the other. Religion may, to be sure, be primarily concerned with man's salvation, but this involves bringing to him and cultivating within him the religious ways of life, individual and social. This function, in turn, is clearly aided or hindered by the political life of any person. Religion, moreover, claims the final loyalty of man, and in the realms of personal and collective ethics seeks to disclose and develop within men, the attitudes, principles and the spirit of the good life. Religion thus conceived cannot, without being false to its purpose, remain indifferent to the political and social conditions that affect each and every citizen.

There are areas of belief in which religion and political theory overlap. To be specific, all the main political philosophies have certain assumptions about the nature of man. This is a legitimate and important aspect of political theory. Another specific set of problems that exists is the mutual concern of religion and political theory; freedom, equality of opportunity and justice. Finally, there is present in every political theory the normative as well as the descriptive element. Political thought, thus, undeniably overlaps with ethical and religious philosophy.[33]

If religion is an act of faith, then that faith must justify itself in action. Religion is a way of life. Religion is the basis of morality; and morality is the yardstick for politics. The sphere of religion is essentially the sphere of morality, and the latter includes the sphere of politics. The link between the three spheres is fundamental, and vital to the understanding of their complementary character as also to their real meaning.[34] Indian political thought cannot be isolated from the main body of Hindu philosophy. In the West, a tradition has been accepted, that is partly Machiavellian, of a science of government which rests upon its own empirical basis. But the great works of Indian polity are, like the political dicta of Aquinas, one facet of a vast and integrated system of reasoning which poses and interprets the very problem of human existence. As Gandhi said, "I claim that human mind or human society is not divided into watertight compartments called social, political and religious. All act and react upon one another.[35]

Political action is human action and therefore, may not be projected apart from the consideration of ethics, as ethics have been elaborated by the religious-philosophical tradition. No one who knows anything about the political developments of Modern India can minimise the importance of the study of the inter-relation between religion and politics in the country. Throughout its long history of several thousand years, Indian culture has been growing and has acquired a very complex, composite, differentiated and variegated structural form.

Used as the term *Dharma*, religion has been the most comprehensive concept in the entire history of Hindu thought, and in the *Aitareya Brahmana,* the king has been called the protector of *Dharma.*[36] The "White Umbrella" was placed on the monarch's head at the time of the coronation as a symbol of sovereign political authority. The ruler so inaugurated was regarded not as a temporal autocrat but as the instrument of *Dharma* or supreme law—although the ancient Hindu state was not thereby a theocracy. Despite certain Machiavellian forms of diplomacy recommended with respect to international relations, such policies were considered primarily as low expedients in comparison with the high ideals of the royal *Dharma*.[37]

The historic Indian culture was well-established by the third century B.C., and the political theories and institutions of the centuries which followed, remained grounded in the classic concepts and practices. The political ideas of the Hindus are to be found in a rich variety of sources ranging from the early Vedas to the writings of Gandhi and Tagore. But the classic theories find their most eloquent expression after the Vedic age, for in the earliest literatures, political thought is represented by occasional passages rather than by organised writings. These include such diverse materials as the sacred law books of Gautama and Manu, the historical tales of the *Puranas,* and the administrative manuals of

Kautilya and his school. Much is reposited in religious and other writings rather than in strictly political studies.[38]

The general thrust of vedic and post-vedic literature was that political power was to operate within a broad framework of social relationship which have essentially a moral foundation. The emphasis was on the unquestionable fact that the interaction between religion and politics was very intimate. While it is true, as some historians like Jayaswal and Beni Prasad have claimed, that politics in ancient India was secular[39] in nature, it would be wrong to infer from this that religion or *Dharma* was not used to legitimise the political authority. The *Brahmin* (Priest) was very powerful in the state structure and forcefully defended his privileges and status. Although the state power was generally in the hands of the *Kshatriyas,* yet the linkage between the secular and the sacred was very intimate.[40]

The relationship between the priest and the ruler is subtly reflected in the former's attempt to sanctify the four *varnas* and project them as some kind of divine dispensation. This sanctification proved very functional to the ruling class and lent order in society. The priestly class and the ruling class joined hands to dominate over the two lower classes: the *Vaishyas* and the *Shudras*. The *Brahmin* projected the ruler and the ruling house as divinely ordained; the *Kshatriyas,* in turn, accorded the top place to the priest in the social hierarchy.

The *Karma* (duty) doctrine enshrined in the *Upanishads* constituted the core of Brahminical doctrine and was used by the rulers to maintain order and civility in society. It sought to explain and justify one's present position in terms of rewards and punishment for one's past acts. Similarly, the concept of *Dharma* was used in a very wide and loose sense, ranging from custom or law to the totality of relationships in which a person stands to society and polity.[41]

In ancient India, there was perhaps more religious freedom, more philosophical inquiry and greater toleration for dissenters' belief than anywhere else in the medieval or modern world. The classical ideal was the completely tolerant secular state, that is, the state made no special concessions to any sect, religious order or belief system; that it provided equality before the law and in all matters temporal for all faiths; that there was no 'established religion; and that all beliefs were equally encouraged and equally promoted. At the same time, the purpose of the state was to assist man in the fulfilment of the ultimate moral purpose of life. The ethical basis of the state was *Dharmarajya*—the rule of *Dharma*. There is no record of religious wars and persecution. To insure impartiality, the king or ruler had a special code of duty called *Rajadharma*, which was different from the *Dharma* of any other individual and which set him apart from all sects in the performance of his duties. He and the state were purposefully precluded from sectarian loyalties, but not from moral purposefulness, so that the state might protect and promote all *Dharmas*. The *Rishis* never taught uniformity. Their ideal for the state as well as the society was unity in diversity, cooperation and harmony.[42]

On first examination such coldly realistic treatises as those of Kautilya and Sukra, one might infer that these are exceptions to the proposition of the relation between religion and politics. But further consideration reveals a careful orientation of the political with the philosophical and ethical tenets of Hinduism. Hindus have one of the world's oldest systems of political science. Their political speculations began at least as early as the second millennium B.C. in the *Rigveda* and continued in other Vedic Samhitas and in the *Brahmans*.[43] Such fundamental questions, as the origin of the social order and the position of the ruler, are raised and answered.

The most important of the various sources are the *Dharmasastras,* which deal primarily with basic law and political theory, and the *Arthasastra* and related materials, which deal with practical politics and administration. Although these comprise distinct literatures, they are not antagonistic traditions, rigidly separated as to type. On the contrary, they are both rooted in the Vedic and later writings and often inter-related in subject matter and treatment. The easiest generalisation is to say that the *Dharmasastras* offer a system of law and organisation for the establishment of the Hindu state and social structure. Whereas the *Arthasastras* provide working manuals to guide the ruler in the conduct of his daily affairs. Both are related primarily to a major aim of the Hindu concept of life. Hindu political thought deals with the problems of *Dharma* and *Artha* which provide the foundations of political and social institutions, but the solution of these problems is essentially only a mean towards ultimate *Moksha.*[44]

The Mauryan period witnessed the emergence of Buddhism, Vaishnavism and Shaivism, but the nexus between religion and politics continued. Indeed, it grew stronger. This nexus touched a new height during the reign of Asoka, when the propagation of *Dharma* became a major part of state policy. The infrastructure of the state was used to preach religious doctrines and these religious doctrines were employed to consolidate political power. The position of the priest remained strong as before, as the whole priestly class was co-opted into political power. According to Kautilya, the power of the *Kshatriya* rulers legitimized by the priest was invincible.[45]

Although some writers have stressed the popular basis of the Hindu King's sovereignty and the recognition of a right of popular resistance to tyranny, the *Dharma* itself was deemed to be the real restraining power over the King's office. Even if mendicants and ascetics engaged in improper proceedings, the king was to restrain them under threat of punishment because if *Dharma* is transgressed then it rebounds to the evil of the ruler. Indeed, the moral behaviour of the ruler may be taken as a cornerstone of Indian though. Like the Confucian political ethic in China and the Platonic in ancient Greece, the Hindu stressed the ultimate importance of individual political morality. The truth is that sacred and secular ideas have always been inextricably intertwined in Indian political tradition.

The ruler and his administration are thereby obligated to conduct the government in accord with the highest ethical principles of the Hindu tradition: to place public welfare and duty above personal desires. And the citizen has, of course, a corresponding responsibility in his own sphere of activity. As Kautilya said: "Harmlessness, truthfulness, purity, freedom from spite, abstinence from cruelty, and forgiveness are duties common to all. Hence the king shall never allow the people to swerve from their *dharma;* for whoever upholds his own duty, ever adhering to the customs of the Aryas will surely want to be happy both here and hereafter. For the world, when maintained in accordance with injunctions of the *Vedas,* will surely progress, but never perish."[46]

Therefore, although the Indian heritage has many facets and apparent contradictions, the core of the tradition is that the problem of government is the ethical problem of the individual projected onto the field of the state. Its solution lies in *Dharma.*

On the eve of the advent of Islam, the country consisted of numerous small and big kingdoms, but all of them were Hindu kingdoms. Their rivalries and occasional battles were seen merely as battles between the two political entities without any religious overtones in them. The situation, however, changed rapidly. The period saw not merely the advent of Islam, but also the emergence of Sikhism and the influx of Christianity. Each of them affected the hitherto existing relations between religion and politics. The armies of Islam brought a 'new vision' of the world and the purpose of life, a rigorous, monotheistic, proselytizing, militant creed of conquest and conversion. The Muslim conquest of India took centuries, but slowly *Swaraj* in India was destroyed and replaced by the Moghul empire.

The Indian culture sought to assimilate the invaders, to create a new synthesis of cultures; but this was impossible. Islam was a closed system. It was accepted or rejected, but never could it be assimilated or harmonized with the polytheism of India.[47] The classical right ordering of the political community was replaced by the 'new ordering' of the conquerors. The regular attacks of Ghazni between A.D. 1001 and A.D. 1026, the destruction and plunder of Hindu temples at Somnath and Kanauj, the connection of indemnities from Hindu population made the interaction of religion and politics extremely intimate. Acts of a purely political nature got projected as of politico-religious nature.[48] And in order to protect the *Aryadharma,* the noble way of life, the social order had to become closed, exclusive, compartmented, for it could not possible save the *Dharma* if it remained open, flexible and assimilative.

Once the Muslim rule was established in India, the rulers began to lean for the strength and survival of their empires on the Muslim population. Islam was adopted as the state religion, and the state acquired a theocratic character. On the other hand, the process of self-defence produced atrophy and the *Varnashramadharma* became the caste system. The social order's struggle to preserve the values of Indian heritage resulted in social disintegration.

From the beginning of the eleventh century to the end of the fourteenth century, the Muslim rulers used their religious identity to muster support in order to maintain and retain political power. The very fact that they vanquished Hindu rulers in bloody battles alienated a large segment of Hindu population from political power. Some of these battles were projected as *Jehads* (holy wars) against the infidels. Moreover, many states in India during this period had predominantly Hindu population but were designated as Muslim states. Islam continued as the state religion and these states were little less than theocracies.

The sixteenth century witnessed the establishment of a powerful Muslim empire at Delhi by Babar, a descendent of Taimur, who used his religion to lay the foundations of his political power. However, it was Akbar, the grandson of Babar, who, after defeating Hemu in a decisive battle, for the first time since the advent of Muslims in India laid down the foundations of a polity without any powerful grounding in religion. For a while, politics was rid of its religious context, and efforts were made to set up a secular polity. Thus, the relation between religion and politics tossed between the various extremes of its connotations. By the end of the Moghul Raj, politics once again began to acquire strong religious overtones. Religion became a mean to control, channelise and legitimize political power, and political mobilization became a process that made people aware of their common religious identities.

Indian society experienced a qualitative structural transformation during British rule, which initiated some of the basic changes in social physiognomy of Indian society, though to subserve its own interest. It would not be wrong to say that in pre-British India there was the near absence of the objective and subjective prerequisites for the emergence of a national culture.[49] The impact of western ideas posed a serious challenge to the traditional Indian society which was marked by many inhuman customs, primitive social usages and irrational beliefs. As against this, the western society appeared to the English-educated Indians, as liberal, rational and humane. Nonetheless, to the orthodox minds, this trend appeared as the beginning of the process of displacement of culture which had overtaken many civilisations, such as Egypt and Greece. However, after a century and half, it was the Indian society that came out triumphant, keeping its cultural identity intact. What was then the secret of this cultural survival?[50]

The Indian society was shaken to its very foundations when placed face to face with the western society and culture. But soon, the instinct of cultural preservation led to the rise of religious revival movements among various Indian communities. Once again religion, or for that matter *Dharma,* became a means for the political mobilization of the masses. It was this remarkable response to the challenge of the West that helped the Indian society to come out unscathed in this cultural encounter, maintaining its cultural identity intact. It is these very religious revival movements that are generally referred to as the Indian Renaissance.

Most of the writers on Indian history and culture, while talking of the Indian Renaissance refer mainly to revival movements among upper caster Hindus only: They overlook the similar movements among other Indian communities. As a matter of fact, the Indian Renaissance was not a single stream but several streams running parallel to each other. Another commonly held belief is that the Indian Renaissance had two broad tendencies—reformism and revivalism. But a close study of the movement reveals that it was predominantly a revivalist movement. Its main objective was the preservation of the traditional Indian social order. Even the reforms that it propagated were expected to maintain and strengthen the traditional socio-religious system so that it could meet the challenge posed by the West. Panikkar regards Indian revival as a part of the Asian revival. In his brilliant analysis of this phenomenon, he observes: "It is not the desire for progress or for betterment that was originally at the root of Asian revival. It was the determination to resist the foreigner who was pressing his attack in all directions—political, social, economic and religious. It was the desire for national strength and not the revolutionary changes that was the main motivation of changes in the Asian communities.[51]

The resurgence movement was a kind of national democratic awakening of the Indian people. It believed in the traditional, organic and associative outlook as against the individualistic, critical, rationalistic and materialistic trends of modern western civilization. It wanted to revive the old scriptures and sometimes offered a scientific interpretation of their teachings.[52] It was not opposed to progress but thought that genuine national progress could be achieved not by opposition to the religious teachings but by a greater conformity to their teachings. However, some of the critics levelled the charges of reactionary conservatism, anti-progressivism and traditional obscurantism against the exponents of Hindu revivalism. Nonetheless, the movement represented attempts to revise the old religion in the spirit of the new principles of nationalism and democracy which were the conditions for the development of the new society. It attempted to build a religious outlook which would build-up the national unity of all communities. The urge to orient towards the past was further accentuated due to the status of the Indian people as a subject nation. The movement thus, being progressive, was an expression of the first national awakening of the Indian people.

Another characteristic of the renaissance movement was that its programme was not restricted to the task of religious revivalism alone, but extended to the reconstruction of social institutions and social relations. This was due to the fact that in India, religion and social structure were organically inter-woven. While rationalizing religion to a greater or less degree, the movement also aimed at rationalizing social institutions and relations to a greater or lesser degree. Nowhere in the world does religion dominate and determine the life of the individual so much as in India. His economic activity, his social life, marriage, birth and death, his physical movements, all are strictly and minutely controlled by religion. It was indispensable for the movement to have an all-embracing programme of religious, social and even political reform. They fought the caste system as much as polytheism and idolatry. They attacked caste privilege as much as the monopoly rights of the *Brahmin* in the sphere of religion. They attacked all this because they were obstacles to national progress which required, as its vital pre-condition, national unity based on the principles of equality and liberty of individuals and groups. The motif of the movement was national advance. The first national awakening of the Indian people took predominantly a religious form.[53]

The movement was national in content but religious in form. The founder of Brahmo Samaj, which inaugurated a new era for the Indian people by proclaiming the principles of individual freedom, national unity, solidarity, collaboration and the democratization of all social institutions and social relations, Raja Ram Mohan Roy, in spite of his rationalist approach, could not overcome his belief in the divinity of the *Vedas*. The Father of Indian Nationalism, as he came to be known, was essentially a democrat and a humanist. In his religio-philosophical and social outlook, he was deeply influenced by monotheism and anti-idolatry of Islam, Deism of Sufism, the ethical teachings of Christianity and the liberal and rationalist doctrines of the West. He tried to interpret and assimilate into himself the highest elements of Islam, Christianity and modern rationalism or humanism, and transformed them into a single creed which he found in the ancient upanishadic philosophy of his own community. He attacked the polytheistic degeneration of ancient Hindu monotheism and idol worship, and stood for a rational approach to religion. He believed that the individual must subject religious principles to the test of his own ethical reason and reject those which contradict the test. Religious renovation, for Raja Ram Mohan Roy, was the vital condition for revising the social structure from a decadent to a healthy basis. The Brahmo Samaj, under him, launched an offensive attack against the caste system branding it as undemocratic, inhuman and anti-national. It crusaded against the evils of *sati* and child-marriage, and stood for the freedom of the widow to remarry and for the equal rights of man and woman. On the other hand, it also valued the modern western culture and organised educational institutions in the country for its spread among the people. The Raja even admired the liberal democratic culture of the West. However, he also launched a protest against the British for restricting the freedom of the press and for excluding the Indian from higher posts.

After Raja Ram Mohan Roy's death in 1833, his disciple, Debendranath Tagore (1817-1905), the father of poet Rabindranath Tagore, led the activities of the Samaj for some time. However, the universal religion which Roy wanted to spread did not find much support from Debendranath Tagore who openly declared the *Vedas* as a divine revelation and the sole foundation of the religious belief of the Samaj. In 1859, when Keshab Chandra Sen (1838-1884) became the joint secretary of the Samaj, he attempted to make the new humanistic movement really national. He believed that the future religion of the world would be the common religion of all nations and all mankind, and declared that the Brahmo religion could be summed up in two concepts—the Fatherhood of God and the brotherhood of man. The progressive ideas of Keshab Chandra Sen estranged him from Debendranath Tagore. As a fallout, in 1865, the Brahmo Samaj was divided into two camps—the conservative and the progressive. The first was called the Adi Brahmo Samaj under Debendranath, and the second, Brahmo Samaj of India under Keshab Chandra Sen.

The Prarthana Samaj came into existence in Maharashtra in 1867 under the guidance of Keshab Chandra Sen. Like the Brahmo Samaj, rational worship of one God and social reforms formed its ideals. It carried the Brahmo Samaj's secular tradition by advocating such social reforms as inter-caste marriages, widow remarriages and improvement of the lot of women and depressed classes. The success of Prarthana Samaj was due chiefly to the towering personality of Justice Mahadev Govind Ranade. He was the first serious thinker in western India to make a dispassionate and sympathetic study of Christianity and to assess its value in the evolution of a new theism. Like Keshab Chandra Sen, Ranade also paved the way for a new religious outlook by giving expression to the spirit of synthesis and integration.[54]

The Arya Samaj founded in Punjab in 1875 by Swami Dayanand Saraswati, though embodying the first upsurge of Indian nationalism, was a movement of quite a different type. It had more of a revivalist character than that of reformation. It declared the *Vedas* infallible and an inexhaustible reservoir of all knowledge. The authority of the *Vedas* was upheld, along with the freedom of individual judgement.

The progressive elements in the programme of the Arya Samaj included the repudiation of the authority of the *Brahmin*, the denouncing of the infinite number of meaningless rites and the worship of the images of different gods and goddesses which split people into numerous belligerent sects and the crusade against the mass of religious superstitions which had kept, for may centuries, the Hindu mind in a state of mental befogging and spiritual degradation. Its slogan 'Back to Vedas' was inspired with the urge to bring about national unity and to kindle national pride and consciousness. However, since it retained its narrow Hindu basis, the national unity it proclaimed could not gather into its fold the non-Hindu communities such as the Muslims and the Christians. It became a semi-rationalized form of Hinduism. One view also holds that the Arya Samaj was intolerant of other religions and religious practices and, perhaps, started the era of militant Hindu nationalism and later inspired the establishment of organisations like the Hindu Mahasabha and the Rashtriya Swayamsevak Sangh.

Theosophy, introduced in India by Madam Blavatsky and Henry Steel Olcott in 1879, and mainly popularized by Mrs. Annie Besant was another religio-reform movement started in India under the impact of the new Indian and international conditions. Theosophy subscribed to the spiritual philosophy of ancient Hinduism and recognized its doctrine of the transmigration of soul. It preached universal brotherhood of men irrespective of distinctions of caste, creed, race or sex. It stood for the development of a national spirit among the Indians. However, it failed to strike deep roots in the country.

The national awakening of the Indian people found expression in the movement inspired by Ramakrishna Paramhansa (1836-1886), a great Hindu saint, in direct line to saints like Chandidas and Chaitanya. It primarily based itself on the principle of devotion or *bhakti*. Its principal propagandist was Swami Vivekanand, a disciple of Ramakrishna, and an intellectual of a very high calibre who, after the death of the saint, founded the mission to propagate his teachings. The Mission aimed at the spiritual conquest of the world for revival of Hinduism.

Vivekanand was the most accomplished and clear-headed representative of Indian thought and culture, the West had ever heard of. After the Parliament of Religions at Chicago was over, an observer was asked why Vivekanand made such a profound impression. The answer was 'because, while every other delegate spoke of the God of his own religion. Vivekanand alone spoke of the God of all. Vivekanand felt that mankind could only be welded together through love and not abstract religious concepts.

Despite the great contribution made by Vivekanand to the cause of secularism, his emphasis on the superiority of Hindu religion and culture over the Christian West has been dubbed as anti-secular.[55]

The presence of the foreign rule, consciously or unconsciously, prompted even a nationalist of high intellectual calibre not only to reject the foreign rule but often also to recoil from the culture of the ruling nation. The very growth of national consciousness arising out of the conditions of the foreign rule, which, on the whole, checked free national development, often urged the nationalist to invoke even the obscurantist and mystical parts of the nation's past culture and attempted to base the democratic and progressive contemporary national movement on them. Politics or, for that matter, nationalism became tainted with religion. Religion became a means of psychological unity fostered by the heritage of historical tradition. The national fervour that emerged was essentially a psychological and spiritual conception. Not only the economic grievances against an alien imperialism and the political desire for autonomous self-determinate existence, but the evolution and manifestation of the soul of a culture were significantly demonstrated in the phenomenon of nationalism. Religion fostered a rallying point to mobilize the masses in the cause of political freedom. Once again there was the reassertion of that deep, unquestioning religiosity, which has all along occupied a place of overriding importance in Indian life.

However, one must also reckon the fact that the British Government attempted to evolve a strategy to exploit the religious identities of the Indians to secure its political power. There were many overt and covert ways in which religious identities of the Indians were used by the British to serve the political interests of the Raj. By and by, the British Government also tried to win over a section of the Muslims so that the Hindu nationalists could be isolated. On the contrary, from the very beginning, the Hindu discourse displayed an unusual feature. Rather than concentrate on the colonial rule and ask whether to ignore, welcome or fight against it, as the Muslims were to do later, Hindu leaders, almost to a man, located and discussed it in the wider context of their social regeneration. The British could not govern India without defining the Hindus and reducing them to manageable categories largely derived from their own ways of thought. The Hindus did not like their essentialist and inevitably biased definition, and had no other way to counter it save by providing an alternative self-definition. The hitherto diffused and vague Hindu self-consciousness thus acquired a corporate articulation during British rule. The Hindu social self-consciousness precipitated simultaneously with the consciousness of colonial rule.[56]

Like critical modernism, critical traditionalism was thus a popular response to the British rule. Though it was mostly influential between 1870-1920, its appeal was not confined to the period. Its merits were obvious. It was articulated by some of the most acute philosophical minds of modern India and had an intellectual rigour and subtlety lacking in its rivals. It developed a coherent and carefully worked out political philosophy grounded in Indian reality, that is, mobilizing mass support against the colonial rule by using religion. It combined respect for tradition with an open-minded approach to modernity, and was less squeamish than the critical modernists about rejecting many a traditional belief and practice.[57]

The characteristics of the phase of resurgence and reaction directed themselves towards making the country more modern and democratic. To persuade the masses to participate in the political agitations was itself a revolutionary step, and in the long run resulted in the national movement becoming more broad-based than before. In India, the creation or facilitating the creation of a new state apparatus and administrative system was not one of the functions which religious reforms were called upon to perform even indirectly, because it was achieved by foreign political penetration into the country. The reformers and revolutionaries used religion and the appeal to the past to bring about changes in the political and even social spheres. The underlying theme that religion and politics were inter-related, witnessed the connection between religious reforms, on the one hand and social and political regeneration of the country, on the other. Religion, thus, played a very important role in the political development of the country. Also see Appendix-I.

REFERENCES

1. N.Q. Pankaj, *State and Religion in Ancient India,* Allahabad: Chugh Publications, 1983, Preface, p. vi.
2. E.W. Hopkins, *Origin and Evolution of Religion,* Delhi: Bharatiya Vidya Prakashan.
3. *Ibid.*
4. J.D.M. Derrett, *Religion, Law and the State in India,* London: Faber and Faber, 1968, p. 56.
5. Mircea Eliade, (ed.), *The Encyclopaedia of Religion,* New York: MacMillan Publishing Company, 1987, Vol. 12, p. 312.
6. George G. Hackman, Charless W. Kegley, Viljo K. Nikander, *Religion in Modern Life,* New York: The MacMillan Company, 1958, p. 6.
7. *Ibid.*, p. 7.
8. *Ibid.*
9. *Ibid.*, p. 8.
10. *Ibid.*, pp. 8-9.

    Also see, James B. Pratt, *The Religious Consciousness,* New York: The MacMillan Company, 1924, p. 2.
11. The word 'religion' has generally been taken as an equivalent for the Sanskrit word *'dharma'*. But religion is merely an aspect of *dharma* and not the whole of it.
12. V.P. Varma, *Studies in Hindu Political Thought and its Metaphysical Foundations,* Delhi: Motilal Banarsidass, 1974, p. 114.
13. T.L. Shay, *The Legacy of the Lokamanya,* Bombay: Oxford University Press, 1956, p. 5.
14. D. Mackenzie Brown, *The White Umbrella: Indian Political Thought from Manu to Gandhi.* Berkeley: University of California Press, 1953, pp. 15-16.
15. Ashis Nandy, *At the Edge of Psychology: Essays in Politics and Culture,* Delhi: Oxford University Press, 1980, p. 49.
16. Rajni Kothari, *Politics in India,* New Delhi: Orient Longman Ltd., 1970, p. 27.
17. *Ibid.*, pp. 27-28.
18. *Ibid.*, p. 28.
19. T.L. Shay, *Supra n.13,* Introduction, p. xiv.

20. Manorama Jauhari, *Politics and Ethics in Ancient India*, Varanasi: Bharatiya Vidya Prakashan, 1968, p. 4.

21. D. Mackenzie Brown, *Supra n.14*, pp. 16-17.

22. The old sense of all-inclusive politics is in turn a corruption of an even older meaning of the word. It clearly originates from Aristotle's *'politeia'*, the sort of constitution in which every citizen had a share, but in the Middle Ages was adapted to distinguish government involving and deriving from the people *(dominium politicum)* from government vested in the King *(dominium regale)*. In this context the word political carries a prescriptive and preferential designation.

23. J.P. Nettl, *Political Mobilization: A Sociological Analysis of Methods and Concepts*, London: Faber and Faber Ltd., 1967, pp. 29-30.

24. *Ibid.*, pp. 30-31.

25. *Ibid.*, p. 115.

26. *Ibid.*, p. 119.

27. Samuel P. Huntington, "Political Development and Political Decay", *World Politics*, April 1965, Vol. XVII, pp. 386-430.

28. J.P. Nettl, *Supra n. 23*, pp. 125-26.

29. *Ibid.*, p. 262-64.

 Also see, Hugh Tinker, *Ballot Box and Bayonet*, London: 1964.

30. Bardwell L. Smith, (ed.), *Religion and The Legitimation of Power in South Asia*, Netherland: E.J. Brill, 1978, Foreword, p. viii.

31. M.M. Sankhdher, *Study of Indian Political Culture: Methodological and Typological Problems*, Ram Avatar Sharma and Sushma Yadav (ed.), *Political Culture in Post-Independent India*, New Delhi: Printlok, 1989, p. 57.

32. George G. Hackman, Charles W. Kegley, Viljo K. Nikander, *supra n. 6*, p. 428.

33. *Ibid.*, p. 429.

34. Frank Thakur Das, *Gandhi on Religion and Politics* Verinder Grover (ed.), *Gandhi and Politics in India*, New Delhi: Deep and Deep Publications, 1987, 88.

35. *Young India* (Ahmedabad), March, 1922, p. 131.

36. V.P. Varma, *supra n. 12*, p. 116.

37. D. Mackenzie Brown, *supra n. 14*, Foreword, p. viii.

38. *Ibid.*, pp. 5-6.

39. A secularized culture cannot retain a sense of subjection to ethical limits.

40. T.R. Sharma, *Religion and Politics in India,* Moin Shakir (ed.), *Religion, State and Politics in India,* Delhi: Ajanta Publications, 1989, pp. 41-42.

41. *Ibid.,* p. 42.

42. T.L. Shay, *supra n. 13,* pp. 21-22.

43. The Samhitas consist of metrical hymns of the *Vedas* in contrast to the *Brahmanas* or prose sections. For an analysis of the political theory in the *Rigveda* and other early works, see, U.N. Ghoshal, *Hindu Political Theories,* pp. 19-35.

44. D. Mackenzie Brown, *supra n.14,* pp. 10,15.

45. K. Antonova, G. Bongard-Levin and G. Kotovsky, *A History of India.* Moscow: Progress Publishers, 1979, Vol. I, p. 74.

46. D. Mackenzie Brown, *supra n.*14, p. 158.

47. T.L. Shay, *supra n.13,* p. 29.

48. T.R. Sharma, *supra n.40,* pp. 43-44.

49. A.R. Desai, *Social Background of Indian Nationalism,* Bombay: Popular Prakashan, 1984, p. 26.

50. K.K. Verma, *Religious Revivalism in Modern India,* K.C. Markandan (ed.), *Concern of Politics: The Indian Context,* Jalandhar: ABS Publications, 1989, p. 162.

51. K.M. Pannikar, *Asia and the Western Dominance,* London: Allen and Unwin Ltd., 1959, Part VI Chapter. I. p. 237.

52. In a letter to Max Muller written on July 26, 1899, Curzon stated: "There is no doubt that a sort of quasi-religious, quasi-metaphysical ferment is going on in India, strongly conservative, and even reactionary in its general tendency. The ancient philosophies are being re-exploited." V.P. Varma, *Modern Indian Political Thought,* Agra: Lakshmi Narain Agarwal, 1986, pp. 372-73.

53. A.R. Desai, *supra n. 49,* pp. 283-84

54. Ibid., p. 285.

55. Ibid., p. 288.

56. Bhikhu Parekh, *Colonialism, Tradition and Reform: An Analysis of Gandhi's political Discourse,* New Delhi: Sage Publications, 1989, pp. 34-35.

57. *Ibid.,* p. 69.

CHAPTER 2

TILAK: RELIGION AND MODERNISATION

One really does not know whether providence have bestowed a special boon on this country. The innate vitality of our age old society is extremely powerful. There is not a single period in its whole history when one exceptionally great personality, or the other, was not born to give an everlasting credit to this nation. Great men have been born here, and they not only freed the country from the evil forces but also dazzled the world at large with their extraordinary calibre in achieving the impossible in most adverse circumstances.

Neither the ephemeral of the West nor the metaphysic of the East, but the impelling need for cultural resurgence has moved men to usher in a breakthrough in revitalizing the ancient and eternal truths in India in the dramatic arena of politics. India has been characterised by certain unique qualities of tolerance and synthesis which have evolved into an integrated way of life. For that matter, religion in India has not been a divisive force but a force of assimilation involving an amazing dialetic. In fact, the Indian culture has been receptive to every new culture that came its way and has drawn the best elements, out of each. Curiously, religion in India was never exclusive and was prepared to shed its dogmatism and rigidity in order to work out a new synthesis.

The national democratic awakening of the Indian people found expression in the religious sphere. The contradiction between the old religious outlook, practices and organization, on the one hand, and the new social and economic reality, on the other, gave rise to various religio-reform movements in the country. These movements represented attempts to revise the old religion in the spirit of the new principles of nationalism and democracy which were the conditions for the development of the new society.

The spirit of nationalism was needed to unite the people into a joint effort to solve problems which had become national due to the political and economic unification of the Indian people, for the first time in their history, under the British rule. Democracy and the principle of individual liberty were also extended, in varying degrees, to the sphere of religion by the reformers and early pioneer nationalists like Ram Mohan Roy, Debendranath Tagore, Keshav Chandra Sen, Telang, Ranade, Fulley, and the founders of Arya Samaj. While these reformers thought that they were returning to the pristine past, in reality, they forged a new society unknown to all past history. Along with a healthy desire for national freedom from the foreign rule, the chauvinist dreams of a spiritual conquest of the world through a resurrected Hinduism were also conceived, and claims of the special 'spiritual genius' were also proclaimed.

In India, the religio-reform movements launched a crusade against medieval religion which sanctified such institutions, as caste, which were a powerful obstacle to the national unity of the Indian people and to the development of the new economy of the country. They attacked polytheism, the practice of meaningless soul-deadening religious rites, and religious dogmas which undermined the critical intellectual power of the people. These religio-reform movements, or the Indian Renaissance as it is known, were national in content but religious in form. It was in the later stages of our national existence, that nationalism found exclusively or predominantly secular forms.

The Indian Renaissance movement had vast repercussions throughout the social and political spheres as well as within the realm of ethics and religion. In this movement, the conflict of civilizations and ways of life began. It stimulated the process of recreation of the classical values. Macaulay had hoped to occidentalize India, but instead, many educated, Westernized Indians began to rediscover the classical Indian philosophy of life. India began its period of renaissance. But Macaulay's aspirations to remake India were also fulfilled by those new intellectuals who reacted in a spirit of imitation, emphasizing the social evils of Hinduism and advocating extreme western-inspired social reforms. The nation was in a ferment of religious, cultural and social activity. New directions were charted. And from this environment, early political awakening of India began. The alliance of foreign rulers with Hindu reformers had proved impervious to the protests of those who valued religious ritual more highly than political independence or social equality. Yet the cry of religion in danger had awakened a responsive chord in millions who otherwise took no note of public affairs. The key to untapped political power, therefore, belonged to the man or party capable of basing a political programme on a religiously motivated movement.[1]

The interest in social reform led many westernized intellectuals to an interest in politics. In trying to enact and realise some of their reform schemes, many sought a voice in political affairs, aspiring to bring about moderate political reforms. Thus, the extremists in social reforms became the moderates of political reform,[2] always along the principles of British political philosophy. It logically followed that social reforms must precede political reforms' to prove India's worthiness for political reforms.

The British had begun to design administrative reforms as early as Queen Victoria's Proclamation of 1858. In 1861, an element of reform was introduced at the lowest levels of local administration. In 1883, the agitation over the Ilbert Bill interested an increasing number of the new intellectuals in political reform. Gradually, the social reformers saw that effective action required a combination and coordination of their social and political programmes. This prepared the ground-work for two Englishmen, Allen Octavian Hume and William Wedderburn, to work with the aid of the most prominent Indian leaders for the formation of an all-India political reform movement. They hoped to organize on a national basis and they believed that the people and the Government would benefit from an exchange of ideas through such an undertaking. They began planning an organisation that would foster cooperation between educated Indians and the British Raj. Subsequently, in cooperation with the liberal Indian intelligentsia, the Indian National Congress was founded in 1885. The Congress could serve as a focal point for national discontent, especially that of the educated classes, and guide this discontent in channels of constitutional movements for the Indian political advance. It could also keep the government informed about the views of the educated classes regarding the measures of the government.

That the Congress was designed as a safety valve for revolutionary discontent was made clear by Hume itself. 'A safety valve for the escape of great and growing forces, generated by our own action, was urgently needed and no more efficacious safety valve than our Congress Movement could possibly be devised.' In his correspondence with Sir Auckland Colvin, Hume remarked, "No choice was left to those who gave the primary impetus to the movement. The ferment due to the creation of Western ideas, education, invention and appliances, was at work with a rapidly increasing intensity, and it became of paramount importance to find for its products an overt and constitutional channel for discharge, instead of leaving them to fester as they had already commenced to do, under the surface."[3]

The political programme of the Congress in the early years of its formation was not concerned with the rallying of mass public support for India's political cause. Rather, it concentrated on representing the advanced case for reform and equitability in administrative matters to the Viceroy, the British people and Parliament. They believed that political reforms would gradually be bestowed as a gift from the British, when educated Indians were able to demonstrate that India deserved such reforms. Their theory of political action was limited to constitutional agitation and concentrated on making appeals for the application of nineteenth century liberal political theories to the administration of the British Indian Empire.

Moderates, as they were called, asserted some of the initial claims on the basis of broad philosophical and religious assumptions, not those peculiar to India. Dadabhai Naoroji, the Grand Old Man of India, could transcend Hindu-Muslim communalism in stating that Indians had as their human right the privilege "to inherit the great blessings of freedom and representation." [4] Surendranath Banerjee, in the year following Congress' birth, stated it more explicitly: "Self-government is the ordering of nature and the will of Divine Providence. Every nation must be the arbiter of its own destinies."[5] Even though the Congress had begun with a mere seventy delegates, messages such as these struck responsive chords. The cry for self- rule found a natural mouthpiece in the Congress, which swiftly moved beyond the hopes for safety valve status.[6]

The moderates prevailed in the early years of the Congress. Prominent among these were Justice Ranade and his loyal disciple, Gopal Krishna Gokhle,[7] who continued to stress social reforms along with political freedom. Ranade was "a constant figure on the Congress platform as a visitor, and he was the power behind the throne, guiding, advising, and encouraging the Congress leaders in their work." His successor, Gokhale, "with his polished speeches, his parliamentary manner, his facts, and his formidable logic, was the westward-looking Indian's pride."[8] So long as men of this temper dominated, the British presence was not essentially under fire. The Moderated Era in Indian politics covered the last two decades of the nineteenth and the first two decades of the twentieth century. The Moderate leaders are now often forgotten, or remembered as soft-headed and weak-kneed men, were naive enough to practise the politics of protest, petition and prayer, and to beg for petty concessions from the British instead of claiming *Swaraj* as their birthright.

This blurred and distorted image of the Moderate Era, partly due to the conscious superiority and almost contempt with which each generation tends to judge its predecessor. But it suffered further damage from the Extremist thunderstorm in 1905-1908 in the wake of the Partition of Bengal, and the Gandhian avalanche of 1919-1920, which was to permanently alter the political landscape in India. The Moderate Era witnessed continual political and social change. It was 'a multiple situation for ever on the move' more like a movie-film than a series of still photographs in a picture gallery.

That British rule would not last forever was foreseen by farsighted members of the ruling race. In 1853, in his remarkable testimony before the Indian Committee of the House of Lords, Sir Charles E. Trevelyan, the brother-in-law of Macaulay, who had served in the civil service of the East India Company, made the startling statement that the British Raj in India was bound to die one day, and that the only question was whether it would die as a result of a revolt at the hands of Indians who subscribed to the 'indigenous' model of political change, or at the hands of English-educated Indians, who subscribed to the new, the British model of political change." Trevelyan argued that if the people of India adopted the British model of change, it would take a long time, and the ultimate severance between the two countries would be neither violent nor harmful to Britain, since cultural and commercial bonds would survive. Events in immediate future were to dramatically confirm Trevelyan's prediction. Within four years came the revolt of 1857. The traditional leaders of Indian society had shot their bolt. Henceforth it was the turn of the English-educated class to try the new, the British model of political change. It sought to meet the West with the weapons borrowed from the West. It ran newspapers and journals: it formed literary and political associations; it sent petitions to the provincial governors and the Governor-General and to the British Parliament. The older leaders of Indian society, the hereditary chieftains, the landlords, the caste, leaders and the merchant-princes, did not fit into this new style of politics, and the initiative passed on to lawyers, teachers and journalists, who knew the idiom of constitutional agitation. The introduction to western learning had sharpened the public conscience of this small English-educated class. It learnt to take a critical look at its social and political environment. Armed with arguments from John Stuart Mill and Herbert Spencer, it learnt to challenge the shibboleths of an entrenched priesthood as well as the pretensions of an alièn and all-powerful bureaucracy.

The first generation of Congressmen was drawn from the English-educated elite. Most of them had their introduction to English literature and politics through the newly established universities. The founding fathers of the Indian National Congress admired the English nation deeply but discriminately. Mahadev Govind Ranade, historian, economist, politician, reformer and judge, perhaps the most versatile and sophisticated thinker of that generation, saw in the British conquest not merely a calamity to be lamented, but an opportunity to be seized. Looking back at the history of his own country, Ranade noted that both Hindus and Muslims had lacked certain qualities. Both had been lacking in the love of municipal freedom, in the exercise of virtues necessary for civic life and in aptitudes for mechanical skills, in the love of science and research, in the love of daring and adventurous discovery, the resolution to master difficulties and in chivalrous respect for woman-kind'. Foreign rule, was, therefore, not merely the cause, but the consequence of the many evils from which Indian society suffered. Ranade conceded that under British rule, the scope for individual ambitions had narrowed, but he felt that the opportunity for the realization of national ambitions had immeasurably increased. India was being roused from the stupor of ages; she had at last a chance of raising herself to the level of the advanced countries of the West. The problem, as he saw it, was one of reactivating 'an ancient but ossified civilization which had been cut-off for centuries from an invigorating contact with the rest of the world'. In this task, India could well look forward to assistance from the British nation. That nation had its own faults and foibles, but its character had been formed by centuries of struggle and self-discipline; it had a 'moral element which inspired hope and confidence in colonies and dependencies of Great Britain'. The British connection was thus part of a disciplining process for India, coming as it did 'through the example of the most gifted and free nation in the world'. Ranade saw the guiding hand of Providence in bringing the two countries together.

Pax Brittanica evoked in educated Indians, feelings of gratitude for the past and hope for the future. They longed for the day when India would, under British tutelage, graduate to self-government like other British dominions. A.O. Hume, who did more than any other single person to set the Indian National Congress firmly on its foundations, expressed the hope in 1888, that in fifty to seventy years, India would achieve 'a status precisely similar to the Dominion of Canada', with her own Indian Parliament, and that the only officials sent out to India from England would be the Viceroy and Governor General.

The meeting of the seventy odd delegates to the Indian National Congress on 28th December, 1885, at the Tejpal Sanskrit College at Bombay (Mumbai), was not the first effort to create a national political organization in India; several earlier efforts had failed and prospects for the survival of the new organization seemed none too bright. Indian nationalism was not the powerful force in 1885, it is sometimes assumed to have been. It was the aspiration largely of English-educated Indians living in the principal towns, who constituted a truly 'microscopic minority'. Lord Dufferin, the Viceroy of India of the day, estimated that in the quarter century from 1853 to 1888, half a million children had a school education of any sort, and the number of graduates turned out by Indian universities was no more than eight thousand. Most Indians continued to think in terms of their region, community or caste; they were conscious of being Bengalis, Biharis, Punjabis, Hindus, Muslims, Parsees, Brahmins, Kayasths, but not of being Indians. The local political associations were proud of the standing they had achieved in the eyes of the public and the government. The British Indian Association of Calcutta, for example, was reluctant to play second fiddle to a new political body with headquarters at Bombay (Mumbai). The Bombay Presidency Association, which was to be the nerve-centre of the Indian National Congress for nearly thirty years, came into existence in 1885, the very year in which the Congress was founded. No wonder W.C. Bannerjee, the first president of the Congress, described one of its main objects as the promotion of 'personal intimacy and friendship, amongst all the more earnest workers in country's cause, and the eradication of all possible race, creed or provincial prejudices.

Since the Congress incurred the displeasure of the government soon after its birth, the feudal elements, the princes, the landlords, the caste leaders, and indeed all those dependent upon the bounty of the Raj, shunned the Congress. Raja Siva Parshad, the Raja of Bhinga and conservative Hindu leaders who had clashed with Sir Syed Ahmed Khan on the Urdu-Hindu issue, called on the Aligarh leader to form a united front against the Congress party. Sir Syed launched the bitterest onslaught on the Congress; he described it as a 'civil war without the use of arms', and considered nationalism and democracy as impossible goals for India. He formed the Indian Patriotic Association, and later the Anglo-Muhammadan Defence Association to conduct a tearing propaganda campaign which succeeded in scaring away the vast majority of the politically-conscious Muslims from the Congress. Even that eminent judge and patriot, Badruddin Tyabji, who presided over the Madras Congress in 1887, was so disconcerted by the heat and dust raised by Sir Syed's campaign that he wrote to A.O. Hume, advising the suspension of Congress meetings for a few years.

The fiercest opposition to the Congress—as may well have been expected—came from the authorities in India. Hume had taken the precaution of discussing his project with Lord Dufferin, the Viceroy, and had secured his acquiescence, if not his encouragement. But Dufferin's attitude changed from a benevolent neutrality to bitter hostility. He began to see in the Congress leaders 'the real enemies of the British'.

Just before his departure from India in 1888, in his St. Andrews dinner speech at Calcutta, he fired a broadside against the Congress. That very year the Congress meeting at Allahabad during the Christmas week became the scene of a tug-of-war between British officials headed by the Lieutenant Governor, Auckland Calvin, and the Congress leaders. The official hostility to the Congress became an open secret.

Among Dufferin's successors, Elgin wavered between indulgence and opposition, but Curzon was implacably hostile. This hostility came to pervade all levels of the official hierarchy, and for obvious reasons. No bureaucracy in the world likes outsiders to interfere in its work. The British bureaucracy in India was proud of its efficiency; its resentment against its critics was in direct proportion to its conviction of its own good intentions and efficiency.

In 1895, Sir George Chesney, a former member of the Viceroy's Council, in an article in the *'Nineteenth Century'*, described the holders of the Congresses as 'a set of inept blundering political charlatans, who have never made one useful or practical suggestion'.

In fairness to the British in India, it must be conceded that most of them sincerely believed that the political system evolved in England in the course of centuries could not be transplanted to India; indeed, such a suggestion struck them as absurd as that of rearing an elephant in the mists of Scotland. They were also convinced that India could not become a nation-state. Sir John Strachey, a former civilian and an ex-member of the Viceroy's Executive Council, began his lecture at the University of Cambridge in 1884 with the assertion that "the first and most essential thing to learn about India is – that there is not, and never was an India', and that it was impossible' that men of Bombay, the Punjab, Bengal and Madras should ever feel that they belong to one great Indian nation." To Strachey and his tribe, 'Indian nationalists were irresponsible demagogues, and their British friends such as Hume and Wedderburn, – at best cranks and at worst traitors'.

Within a couple of years of the establishment of the Congress, its leaders saw that the official mind in India was like a rock, which was impossible to penetrate, and that the Congress, if it were to survive as a political body, would have to address itself to public opinion in Britain over the heads of its agents in India. This strategy necessitated not only the setting up of the British Committee of the Congress in London, spreading its opinion with its journal *India*, but with the modulation and presentation of Congress policies so as to win the support of Liberal opinion in Britain. The British Committee (including such veterans as Hume, Wedderburn, Dadabhai Naoroji and W. C. Banerjee) kept its fingers on the pulse of British opinion. Its task was rendered difficult by the turn of the electoral wheel in Britain. In 1886, a few months after the establishment of the Congress, the Liberal Party on which Congress leaders had pinned their hopes, was voted out. What followed was a long period of nearly two decades of Tory ascendancy in Britain, marked by the resurgence of jingo imperialism, and an intense competition between European powers for trade and territories in Asia and Africa.

In the face of the hostility of Anglo-India and its conservative allies, the paramount concern of Congress leaders was to protect the organization from internal erosion and external assault. They skilfully skated past the issues which could divide and weaken their ranks. Despite the taunts of their critics, they kept social reform off the Congress agenda; most of them held radical views on the reform of Indian society, but they knew that it was an explosive issue which stirred fierce prejudices and animosities. Dadabhai Naoroji told the second Congress (1886) that theirs was a political body, representing the political aspirations of the Indian people and must, therefore, confine itself to questions in which the entire nation had a direct interest. The Congress leaders were equally careful in treading on the delicate ground of religious controversy. They were taken aback by the violent opposition of Sir Syed Ahmed Khan, but they tried to disarm Muslim fears with a self-denying ordinance, barring discussion at Congress sessions of any proposal to which the delegates of any religious community as a body were opposed. The Congress leaders tried to soften inter-provincial jealousies by rotating the venue of the annual sessions among the principal towns of India, and by bearing in mind the claims of different communities and regions while choosing the Congress president of the year.

The informal and flexible structure of the early years helped the Congress to escape the process of splintering, to which nationalist movements are prone. A certain continuity was ensured by A.O. Hume, who acted as a one-man secretariat of the Congress for the first seven years, and then by D.E. Wacha and Gokhale, who acted as joint secretaries. And the main direction of the Congress policies for nearly thirty years remained in the hands of a coterie of leaders in London, Calcutta and Bombay, bound to each other not only by devotion to a common cause, but ties of friendship. They knew that any setback to Congress would be a victory for its Anglo-Indian adversaries. Whenever there was an open rift, for example, in Poona in 1895 on the holding of the social conference in the Congress pavilion, the Congress leadership used all the resources to bring about a compromise. It was important for the Congress to be able to speak with one voice both to the people and the government. Only once-at the Surat session in December, 1907, it was unable to do so. It is significant that the Surat split between the Moderates and the Extremists struck Lord Minto, the Viceroy of the day, as 'a collapse of the Congress' and 'a great triumph' for us.

While the Congress leaders had to guard against fissiparous tendencies, their immediate problem was to parry the attacks of the British bureaucracy in India. They deliberately adopted a low profile so as not to provoke a repression which the infant political body was in no position to withstand. They adopted a tone of sweet reasonableness. At the very first session, when Dadabhai Naoroji suggested that the Congress should 'clearly and boldly' declare its objects, the majority of his colleagues preferred caution to candour; the Congress refrained from precisely spelling out its ultimate aims. It had good reasons for not inscribing 'Home Rule' or 'self-government' on its banner. Significantly, even as late as in 1899, when the Congress gave itself a written constitution for the first time, it defined its aims vaguely as the promotion by constitutional means of 'the interests and well-being of the people of the Indian Empire'. In those early years 'moderation' was the watchword. 'If we honestly expect that the English nation will do its duty towards us', Dadabhai Naoroji told the second Congress, 'we must prove worthy by showing that we are never unreasonable, never violent, never uncharitable. We must show that we are earnest, but temperate, cognizant of our rights, but respectful of those of others; expecting the fairest construction of our own acts and conceding these to those of others."

In June, 1904, Dadabhai Naoroji declared at a meeting of the London India Society, that there was 'one remedy for the present dishonourable, hypocritical and destructive system of British rule in India, and that was self-government under British paramountcy'. Six months later, a Congress president, Sir Henry Cotton, for the first time defined the goal of the Congress 'as a United States of India on a fraternal footing with the self-governing colonies. Such a pronouncement may not sound revolutionary today, but it had never been made before so unequivocally from the Congress platform. In June, 1905, Gokhale incorporated the ideal of a self-governing India in the constitution of the Servants of India Society, and expounded it with great clarity, conviction and courage during his visit to England just before the general election of 1905.

It is important to remember that this change in the Congress stance took place before the Partition of Bengal raised the political barometer in India. Congress veterans saw the partition as an aberration of the reactionary Tory regime, but this regime was on the way out. 'Our day of emancipation, Dadabhai wrote to Gokhale on 26 November, 1905,' 'is much nearer than many of us imagine.' A wave of hope ran through nationalist India. For the first time since the Congress movement began, the Liberal Party had come into real power in Britain with a comfortable majority. In his presidential address to the Benares Congress, Gokhale hailed the new British Prime Minister, Campbell-Bannerman, as a 'tried and tested friend of freedom', and John Morley, the Secretary of State for India; as 'the reverent student of Burke, the disciple of Mill, the friend and biographer of Gladstone'. 'A more gratifying combination of circumstances, Gokhale added, 'could not be conceived and it now rests with us to turn it to the best advantage we can for our motherland.

The Congress veterans did not like the Partition of Bengal at all, but it seemed to them that an agitation against it was unnecessary after the installation of a Liberal government in Britain. It was important to undo the wrong that Lord Curzon had done to Bengal, but was it not more important to seek constitutional reforms which would make such wrongs impossible in future? The Congress leaders did not like the cry of universal boycott. They feared that it would give a handle to Anglo-Indian enemies of constitutional reforms for India, who never tired of portraying educated Indians as perverse and irresponsible. Obviously, it was in the interest of the Indian people to preserve, and if possible to increase, whatever little powers of administration and control they possessed rather than give up what they had won after years of struggle. The rapier-thrusts of Aurobindo Ghose and Tilak in *Bande Mataram* and *Kesari* seemed ill-conceived. To flatly question the right of the British Government to rule India, and the right of the leaders of the Congress to speak for the Indian people, was only to make the task of the new Liberal government in England even more difficult than it was. The Indian educated classes had learnt to admire the Liberal Party as the party of Ripon, Bright, Bradlaugh and Gladstone. They had no doubt that the Liberals would enable India to share the common heritage of freedom.

The decade 1905-1915 was ideal for the realization of the dream of the founders of the Congress—the Moderate dream in which Britain was seen as India's political mentor. Slowly but steadily the people of India were to be associated with the governance of their country; as they learnt to shoulder the responsibilities entrusted to them, more and more power was to devolve upon them until India acquired the status of a self-governing dominion within the British Empire. The Moderates looked upon the British Empire very much as we look upon the United Nations today. The

Empire seemed not only a guarantee of security in a world made increasingly insecure by the competing imperialism of Germany, Russia and Japan; it was also a valuable link with the western world for those cultural, technological and commercial interchanges which were essential to really usher India into the twentieth century.

Throughout this period, a Liberal government was in power in Britain, and Indian politics was dominated by the Indian Liberals, the Moderates. The Moderate leaders did all they could to create the right atmosphere in India to enable the Liberal Party in Britain to do something big for India: they fought and even expelled the 'Extremist' party in the Congress when its propaganda seemed likely to hurt the cause of reform. The Moderate dream was, however, not realized. The constitutional reforms were not only delayed, but doled out in pitifully small doses. One by one the idols of the British Liberals fell from the Moderate pedestal.

Despite disappointments and set backs, the Moderate leaders did not give in to despair. For one thing they found it difficult to shed their belief that 'the genius of the British people... as revealed in history is on the whole, made for freedom, for constitutional liberty'. For another, they could not forget the modest beginnings of political life in their own lifetime. 'What a wonderful revolution we have seen! 'Romesh Dutt wrote just before his death in 1909 to Surendranath Bannerjee. Dutt and Bannerjee had grown up in a society in which political aspiration, let alone political agitation, was virtually unknown. The sense of Indian nationality was submerged under a welter of sectarian and regional loyalties, the press was neither vocal nor free, there were a handful of Indians in the Civil Service, and none in the provincial and central executives, municipal bodies were run by officials, and the legislative councils were packed with British officials and their nominees from the titled Indian gentry. In less than fifty years the Indian political landscape had been transformed. National consciousness had been quickened; the press had become a power in the land; there were some Indians in the superior ranks of the civil service, and some of them sat even in the executive councils of the Governors and the Viceroy; the local bodies had been reorganized on a popular basis, and legislative councils had a sizeable Indian element.

The Moderate leaders were not daunted by the pronouncements of British statesmen that India was unfit for self-government. In 1912, after the Liberal Secretary of State, Crewe, had made such a statement, Gokhale told a meeting organized by the Indian residents in London that 'these matters were not so much in the hands of English statesmen as they were in their (Indians) hands', that there were forces mightier than any statesman, mightier than all statesmen put together that were moulding the destinies of all the East, and of India among Eastern nations.' Gokhale's prophecy was to come true five years later in August, 1917 when Edwin Montagu, the Secretary of State for India, declared that the policy of 'His Majesty's Government...is that of increasing association of Indians in every branch of the administration, and gradual development of self-governing institutions with a view to the progressive realization of responsible government in India as an integral part of the British Empire.'

Montagu's declaration was only the enunciation of a goal and did not prescribe a time-table for the devolution of power to Indian hands. It was hailed in India as a landmark in Indo-British relations. It came too late to save the Moderates' credibility and control of the Congress, which had been undermined by the small political gains they had been able to show for their pains. The death of

Gokhale and Pherozeshah Mehta in 1915, fatally weakened the Moderates. In 1916, Tilak and his adherents rejoined the Congress and made themselves felt. Two years later, there was another split in the Congress, a sort of reversed Surat; it was now the turn of the Moderates to be squeezed out of the Congress. The Moderate Era in Indian politics was coming to an end. Henceforth the Moderates or the Liberals as they came to be called continued to figure on the political stage as individuals, but were never again a dominant factor in national politics.

It must be remembered that in the 1890s, as Tilak's extremist persuation moved more into the ascendancy, the Government's position towards Congress had already begun to harden. With Muslim representation dwindling to insignificance, Congress also assumed a more specifically Hindu religious base. The militant nationalists revived the memories of the Vedic past of the Hindus, the great phase of the reigns of Ashoka and Chandragupta, the heroic deeds of Rana Pratap and Shivaji, the epic partiotism of Laxmibai, the Queen of Jhansi and the leader of the National Revolt of 1857.

The philosophers of militant nationalism believed in the special genius of India. They propounded that the Indian people were endowed with a special spiritual consciousness. "The Hindus constitute a distinct people. The regulative idea in the evolution of Hindu character, the idea which has given a peculiar shape and colouring to the entire history of the race, is their innate consciousness of the spiritual and the eternal."[9]

The extremists, Lala Lajpat Rai (Punjab), Bipin Chandra Pal (Bengal), Aurobindo Ghose (Bengal) and Bal Gangadhar Tilak (Maharashtra) and a host of their supporters and followers, criticized the timid, westernized political programme of the Moderates and conceived of a new dynamic platform of Indian political action. However, it was Tilak's famous slogan *"Swaraj* is my birthright and I will have it" that thrilled the whole of India. To his generation, it was the flaming torch which led them out of the darkness and frustration of the period, into light and liberty and life.[10] Bal Gangadhar Tilak lived in a dynamic era of India's history and made his contribution in dynamic terms. He was, in the words of Mahatma Gandhi, "the Maker of Modern India."[11]

The extremists believed that the moderates were always ready to bark at the British bureaucracy about poverty, pestilence, ignorance and even imperial exploitation; but they were not prepared to take the next step and bite the wrong-doer if it were necessary. Men like Gokhale, Madan Mohan Malviya and Sir Pherozeshah Mehta made, on occasion, eloquent and fiery speeches, but their British listeners well knew that their fire did not burn; they flourished swords, but they had no edge on them. And how could the rulers take the Moderates seriously when they were convinced that the spiritual basis of these men's politics was fulsome adoration of the British way of life, and above all, a sincere belief that the British ruled India by Divine dispensation? Even a man like A.O. Hume, a life-long member of the Indian Civil Service and known for his moderation, advised the leaders of the Indian Congress to adopt a more vigorous policy. He told them that merely meeting once a year in the Christmas vacation, passing a few resolutions and sleeping over them for the rest of the twelve months would achieve nothing. He said, "You meet in Congress, you glow with a momentary enthusiasm, you speak much and eloquently; but the Congress closes and every one of you goes off straight away on his private business! Years ago I called on you to be up and doing; years ago I warned that 'Nations by themselves are made', and have you heeded these counsels? You have, indeed, ever eagerly clamoured for and vainly clutched at the Crown but how many of you will touch the Cross even with your finger-tips?"

This challenge, it should be remembered, was issued to the leaders of India by no less a person than the Father of the Congress. But the leaders who controlled the organization would not or could not take it up. Sir Pherozeshah Mehta, the "Lion of Bombay", spoke for the Moderate Party in words which he called "the confession of faith of a devout and irreclamable Congressman". He said, "I am an inveterate. I am a robust optimist like Mahadeo Govind Ranade. I believe in divine guidance through human agency... My steadfast loyalty (to the Crown) is founded upon this rock of hope and patience; seeking the Will of Providence, like Oliver Cromwell, in dispensations rather than revelations, seeing God's will like him in fulfilment of events. I accept British rule... as a dispensation so wonderful, a little island set at one end of the world establishing itself in a far continent as different as it could be, that it would be folly not to accept it as a declaration of God's will."

Sir Pherozeshah Mehta was the high priest of the Moderate Party and Gokhale was his staunchest follower and henchman. Between them and Tilak there was hardly any common ground. Mehta and Gokhale regarded the conquest of India as God's will; Tilak regarded it as curse. They welcomed the British rule; Tilak hated it. They wanted the Empire to last for ever; Tilak wished to see its end without delay. The Moderates were prepared to wait indefinitely for the attainment of their ideal, namely colonial self-government; the New Party, however, was impatient to reach the goal of *Swaraj*, by which they meant complete independence. One would have thought that in the natural evolution of things, the Moderates, in response to the rising tempo of the movement, would slowly move nearer to the position of the New Party; after all both wings of the National Congress were agreed on the need for the salvation of India. But they were unfortunately, widely separated in their approach to and treatment of the basic situation. The old methods of petitioning the bureaucracy or their masters in London had yielded little if anything by way of political rights. The 1892 Council's Act was trotted out by the Moderates as a great triumph for their constitutional agitation. But in reality what did it amount to? A few non-official members were nominated by the Governor of the province or the Viceroy of India after their so-called "election" through district boards and municipalities. The Governor had the right to reject the "elected member", and this effectively killed any idea of democratic franchise. Once elected, a member could ask questions and make speeches but could neither ask supplementary questions nor criticize the budget. There are on record scores of members' questions which the executive Member of the Government disposed of by the most expressive monosyllabic reply—"Yes" or "No". Many a time the popular members used to get so furious at this sort of treatment that they walked out.

Tilak, who was elected to the Bombay Council twice, once in 1895 and again in 1897, had first-hand experience of the way business was conducted there. He exposed the sham nature of these councils when five eminent members unanimously opposed a bill in 1994 and were rebuked by the Executive Members as men who did not know their own people. On another occasion Pheroz Shah Mehta had asked a question on a matter which was causing great inconvenience to the people. The Government reply was a plain "No". The popular members were stupefied by this ridiculous reply but could do nothing—they were debarred from asking a supplementary question or raising the issue again on a motion for the adjournment of the House.

Tilak was determined to expose the spinelessness of the Moderates and so prevent general acceptance of their ineffective political policy. Accordingly, early in 1907, he initiated an important public discussion on the vital issue of "Constitutional Agitation" in India.

The Moderates were doing all they could to prevent the country from following the lead given by Dadabhai Naoroji, and from supporting the Swadeshi-Boycott movement. In his own contribution, three articles on "Constitutional or extra-Constitutional agitation", Tilak dealt not only with the arguments the Moderates were already putting forward, but also with others which he thought they might bring out later to support their attitude. His articles (*Kesari*- February 12th, February 19th and March 5th, 1907) are a masterly exposition of the fundamentals of the politics of a conquered country, showing the vital difference between the concepts of legal and constitutional agitation and demonstrating how his programme of passive resistance or non-co-operation was the only one suitable to the conditions then prevailing in India.

In February 1907, Gokhale had delivered a series of lectures at Allahabad in which he put forward at some length his ideas on constitutional methods and by inference tried to show the futility of passive resistance as advocated by Tilak and his New Party. Gokhale had posed the question: "What is constitutional agitation?" and had answered it thus: "Constitutional agitation was agitation by methods which they were entitle to adopt to bring about the changes they desired through the action of constituted authority. Thus defined, the field of constitutional agitation was a very wide one. But there were two essential conditions—one, that the methods adopted were such as they were entitled to employ, and second, that the changes desired must be obtained only through the action of constituted authority by bringing to bear on them the pressure of public opinion." Gokhale next proceeded to point out that the loose talk in which some people indulged, namely, that constitutional agitation had failed in India, was unjustified.

Tilak in his article of February 12th boldly declared that "the Congress agitation based on the so-called 'constitutional methods' is a sheer waste of time. The continued stress laid on these methods has misled the country and wasted these valuable twenty-one years. We venture to suggest that although the word 'constitutional' has been paraded so often by our leaders, they have made the grievous mistake of misunderstanding its origin and application. Theirs is a case of following blindly the phraseology appropriate and applicable to English politics but totally inapplicable to Indian conditions. In England, an unpopular Act of the Government in power could be repealed by the people's vote. The people have democratic means of changing the Government; the Government is answerable to the country and if it fails to convince the electorals it stands condemned and is thrown out. Is there anything of this kind in India? Can Mr. Gokhale or his Moderate Party show us the constitution of India which could confer this right on the people?

"The Government of India is the creation of the British Parliament, and is theoretically responsible to that Parliament and not to the people of India. The naked truth of the Indian situation is that the right to punish anyone who goes against the Government of India rests with the Government, and the rules and regulations about it are to be found in the Indian Penal Code. In all seriousness one can suggest that what Gokhale calls India's Constitution is really the Indian Penal Code. If he had his Moderate friends suggest that our agitation should be within the four corners of that Code we can appreciate the argument—then it will mean that it should be legal and legitimate – that is perfectly under-standable." No one for a moment suggested, Tilak asserted, that the Indian agitation should resort to arms or become illegal, but then "it would be more honest and realistic to ask the people to be legal in their agitation, the scope of which can be determined by circumstances, but it is futile and misleading to call it constitutional".

Tilak elaborated his views in the other two articles which can be summarized as follows. In the first place India had no Constitution of her own; the Indian Government was created by the Statutes of the Parliament of Great Britain and was not responsible to the people. Therefore the talk of bringing about constitutional changes through the action of the constituted authority was moonshine. In the second place the Indian people had no law-making powers. Government officials had the sole authority to make and unmake laws, and if they so desired they could put an end to all forms of agitation and deprive the people of even their elementary rights of free association and free speech; they could easily penalize all political activity in the country. India's officialdom was an autocracy and in fighting such an autocracy it was not always possible to follow methods that would be described as legal; for such a description or interpretation was liable to be changed according to the whims of the bureaucracy. Tilak argued that not law but justice, morality, and equity should be the guiding principles of Indian agitation. Constitutional and law-abiding methods against an alien bureaucracy which possessed almost absolute and autocratic power could only lead to political suicide.

These articles by Tilak furnished the *raison d'être* for the militant programme of the New Party and effectively squashed the arguments of the Moderate Party.

In reality the New Party (which came to be known as Extremists) and the Moderates differed little in their ideals; it was in the methods to be used in the day-to-day working of the political programme that the fundamental cleavage between them lay. At this time the well-known British author and journalist, H.W. Nevinson, was touring India and secured an interview with Tilak, a part of which is worth quoting as emphasising this difference in methods. He quotes Tilak thus: "It is not by our purpose, but by our methods only that our party has earned the name of Extremist. Certainly there is a very small party which talks about abolishing the British rule at once and completely. That does not concern us; it is much too far in the future. Unorganized, disarmed, and still disunited, we should not have a chance of shaking the British suzerainty. We may leave that sort of thing to a distant time. Our object is to obtain eventually a large share in the administration of our country.

"What we aim at doing now is to bring pressure on the bureaucracy; to make it feel that all is not well. Of late the attitude of our British officials has greatly changed for the worse. They no longer speak of educating us up to freedom, as the great Englishmen like Elphinstone did in the past. They appear to agree with *The Times* that our education in subjects like English history must be checked, because it is dangerous for 'natives' to learn anything about freedom.

"The immediate question for us is, how are we to bring pressure on this bureaucracy, in which we have no effective representation, and are debarred from all except subordinate positions? It is only in our answer to that question that we differ from the so-called Moderates. They still hope to influence public opinion in England by sending deputations, supporting a newspaper, and pleading the justice of our cause. Both parties, of course, have long given up all hope of influencing. Anglo-Indian opinion out here. But even in England we find most people ignorant and indifferent about India, and the influence of retired Anglo-Indians at home is perpetually against us. When Lord Cromer said the other day that India must be no party question, he meant that Liberals should support the bureaucracy as blindly as the Tories. The history of the last year has proved to us how unexceptionably they fulfil that duty.

"Under these disappointments we Extremists have decided on other methods. It is a matter of temperament, and the younger men are with us. Our motto is 'Self-reliance not Mendicancy'."

Then Tilak turned to the question of the Extremist programme. "Besides the ordinary Swadeshi movement," he said, "we work by boycott and passive resistance. Our boycott is voluntary. We do not advocate picketing or compulsory prevention from the purchase of foreign goods. And in passive resistance we shall simply refuse to notice such measures as the Seditious Meetings Act. But we do not care what happens to ourselves. We are devoted absolutely and without reservation to the cause of the Indian people. To imprison even 3,000 or 4,000 of us at the same time would embarrass the bureaucracy. That is our object—to attract the attention of England to our wrongs by diverting trade and obstructing the Government."

The New Party's conclusion that it was impossible to gain any concessions by petitions and prayers was the prime difference between the Moderates and Progressive parties. Tilak did not believe in philanthropy as a principle of British politics. "There was no instance in history," he said, "of one foreign nation ruling another for the benefit of the other and not for its own profit. The rule of one nation by another was in itself unnatural." He granted the efficiency of the

British Government and the excellence of its methods for its own purpose, but these methods and that efficiency did not work for the interests of the people of the country. "A good foreign government was less desirable than an inferior native government," was his considered opinion.

The Moderates had always had faith in the British Government but very little faith in themselves and their own people in India. They believed that England's heart was good, sympathetic and generous, and that she meant to, and would, grant India self-government. This was not at all the New Party's belief. Tilak had said at Calcutta, "We believe in Lord Morley and in the genuineness of his profession as a philosopher. The old school (the Moderates) thinks that politics could be governed by the dictates of philosophy; we hold that politics and philosophy are two different things and ought not to be mixed up together. The old school thinks that concessions could be secured by logical persuasion. We believe they can be won only by hard work and sacrifice!"

Tilak's exposition of the fundamental differences between his New Party and the Moderates attracted immediate attention all over the country. His succinctly expressed view that "India's only Constitution is the Penal Code" echoed through India. His articles were translated and published in Calcutta, Ahmedabad, Allahabad, Benares, Lahore and Madras and in many other towns, and special pamphlets were issued by his followers in various parts of the country.

Before the Moderates had time to recover from Tilak's attack on their ideals and methods of constitutional agitation he delivered another blow which knocked the bottom out of their political philosophy. Ever since the Congress was founded in 1885 (and even before) the old school had made Queen Victoria's Proclamation of 1858 the sheet-anchor of their political creed. Tilak also used to refer to it occasionally in order to prick the British conscience—but more often as a peg on which to hang his arguments than as an indication of his own faith in it. In June 1907, he gave his interpretation of the true meaning and purpose of the Proclamation, and this, like his exposition of "constitutional agitation" a few months earlier, shook the Moderates and the country.

Some time before this a private letter, written by Lord Lytton the Viceroy of India (1876-80) to the then Secretary of State for India, had come to light. In it he said that "claims and expectations of complete equality and admission to offices as promised by the Proclamation of 1858 can never be fulfilled. Governments of England and India appear unable to answer the charge of breaking to the heart the words of promise they have uttered to the ear". Lord Curzon for his part had also stated: "The highest ranks of civil employment in India must as a general rule be held by Englishmen, for the reason that they possess, partly by heredity, party by upbringing, partly by education, the knowledge of the principles of government, the habits of mind, the vigour of character, which are essential for the task, and that, the rule of India being a British rule, and every other rule being under the circumstances of the case impossible, the tone and standard should be set by those who have created and are responsible for it." This was the first direct contradiction to Queen Victoria's Proclamation which guaranteed equality of status to Indians in all branches of the administration. Such a statement not only added insult to injury but was a challenge to the intelligentsia of India. It is small wonder, then, that some of the educated Indians took up the challenge and began anti-British activities.

Tilak took full advantage of the fact that servants of the Crown, holding the highest positions, had expressed themselves in such terms about the Proclamation, and proceeded to put his own interpretation on it. He boldly declared that the 1858 declaration was, contrary to what many people thought, not a contract between the Sovereign and the subjects at all. "In my view," he said, "the Proclamation is not a contract but a statesmanly sop to pacify the people of India who had rebelled against the British—indeed it was a piece of cheating. Contracts are made between equals, not between the weak and the strong. Contractual relationship between the ruler and the ruled is a western concept and is useful to give a practical basis to any government... The King is divine, they say; all right, agreed! But I ask you, what are the subjects? Are they not divine?... Our ancient scriptures and law books accept the principle of the King's divinity but they do not allow him absolute and arbitrary powers. When the King's rule becomes unjust and oppressive he ceases to be divine. The moral of it all is that oppression and injustice cannot be justified even if the divinity of Kingship is accepted."

Then he went on to answer Anglo-Indian critics who had called the members of the New Party revolutionaries: "It is true that what we seek may seem like a revolution; it is a revolution in the sense that it means a complete change in the theory of the government of India as now put forward by the bureaucracy. It is true that this revolution must be a bloodless revolution, but it would be folly to suppose that if there is to be no shedding of blood, there are also to be no sufferings to be undergone by the people. These sufferings are bound to be great and the sacrifices supreme. You can win nothing unless you are prepared to suffer and sacrifice. An appeal to the generosity and good feeling of the rulers has been found everywhere to have but narrow limits. Our demands and our intentions are legitimate; they are constitutional and supported by history. They are also natural to human nature and, above all they are in accordance with God's will and creation."

While Tilak carried on his campaign against the "dependent philosophy and mendicant mentality of the Moderate Party", he never neglected the more dynamic aspect—fighting the people's apathy and indifference to their conquered status and poverty. He toured Maharashtra, besides visiting the provinces of Berar, Bengal, and the United Provinces, to rouse the people to boycott British goods and buy only Indian goods "even at a sacrifice". His speech at Pandharpur—one of the famous sacred places in Maharashtra—and another, addressed to the workers of Bombay, are particularly noteworthy. In them he expounded *Swadeshi* in the wider context of self-government. *Swadeshi,* he said, was a compound word—Swa means "my own" and Deshi means "belonging to country". His message, he explained, really meant that not only should the people buy home-made goods and boycott British goods but they should also demand a government of their own—a government by the people and for the people. "This subject of home-rule or *Swaraj* must be discussed from village to village," he told his audience. "The people must not keep quiet. All you people, workers and peasants, you must come forward boldly and declare that your condition under the present administration is most deplorable and unbearable. I know you have no weapons, but you do not need them; you have something else more powerful and effective than arms—it is the weapon of boycott. Refuse to buy British goods, and so teach them a lesson. And above all remember the country is ruled by the British because you co-operate with them. If you withhold your co-operation the administration must cease to function—I dare say it will collapse."

In his Bombay address to the workers he exhorted them not to allow themselves to be divided by the advice of self-interested people. "Do not heed those who tell you," he said, "that the *Swadeshi* movement is a sort of fad of the *Brahmans;* they tell you this to create caste hatred and differences amongst you. If you think for a moment, you will realize that the real benefactors of *Swadeshi* are yourselves, the workers in the country. Look at me. My clothes are of cloth made by you, the wages for which are earned by you, which means it is you who reap the direct benefit of the *Swadeshi* movement. The true meaning of *Swadeshi* is that there should be more and prosperous industries, in our country, so that you people can get more and better jobs and wages."

This homely and direct way of explaining the basic ideas of the New Party brought thousands of people under Tilak's banner and the party's popularity, prestige and power grew enormously.

In Bombay, Tilak set up the "Swadeshi co-operative stores" with the help of Sir Ratan Tata, Sir Manmohandas Ramji, and other influential Gujaratis, Bhatias and Marwaris. He also encouraged and gave a tremendous fillip to the Paisa Fund, a movement started in 1905 by a Mr. A.D. Kale. Tilak became its treasurer and he was proud to tell an audience in Bombay (February 10th, 1907) that the fund had risen from Rs. 2,000 to Rs. 8,000. Further research into the Indian glass industry and grants for technical study abroad by Indian students were two of the purposes for which the money was used. Financial help was also given to village weavers, and small cottage industries were promoted and encouraged. At the same time Tilak was also engaged in collecting funds towards the establishment of national schools, which he later developed into Samarth Vidyalaya of Talegaon.

Tilak's campaign, urging the people to buy Indian-made goods, naturally led to the encouragement of Indian industries. In *The New Spirit in India* Nevinson records the spread of Swadeshi in the following words: "Such was the movement which I found speeding up the eighty or ninety cotton mills in Bombay, because work as they might, they could not keep pace with the demand from Bengal... The movement was spreading to all kinds of merchandise besides cotton. In Calcutta they had started a *Swadeshi* match factory, in Dacca soap factory and tanneries. In all Indian towns you will now find *Swadeshi* shops where you may buy native biscuits, cigarettes, scents, toys, woollens, boots and all manner of things formerly imported. Nearly all the trade advertisements in Indian papers are now *Swadeshi*." The imports of British goods began to decline rapidly; during one month, May 1907, *The Times* of London reported, "Indian imports of Manchester piece goods declined by 42,492,500 yards".

Another important event of the year was the Indian visit of Keir Hardie, M.P., the founder of the Independent Labour Party. He came to Poona in October 1907, and was received by Tilak and forty prominent citizens. He paid a special visit to the *Kesari* office and later attended a reception in his honour organized by the Sarvajanik Sabha, at which he was presented with an address. The tone and the language of the address bore the unmistakable imprint of Tilak's personality and became the subject of comment in newspapers. In the address Tilak requested Keir Hardie to use his influence to convince the British electorate of the justice of the Indian demands, but also pointed out that the "New Party is not going to depend any longer on the Liberals or other political parties in England to achieve its objective of *Swaraj*. India has now adopted a programme of self-reliance and is confident of reaching her goal." The guest was very pleased with this refreshing note of self-help which was something different from the addresses he had received in Calcutta and elsewhere. In reply Keir Hardie said "My sympathies were always with India, but now they have grown a hundred-fold. I will call a special conference of the Labour Party and tell them all about you and your condition." When he returned to London he particularly remembered his visit to Shivapuri and other villages near Poona, made in the company of Tilak and N.C. Kelkar, for there he was able to get into direct touch with the villagers and learn something about the poverty of the peasants under the British Raj. Another vivid memory which stayed with him was of the close watch kept on him in Poona by the C.I.D.; it so enraged him that he publicly threatened to expose these "un-British" methods on his return to England.

This contact which Tilak made, through its founder, with the Labour Party of Britain was maintained throughout his political career. Later when he visited England in 1918, the Labour Party was one of the political groups which offered its co-operation to him in his home-rule agitation.

The Moderates for their part were not sitting idle all this while. In their own way they were busy intriguing and manoeuvring, finding ways and means of undermining the growing influence of Tilak. They were thoroughly disturbed by his popularity and prestige and the power of his propaganda, and became more determined than ever to thwart him.

Their determination to keep the Congress aloof from the ideology of the New Party first became apparent at Surat where the Bombay Provincial Conference was held at the end of March 1907, under the presidency of Sir Bhalachandra Krishna Bhatavadekar, a staunch Moderate and a blind follower of Mehta. His presidential speech was typical both in his servility to the Government and his resentment towards the New Party. He said, "Public workers must be honest; they must avoid ostentatiousness and devote themselves to truth. Petitions to the Government should be short and moderate in tone. The Government may be committing mistakes but they can be rectified only by rousing its sense of justice and sympathy. The present Government of India is liberal and reasonable. Not only this but in my view, we can hardly expect a better government for many years to come. Our efforts must be persistent but we must not spoil our cause by impatience and extremism." And all this when the Government was busy furbishing its armoury of repressive measures! Sir Bhalachandra refused to allow resolutions on *Swadeshi* and boycott to be moved and in justification of his action he said that an industrial and not a Provincial conference was the proper place for such resolutions.

Opposition to the New Party and its programme was shown at other conferences held under Moderate leadership. At Raipur, at the Provincial Conference of Nagpur and Berar, Rao Bahadur Mudholakar, the president, refused to allow the singing of *"Vande Mataram"*, a Bengali song which had attained the status of India's national anthem. The slogan "Moderation is our Motto" greeted the delegates as they entered the conference hall.

There was heated discussion on the resolutions for *Swadeshi* and boycott, but here again the President disallowed the resolutions. At the United Provinces Provincial Conference, held at Allahabad under Pandit Malaviya, the two parties again clashed. After the president had stopped two hundred delegates of the New Party from attending, the "rump" conference passed a few ineffectual resolutions. The conference itself was attended by a mere few scores of delegates, but outside the hall, Lajpat Rai, one of the leaders of the New Party, was able to draw audiences of ten thousand and more people. What was true of this conference was also true of conferences in Bengal and other provinces. The popular support was unmistakably for the New Party's programme which reflected the fighting spirit of the people. By contrast the speeches, the attitude and the resolutions of the Moderate Party were so mild and uninspiring that they could hardly claim to represent anybody except themselves.

For three decades prior to Gandhi's rise to political eminence, the myth of the Lokamanya, derived from the political career of Bal Gangadhar Tilak, was one of the most powerful political myths in India. Lokamanya (one who is revered by the people) stood for a more practical, pragmatic approach to politics and seemed to epitomize a more earthy and aggressive tradition. In a society that was undergoing rapid change, myth-making, or the cross-fertilization of myths, was a significant activity, whereby a leader defined his position in terms of the great epics, heroes and values of the past.[12]

Lokamanya Tilak has been acclaimed as the first Indian nationalist who bridged the gap between the elitist Indian National Congress and the more traditional masses. It has been argued that Tilak achieved his success for several reasons. A forceful and charismatic personality enabled him to epitomize the struggle for Indian independence and develop cadres of supporters who looked to their leader for inspiration. He linked the nationalist movement with religion and traditional heroes and succeeded in wooing orthodox leaders, peasants and artisans to the cause. He was an educated Indian who valued such modern ends as industrial progress and the establishment of a nation state, and he made use of modern techniques of propaganda, such as the press. Tilak has been acclaimed as a leader who could tap the forces of modern, traditional and charismatic authority.

Precisely because of these unique characteristics, historians have continued the process of the canonization of this "superhuman" politician. Tilak was the divine potter, the "Hercules and Prometheus of Modern India",[13] who fashioned mass movements out of the shapeless clay of inertia. He was the master strategist who welded the diverse elements of Indian society in the common struggle against the British. Specially, he succeeded in "tapping and bringing together the hitherto ignored urban and peasant lower classes" into the elitist Congress movement.[14] A brilliant tactician, he combined religion with politics, and tradition with modernity, and was thus able to bridge the gap between the westernised elites and the traditional masses. He was orthodox and yet in favour of reform; a spokesman of the *Brahman* community, he was revered also by the *non-Brahman* masses; he was an apologist for Hinduism, yet respected by people of other religions.[15]

Tilak knew that once the spiritual and religious springs of India's great past were revitalized, the greatness and glory of Her future were assured. To him, India seemed to have a character, a tradition, a personality. What mattered to him was the preservation of those-ways of living which are peculiar to India, through which alone, he said, she could rediscover her soul, her strength and attain her emancipation.

Tilak did not belong to the category of those political philosophers who had visualised the picture of a perfect political society, its features or possibilities. His political thinking narrowed down to a single problem, namely, the political emancipation of his country. Hence, his ideas were dominated by an element of great realism as the term "responsive" or "conditional" cooperation to the government implied. That is why Hugh Tinker writes that the national movement in India has been distinguished from almost every other search for independence and national identity by the quality of the intellectual debate which went on among the political leaders about the nature of freedom, the character of nationhood, and the obligations of individuals to society, more because of the intimate association of religion with politics.[16]

Although Tilak was a national figure who epitomized the Indian struggle against the British in his days, he was primarily a Maharashtrian politician deeply imbued with the cultural traditions of the region. His influence at the national level was based on a sizeable local following achieved by the development of a style of politics in harmony with the religion. Tilak was the embodiment of the spirit and character of his own Maharatha race, 'rugged, strong and sturdy people, democratic in their very fibre, keenly intelligent and practical to the very marrow; following in ideas, the drive towards life and action; capable of great fervour but not emotional idealists. To these qualities, he added the lucid simplicity of genius, intensity of purpose, and an inner strength based on conviction.

On the personal front, Tilak was a Vedantist—a believer in the 'advaita' philosophy. His concept of freedom as man's natural or birth-right was based on the non-dualism of the *Vedanta.* According to it, all men are portions or aspects of the Absolute and hence all have the same autonomous spiritual potentiality. *Vedanta* philosophy therefore, made him an uncompromising champion of freedom. "Freedom was the soul of the Home Rule Movement", he said. "The divine instinct of freedom never aged. Freedom is the very life of the individual soul which Vedanta declares to be not separate from God, but identical with him. This freedom was a principle that could not perish." Tilak's treatment of freedom as a divine attribute gave a philosophical foundation to the political struggle for liberty in which he was engaged. *Vedanta* not only formed the source of an urge for freedom; it also provided the necessary justification for its attainment as well. In Tilak's case, however, he relied, to a large extent, on his own interpretation of the religious texts to provide his political methods with a philosophical basis. He firmly believed that "the canons of interpretations of a text are no less important than the text itself, and the real mischief arises from not constructing the text in this respect as it should be."[17]

Tilak shaped his ethical formula on the premise that "in finally deciding questions of ethics, one has to pay more special attention to the pureness of the Reason of the doer, than to the external result of his Actions." This brought him to the following conclusion: "If the Reason is sinful, the Action will be sinful; but, from the fact that the external Action is bad, one cannot draw the conclusion that the Reason also must be bad; because that act may have been performed by mistake, or as a result of a misunderstanding, or as a result of ignorance; and in these cases it cannot be said to be ethically sinful.[18] According to this interpretation, it was the motive rather than action itself which determined sinfulness. Applying this formula, Tilak could justify even political assassinations such as those committed by the Chapekar brothers[19] and the Bengal terrorists. They believed that they were performing a beneficient act, rather than an act of personal vendetta or revenge.

As a child, Tilak learnt the values of the *Bharatdharma* in his home at Ratnagiri. His father was an educator, and he carefully tutored the boy in Sanskrit and Mathematics. Little is known about Tilak's mother, except that she was a devout and religious woman, who died in 1866 when Tilak was just ten years old. However, T.L. Shay opines that his mother helped Tilak mould his firm character and taught him the values of his classical heritage.[20] From both parents he learnt a healthy veneration for spiritual values, and he shared the history of the Marathas, in that he was heir to a glorious martial tradition. His religious or spiritual orientation, the product of his family's devoutness, was apparent in his later writings, as when he wrote, "The greatest virtue of Man is to be filled with wonder and devotion by anything in the animate and inanimate creation that suggests inherent divinity."[21] He also made continuous reference to the great Shivaji and the history of his Maratha people, the fiery tradition of their independence, their war against the Mughal Empire to restore *Swaraj* and to save the *Dharma*. Thus, from his childhood, he inherited a vision of a new India arising, firmly based on the spirit and traditions of Her civilization and Her glorious past.

The early phase of Tilak's life was devoted to educational and journalistic activities. He, alongwith Agarkar, joined Chiplunkar in his mission to mould the youth of the country. The New English School was opend on January 1, 1880 by Vishnushastri Chiplunkar in partnership with Tilak, Agarkar and Namjoshi. "No school through the length and breadth of India perhaps can boast of a group of founders of such great personality. The rejuvenation of the land of their birth was their goal and they looked upon education, properly conceived and properly conducted, as the surest way leading to it."[22] The cardinal aim of the founders was to make education as inexpensive as possible because the mass of the people were very poor. But they took care to see that cheapness was not achieved at the expense of efficiency. Although men like Chiplunkar and Tilak were deeply religious, they made no provision for moral and religious instruction. Sectarian and denominational appeal had no place in the minds of the founders, who worked on a perfectly secular basis. Breathing and living patriotism, they hoped to mould the characters of their pupils by their own examples. They had not merely opened a school for teaching students: they had started a new school of thought, a new way of life.[23]

The political events of the last decade of the nineteenth century, marked by the British atrocities, fired Tilak's imagination by the idea of an armed revolution to throw off the British rule. But he soon realised the futility of following such a course without first enlisting the people's support. Tilak was too profound a student of history not to appreciate that abortive revolutions did more harm than good to a cause, for such a setback creates despondency and inertia which are not easy to dispel. A revolution is the physical expression of the inner drive towards radical change. In 1880, this drive towards change was becoming evident in the academic discussions of the educated, but its faint echoes reached no further than the drawing rooms of the intelligentsia of India as they were few. Outside these narrow limits there was no contact with—and therefore no hope of response from—the Indian people as a whole. Tilak therefore believed that a renaissance movement was absolutely necessary before a revolution could be thought of.

The other important area in which Tilak involved himself was journalism. Tilak was convinced that the newspaper, like the progress of education, could be a big factor in promoting political awakening among the people. From his student days, he had seen how Anglo-Indian newspapers and journals were serving as a useful medium of support for the colonial rule, and had a pronounced imperialist bias. The national newspapers, excepting a few in Calcutta, were struggling for existence, and although Poona had several newspapers, none of them was performing that function which Tilak and his associates wanted an Indian newspaper to perform at that time.[24]

It was in order to lay the corner-stone of a future revolution that Tilak and his co-workers decided to launch two newspapers, the *'Kesari'*, published in Marathi, and the *Mahratta* in English. They wanted these weeklies to act as an instrument of enlightenment, and the prospectus of the *Kesari,* published in October 1880 stated, "The evils of flunkeyism and flattery have been growing since the beginning of the Imperial rule and surely every honest man will admit that these are harmful to the true interests of our country."[25]

Kesari was to cater to the need of "the mass of ignorant population, who have generally no idea of what passes around them and who therefore must be given the knowledge of such topics as concern their everyday life by writings on literary, social, political, moral and economic subjects." The *Mahratta*, on the other hand, kept in view "the more advanced portion of the community, who require to be provided with material for thinking intelligently on the important topics of the day."[26] One of the *'Mahratta'* articles, urging education of the people in a spirit of nationalism as the main requisite for attaining the desired political goal, subsequently became one of the guiding ideas of Tilak's whole social and political activity.[27]

In the meantime, two other significant developments had occurred. The first was that Tilak had entered the lists of public debate and activity on matters of social, religious and educational reform through the Deccan Education Society; the second was his involvement in political life. With regard to the first, the major reform issues of Tilak's time concerned with such subjects as female education, the age of female consent in marriage, and widow's rights. The details of his arguments against such reforms are less important here than is the basic position from which Tilak advanced these arguments. Fundamentally, he opposed any reforms that might be imposed upon the Hindu community by British law. He claimed that he did not resist reform *per se,* only that it should arise in conformity with *Dharmasastra,* out of an educated Hindu community. Thus religious, social and educational reform proposals were to be judged in the light of Hindu religious tradition. Furthermore, Tilak's knowledge of Hindu scriptures enabled him to argue authoritatively on the relative merits of existing practices and demerits of proposed reforms. This attitude won him the support of much of the orthodox Hindu community which felt threatened by various reform proposals. He became not only the defender of the tradition, but also a leader in the counter-attack against foreign interference. However, Tilak's opposition on many religious grounds seemed a cynical exercise in political opportunism.[28]

Nonetheless, Tilak prepared the ground for his organisation and directed his attention to the work of bolstering the Hindu ego, and enhancing his own prestige among his orthodox compatriots. He was able to further these aims simultaneously by writing his first book, *'The Orion,'* subtitled *"Researches into the Antiquity of the Vedas"*, in 1893. The estimate of Vedic antiquity then generally current amongst Vedic scholars was based on the assignment of arbitrary period of time to the different strata into which the Vedic literature is divided; and it was believed that the oldest of these strata could not, at the best, be older than 2400 B.C. In *'The Orion'*, Tilak tried to show that all such estimates, besides being too modest, were vague and uncertain, and that the astronomical statements found in the Vedic literature supplied far more reliable data for correctly ascertaining the ages of the different periods of Vedic literature. Even Max Muller argued that "for a study of man, or, if you like, for a study of Aryan humanity, there is nothing in the world equal in importance with the *Veda*."[30] Tilak argued that the hymns of the *Rigveda* before 4000 B.C. In support of his theory Tilak cited old traditions of the Parsees and the Greeks which are strikingly similar to traditions mentioned in the oldest Vedic works; in particular he infered from the Greek legend of Orion (the name Orion has the same root as the Greek word for "beginning") that these legends arose during the period before the Greeks separated from the Hindus.

Tilak's theory, which put the antiquity of the *Vedas*–therefore the antiquity of the Aryan civilization–back to 4000-5000 B.C. startled the western world. But the masterly way in which he argued his case and the weight of evidence he produced in support of his theory forced many sceptical spirits to admit that the theory was substantially sound and must therefore be reckoned with. Eminent scholars in Europe and America praised Tilak's work highly—Max Muller, Jacobi, and Weber were particularly appreciative of the author's learning and originality. Dr. Bloomfield of John Hopkins University in an anniversary address spoke of Tilak's book as "un-questionably the literary sensation of the year. History, the chronic readjuster, will have her hands uncommonly full to assimilate the results of Tilak's dicovery and arrange her paraphernalia in the new perspective". He has recorded his reactions on receiving *Orion*. He glanced through the introduction, where Tilak "blandly informs us that the age of the *Rigveda* cannot be less than 4000 B.C. and that the express records of the early Hindu antiquity point back to 6000 B.C. Having in mind the boundless fancy of the Hindu through the ages and his particularly fatal facility for 'taking his mouthful' when it comes to a question of numbers, I proposed to myself to continue to turn the leaves of the book with the amused smile of orthodoxy befitting the occasion. But soon the amused smile gave way to an uneasy sense that something unusual had happened. I was first impressed with something leonine in the way in which the author controlled the Vedic literature and the occidental works on the subject; my superficial reading soon gave way to absorbed study and finally, having been prepared to scoff mildly, I confess that the author had convinced me in all the essential points.

In this second work, *The Arctic Home in the Vedas*, Tilak used geological analysis to locate the original and civilized Aryans in the northern polar regions prior to 8,000 B.C. His conclusions were based on his Vedic research, supported by recent discoveries in geology and archaeology. The arctic regions, though now desolate and unfit for human habitation, enjoyed, before the glacial epoch, a mild and temperate climate. There are references in the *Vedas* to astronomical phenomena peculiar to the North Pole such as night and day each of six months duration. On the hypothesis of a long night of six months, Tilak lucidly explains the anxious wait for the dawn and the rapturous utterances upon its arrival. Corroborative evidence from the *Zendavesta*, the sacred book of the Parsees, is also cited.

The principal theme of *The Arctic Home in the Vedas* can be stated in Tilak's own words: "The beginnings of Aryan civilization must be supposed to date back several thousand years before the oldest Vedic period; and when the commencement of the post-glacial epoch is brought down to 8000 B.C. it is not at all surprising if the date of primitive Aryan life is found to go back to it from 4500 B.C., the age of the oldest Vedic period. In fact, it is the main point which the present volume seeks to establish. There are many passages in the *Rigveda*, which, though hitherto looked upon as obscure and unintelligible, do, when interpreted in the light of recent scientific researches, plainly disclose the Polar attributes of the Vedic deities, or the traces of an ancient Arctic calendar; while the *Avesta* expressly tells us that the happy land of *Airyana Vaejo*, or the Aryan Paradise, was located in a region where the sun shone but once a year, and that it was destroyed by the invasion of snow and ice, which rendered its climate inclement and necessitated a migration southward. These are plain and simple statements, and when we put them side by side with what we know of the glacial and the post-glacial epochs from the latest geological researches we cannot avoid the conclusion that the primitive Aryan home was both Arctic and inter-glacial."

Tilak's theory about the Arctic home of the Aryans was so startling in its nature that it did not gain easy acceptance by scholars, though it was acknowledged that he had made out a strong case. The most important testimony came from Dr. F.W. Warren, author of *Paradise Found* and President of Boston University, who wrote in the *Open Court Magazine* of Chicago: "In the judgement of the present writer the array of evidence set forth is far more conclusive than any ever attempted by an Indo-Iranian scholar in the interests of any earlier hypothesis. Absolute candour and respect for the strictest methods of historical and scientific investigation characterize the discussion throughout. This results in part, no doubt, from the fact that the author's own attitude of mind was at the outset highly sceptical. He says: 'I did not start with any preconceived notion in favour of the Arctic theory;nay, I regarded it as highly improbable at first; but the accumulating evidence in its support eventually forced me to accept it." Dr. Warren concludes: "It is hard to see how any candid mind can master the proof produced without being mastered by it in turn. Whoever will master this new work, and that of the late Mr. John O' Neill on *The Night of the Gods* will not be likely ever again ask,.where was the earliest home of the Aryans?"

Orion and *The Arctic Home in the Vedas* established Tilak's reputation as a scholar with an unusual insight and understanding of Vedic literature, and many Orientalists expressed the hope that he would continue his work of unravelling mankind's past and add to the stock of knowledge on subjects which can be tackled only by men of his calibre and breadth of vision. Whether or not his theories about the antiquity of the Vedas and the original home of the Aryan race stand up to the test of time and scientific research, there can be no two opinions that his writings have influenced and helped the course of Indo-Indian research and opened new, wide vistas in this field. It is a tribute to Tilak's work that so far no scholar of eminence has made any serious attempt to refute his conclusions; this suggests that, on the evidence and data at present available Tilak has said the last word.

Tilak's other contributions in the same field are his essays on *Vedang Jyotish,* or Vedic chronology and calendar calculations in the *Vedas.*

These books were written and published in English and consequently attracted the attention of the outside world. Curiously enough, *Orion* and its sequel *The Arctic Home in the Vedas* would probably have never been written but for Tilak's study of the *Gita.* In the preface to *Orion* he mentions that the words "Màsànàm Màrgasirso' ham" in the *Gita* first led him to Vedic research which in turn yielded the vital discovery that *Mrigasirsa* in the *Rigveda* and the *Orion* of Greek legend were the same. Having stumbled on this valuable clue, Tilak's ever-questing mind dug deeper still into the *Vedas* and discovered the Arctic Home of the Aryans. It has been suggested that these works achieved the practical goal of providing Hindus with an ancestry that placed them second to no culture or civilization. After all, Tilak's one and only aim was the political emancipation of the nation through mass-mobilization by psychologically uniting them on the platform of religion. The secret of Tilak's hold on the masses lay in his deeply-held respect for the religion of his forefathers. All that was ancient and truly noble in the Hindu tradition was sacred to him. Indeed, his profound reverence for and knowledge of the *Vedas* were his sheet-anchor amid all the social and religious upheavals of his day, which only too easily became tempestuous storms at the slightest change in the atmosphere.

In the meantime, because many of the issues that concerned Tilak and on which he had expressed himself in *Mahratta* and in his reform activities, had clear political implications; they marked Tilak's formal entry into politics. *Swaraj* was the most obvious of these. It was inevitable then that Tilak should move into the field where he could apply direct action towards the realization of his objectives. In 1889, he participated in the meeting of the Bombay Provincial Conference of the Indian National Congress. He was elected a delegate to the meeting of the Congress itself in the same year, and so began the political involvement that was to last the rest of his life.

From this time onwards, there is constant evidence of Tilak's endeavours to awaken in India, feelings of pride and self-sufficiency in her ancient culture and traditions, and to build on these feelings a pragmatic political programme. As Aurobindo Ghose said, "To bring in the mass of the people, to found the greatness of the future on the greatness of the past, to infuse Indian politics with Indian religious fervour and spirituality, are the indispensable conditions for a great and powerful political awakening in India. Others—writers, thinkers, spiritual leaders—had seen this truth. Tilak was the first to bring it into the actual field of practical politics.[31]

A brief examination of some of this evidence will help illustrate the role played by Tilak's work on the *Bhagavadgita*. The *Bhagavadgita* is perhaps the strongest and most comprehensive production of Indian spirituality and justifies to that spirituality by its own authoritative ancient message, the sense of the importance of life, of action, of human existence, of man's labour for mankind which is indispensable to the idealism of the modern spirit. But, where, in all the political activity does the *Gita* fit in? Perhaps in Tilak's creed and testament: "I regard India as my motherland and my Goddess, the people in India are my kith and kin, and loyal and steadfast work for their political and social emancipation my highest religion and duty."[32]

By Tilak's own account, as a boy, he was often told by his elders that a strictly religious and really philosophic life was incompatible with the hum-drum life of every day. If one was ambitious enough to try to attain *Moksha,* the highest goal a person could attain, then he must divest himself of all earthly desires and renounce this world. One could not serve two masters, the world and God. [33] Tilak understood this to mean that if one would lead a life which was the life worth living, according to the religion in which he was born, then the sooner the world was given up the better. This set him thinking. The question that he formulated for himself to be evolved was: "Does my religion want me to give up this world and renounce it before I attempt to, or in order to be able to, attain the perfection of manhood?" In his boyhood, Tilak was also told that the *Bhagavadgita* was universally acknowledged to be a book containing all the principles and philosophy of the Hindu religion, and he thought, if this be so he should find an answer in this book to his query; and thus began his study of the *Bhagavadgita.*[34]

Tilak approached the book with a mind prepossessed by no previous idea about any philosophy, and had no theory of his own for which he sought any support in the *Gita.* A person whose mind is prepossessed by certain ideas reads the book with a prejudiced mind. Tilak dealt with this topic in his book, *Gita Rahasya.*[35] He emphasized that if one wants to read and understand a book, especially a great work like the Gita, one must approach it with an unprejudiced and unprepossessed mind. Also, one must take into consideration the time and the circumstances in which the book has been written. In short, the book must not be read devoid of its context.

Tilak wrote the *Gita Rahasya* in 1910 in 108 days (although he was not able to publish it until June, 1915 when he came out of jail). The conclusion he reached after a prolonged study was that the Gita "advocates the performance of Action in this world even after the actor has achieved his union with the Supreme Spirit by knowledge or devotion and that Action is necessary to keep the world moving along the right path of evolution, which the Creator has destined the world to follow."

Tilak started his study of the Gita to find an answer to the problem whether it was necessary to renounce the world in order to attain divine bliss and peace. In search of a solution he read all the learned expositions of the *Gita* both from the East and the West but got no satisfaction from any of them. He found that the various commentators had all approached the *Gita* with preconceived ideas: "They do not want to know what the *Gita* says but want to find out if there are any principles in the *Gita* which will support their own pet theories or ideas." Tilak discarded them all and approached the book with an open mind, "prepossessed by no previous ideas about any system of philosophy" as he had no theory of his own for which he sought support in the *Gita*. This scrupulously objective approach led him to the conclusion that the main theme of the Gita was the Activist philosophy of life. In the *Gita Rahasya* he has exhaustively examined the various philosophical systems propounded by Socrates, Plato and Aristotle in ancient Greece, and Mill, Bentham, Green, Spencer, Comte, Kant, Nietzsche, Schopenhauer and others in the modern world.

He compares them with the great philosophies of the East: those of Buddha, Shankar and Ramanuja in India and that of Confucius in China; and all of them to the ethical and metaphysical principles embodied in the *Gita*.

He did not blindly accept what was already established; nor did he slavishly adhered to authorities, either Western or Eastern, in the interpretation and exposition of the Gita. A rigid rationalist by conviction, he applied a simple but convincing test to prove his theory. The test which he applied to the *Gita* was to examine its beginning and its end. The *Gita* begins with the arrival of Arjuna on the battlefield to fight the enemy. At the crucial moment he is assailed by doubts and perplexities as to his duty, and is plunged into confusion and dejection. On the one hand the religion of the warrior was bidding him, "Fight!" and on the other hand, devotion to his teachers, love for his relatives and other natural bonds were holding him back. If he fought he would be killing his own kith and kin; if he did not he would be failing in his duty as a warrior. The strain of making the decision proves too great for him. He becomes faint, the bow drops from his hand and he falls to the ground, crying, "I shall not fight! It would be better for me to be a beggar, crying for feed to stay my hunger, than to win the kingdom by committing such terrible sins as killing my own relatives and wiping out the whole clan. It does not matter if my enemies, seeing me unarmed at this moment, come and kill me; I do not wish to enjoy a happiness which is steeped in the blood of my brethren killed in warfare and burdened with their curses. It is true that it is my duty to follow the warrior religion, but if on that account I have to commit such terrible sins as killing my own people then let the warrior-religion and the warrior-morality go to perdition". With his conscience disturbed by these problems and uncertain as to his duty, he surrenders to Sri Krishna and begs him to show him the right path—"I am your pupil, please guide me." Sri Krishna counsels Arjuna what to do; and the confused warrior throws off his depression, takes up his bow, fights the enemy and wins the battle.

The *Gita* is the discourse between Arjuna and Sri Krishna. It ranges widely over the spiritual, moral and metaphysical aspects of life, leading to man's ultimate development and fulfilment in unity with God. It deals with man and his place in the cosmos; his duty to his fellow beings; the right and wrong approach to creation around him; the consideration of the forces of good and evil; the principle of *Lokasamgraha,* or the greatest good of the greatest number; violence and non-violence; truth and untruth—absolute and conditional; meritorious and sinful conduct; and a whole host of bewilderingly complex and intricate relationships which man must enter into in his mortal existence and their effect on his life hereafter. The sum total of this philosophical discourse is to impress upon Arjuna the importance of so conducting himself in this world that he can ultimately reach the highest stage of human development and become one with *Brahman* or the Supreme Spirit. Sri Krishna expounds three ways of reaching this stage of perfection; by knowledge through meditation, through devotion, and through the performance of one's duty. All the paths are of equal importance and value in the spiritual development of man and any one of them will enable him to reach the final stage of *Moksha* (freedom from worldly bondage) and the state of eternal, true bliss.

Tilak accepts all this. The main—and fundamental—difference between him and other commentators on the interpretation of the *Gita* lies in the answer to this question: Is a person who has attained the highest state of perfection by following any one of the ways, under an obligation to work for the world? Great philosophers and thinkers like Shankar and Ramanuja have maintained that a liberated soul (Muktàmà) has no need to perform any worldly deeds. They hold that man's highest duty is to himself, namely to strive for spiritual development, which would lead him to the fulfilment of his union with the *Brahman*. Once that union or oneness is attained he is free from all obligations. This is the doctrine of *Sanyas* or complete renunciation. Tilak maintains that this doctrine is contrary to the fundamental concept and origin of the cosmos which is willed into existence by the *Brahman*. Action or Duty is part of the Divine Will and the liberated soul cannot escape it. There is a vital difference, however, between the Action of an unliberated soul and the Action of liberated soul. The first is actuated by worldly desires and is attached to the fruits of his Action which may lead to possession, greed, anger, hatred and conflict. The Action of the second is pure, performed in a spirit of dedication and therefore without desire and attachment to the fruits of Action. His Action is not undertaken for his own benefit but solely to fulfil the Divine Will, the primeval Energy which is the cause as well as the effect of the cosmos.

This conclusion differs from almost all other commentators, who have given their judgement in favour of complete inaction once the individual has attained *Moksha* (freedom from worldly bondage) and unity with the Eternal Spirit. Tilak believes: "There is a fundamental unity undelying the Logos, Man, and the World. The world exists and continues to exist because the Logos has willed it so. It is His Will that holds it together. Man strives to gain union with God; and when this union is achieved, the individual will merges in the Universal Will." If man seeks unity with God he must necessarily seek unity with the world around him and work for it. If he does not, then his unity with God is imperfect, "because there is union only between two elements (Man and God) out of three, the third element—the World—being left out. And no unity is perfect except the unity of the fundamental trinity." He declares: "I have thus solved the question for myself and I hold that serving the World and thus serving His Will, is the surest way of salvation, which can be achieved by remaining in the World and not going away from it."

The whole setting and tenor of the *Gita* supports Tilak's view. As a result of Sri Krishna's teaching Arjuna does not retire to the woods to contemplate the Eternal but goes into action. The message of *Gita* enables him to realize that it is not action that is forbidden but interested action. It is wrong to shrink from one's appointed duty, afraid of the consequences. "The *Gita* asks us to work in imitation of the Lord, for the purpose of *Lokasamgraha* or the greatest good of the greatest number—the unification of humanity in universal sympathy. The *Gita* is designed to provide a solution to all human problems. It reconciles and harmonizes spiritual freedom with work in the world."

This activist philosophy of the *Gita,* Tilak not only preached but practised throughout his life. His bold stand against making wisdom or *Jnana* an end in itself and, instead, establishing the supremacy of *Karma,* or Action, over all other forms of Divine worship provides a novel theme in philosophy and has profoundly influenced eminent thinkers in India. Whether the author of the *Gita Rahasya* had meant it or not, his message has given young India a new ideal to work for, the ideal of selfless and disinterested service to humanity.

Tilak commented that the *Gita* advocates the performance of action in this world even after the actor has achieved the highest union with the supreme Deity by *Gyana* (Knowledge) or *Bhakti* (devotion). This action must be done to keep the world going by the right path of evolution which the creator has destined the world to follow. In order that the action may not bind the actor, it must be done with the aim of helping his purpose, and without any attachment to the coming result. Tilak held this to be the lesson of *Gita*. There is both, the *Gyanayoga* and the *Bhaktiyoga*, but they are both subservient to the *Karmayoga*.[36]

The independent, impartial conclusion reached by Tilak was that the *Gita* teaches the philosophy of Energism or *Karmayoga*. *Karma*, according to Tilak, includes all conceivable actions of the human being—physical, mental, social, vocational, religious, secular, and so forth; all action in the animate and inanimate world; even the mere fact of being alive.[37] Apart from this, Tilak remained most concerned, however, to refute any interpretation that encouraged the *gyanayogis* to give up worldly life and renounce all action. Furthermore, Tilak also alleged that there was a fundamental flaw in the doctrine that supposedly demands the renunciation of action when it is not possible to do so while alive. He claimed that the *Gita* solves this problem by revising the concept of renunciation in the light of its doctrine of action. With this interpretation, Tilak held that in the *Gita* there is no real difference between *true sanyasa* and *Karmayoga*.[38]

The discussion of *Gita Rahasya* was intended to show that the text appealed personally to Tilak, and that it also suited the cause of religious nationalism that he espoused. Gita was an ideal text with which Hindus could identify and in which they could base and legitimize their religious and political aspirations. Tilak was always legalistic in his attitude towards religion. Tilak's approach to religion was fashioned by his rationalist and activist outlook. His approach to the Hindu tradition was "frequently analytic emphasizing praxis, the formal and behavioural side of religion." By contrast, Ranade and Gandhi were more attuned to emotional religion, the religion of the heart, *bhakti*. Thus the terms "orthodoxy" and resuscitation of tradition" had different meanings for them.[39]

A greater part of Tilak's success as a politician was due to his ability to play a mixed role and speak in different social and religious terms to various groups. Thus, in 1891, when he was wooing the orthodox party, he spoke in traditional language; at other times he was a spokesman for reform and modernity. In 1893, following the communal riots, he spoke in a Hindu voice, whereas at other times he wooed the non-Hindus.

It would be important to mention here that Tilak was dubbed anti-Muslim because he stood up for the Hindu community when the Muslims in Poona and other cities caused riots by attacking Hindu temples and processions. Serious disturbances took place in Bombay and Poona in 1893 and 1894, and resulted in the death of nearly seventy-five people and serious injury to three hundred others. From the outset, Tilak pointed out that there were three, and not two, parties concerned in the Hindu-Muslim disputes: the Hindus, the Muslims and the foreign government. Until and unless the government was prepared to hold the balance and act impartially, the two communities were bound to feel unsure about their position.

Tilak strongly criticised the Government's partiality to the Muslims, and he accused it of practising the policy of "divide and rule", and exposed the hollowness of the Government's appeal to the leaders of the two communities for conciliation. Tilak declared that the real dispute was not between the educated leaders of the two communities: but that it was found among the uneducated and the illiterate. If such people were to be kept under control, the Government ought to abandon the policy of favouring one at the cost of the other. The rigours of law were to be applied to both equally and impartially.

The year 1916 was the most eventful year in Tilak's career. The early part of the year saw the foundation of the Home Rule League, its phenomenal success, the presentation of the public purse on Tilak's sixty-first birthday, and his legal victory in the last sedition trial. In the second half of the year, comes the session of the Lucknow Congress, which marked the zenith not only of Tilak's life, but also, perhaps, of the history of the Congress, an organization which only twelve months before, at Madras, was at its lowest ebb with an attendance of barely a few hundred delegates.

Tilak, who had previously borne a reputation for intransigence in politics, appeared in the role of a constructive and conciliatory statesman. The days of fiery speeches and denunciations were over; a new phase of compromise and responsive co-operation began. He was seen at his best at the Lucknow Congress which marked a definite stage in political evolution of India.

From the Surat split until the Lucknow session the Indian National Congress was completely controlled by the Moderates, who, true to their reformist attitude, limited its activities to meeting once a year and passing resolutions on such subjects as: Improvements in the Council Regulations; the creation of Executive Councils in the United Provinces and the Punjab; the prevention of the extension of communal representation to local bodies; the abolition of the system of indentured labour and the removal of intolerable restrictions and humiliating conditions imposed on Indians in South Africa.

The net result of the Congress action up to the end of 1916 may be summed up as virtually nil. The Congress was unable to secure any material improvement in the condition of Indians; the Council Regulations remained unchanged; the United Provinces and Punjab were still without Executive Councils; the principle of communal representation had been extended to municipal bodies—at least in one province; the Secretary of State for India's Council continued to function as before; the Press Act was still on the Statute Book and continued to strangle public opinion in the country by inflicting heavy penalties on the Nationalist section of the Press; the Arms Act remained unaltered. In one word, the Congress resolutions had proved utterly ineffectual. The only exception to this otherwise dismal record was the acceptance by the Government of the demand for the abolition of the system whereby, for over seventy-five years, indentured labour had been exported to the Crown Colonies. On the other hand, however, the Government of India showed little interest in the humiliating treatment meted out to Indian Nationals in South Africa. Such was the depressing balance sheet of Congress achievements up till 1916, when once again it met at Lucknow under the presidency of the Moderate leader Amvika Charan Mazumdar.

But all this changed after the Lucknow session. The Congress ceased to be a merely deliberate body and became an active agitational organization and devoted its entire time to making the people conscious of their political rights and responsibilities.

Earlier in the year the Government of India prepared a dispatch to the Secretary of State in which a number of reforms were suggested. This struck Tilak as a good opportunity to put the public view-point before the Secretary of State through the medium of the non-official members of the Central Legislative Assembly. At his urging, Jinnah and other members prepared a memorandum demanding council reform, which was signed by all nineteen non-official members of the Legislative Assembly.

This was the first united demand for *Swaraj*, the first occasion when Muslims and Hindus, Moderates and Extremists, Parsees and others spoke together with one voice to demand vital reforms.

Tilak took care to see that all the members spoke with one voice. His success prepared the ground for the triumphal session of the Congress at Lucknow, for Jinnah was, so to say, already committed to sign the Congress League scheme, at Lucknow.

Tilak travelled to Lucknow with more than 300 delegates in a special train – the "Home Rule Special" – arranged by two of his followers, Dr. D.D. Sathe and Dr. Velkar. He left Bombay on December 26th and newspaper correspondents have given a vivid description of how he was honoured, garlanded and wildly cheered all along the route. Previously he was respected for his learning, worshipped for his saintly character, and admired for his courage; now in 1916 he had become the apostle of national liberation and thousands of people, young and old, wanted to catch a glimpse of him. They waited for the special train in the cold, and in pouring rain. His long years of suffering for the country had raised his reputation all over India to the point where he was the people's guide and philosopher.

When the special train reached Lucknow it was met by the city leaders and by thousands of admiring men and women. Their enthusiasm knew no bounds; they besieged Tilak's car, showering lilies and roses on him and offering countless bouquets and garlands. Carried away by their enthusiasm, the people purposely punctured the tyres of his car and bore him off to a carriage which they drew through the streets of the city, shouting his slogan – "*Swaraj* is my Birthright and I shall have It." It took a full three hours for the procession to reach Chedilal Dharmshala – where Tilak was staying during the Lucknow session – a fine airy building with a large quadrangle which became, as it were, a temple for the Nationalists and the Lucknow people alike.

On December 28th the Congress opened and the ovation Tilak received was, according to a contemporary account, beyond description. His appearance on the Congress platform had a tremendous effect—it changed the whole atmosphere. The long-felt sense of frustration gave place to a feeling of hope and buoyancy.

Tilak spoke on the main resolution on self-government and in acknowledgement of the tremendous reception which he received on rising to address the meeting he said: "I am overwhelmed by the warmth of your reception and I feel deeply grateful to you for it. However, allow me to say that your reception is really more for the principles I have been fighting for all these years than for me personally. The resolution which I wish to support embodies all those principles, it is the resolution on self-government."

Explaining the resolution, he went on, "It may not be *Swaraj* in the widest sense of the word but it is far better than *Swadeshi* and boycott. It is in fact a synthesis of all the Congress resolutions passed during the past thirty years—a synthesis that will help us all to proceed to work in a definite and responsible manner. We cannot now afford to spend our energy on all thirty resolutions—public service resolutions, Arms Act and sundry others. All that is included in this one resolution on self-government, and I would ask every one of you to try to carry out this resolution with all your effort, might and enthusiasm."

On the question of Muslim representation in the Central and Provincial Councils he was more than generous, He declared, "It has been said by some that we Hindus have yielded too much to our Mohammedan brothers. I am sure I express the feelings of the Hindu community all over India when I say that we could not have yielded too much. I would not care if the rights of self-government are granted to the Mohammedan community only. I would not care if they are granted to the Rajputs. I would not care if they are granted to the lower and the lowest classes of the Hindu population, provided the British Government considers them more fit than the educated classes of India for exercising those rights. I would not care if those rights are granted to any section of the Indian community. The fight then will be between them and the other sections of the community and not, as at present, a triangular fight. When we have to fight against a third party, it is a very important thing that we stand on this platform united; united in race, unite in religion, united as regards all different shades of political creed. That is the most important event of the day."

It is no secret that but for Tilak's presence, his towering personality and the great prestige he commanded, the Congress would never have accepted the communal part of the resolution.

In the first place, all were agreed that the separate representation of Mohammedans was a dangerous principle. Then again, even if this principle were conceded, it would be a ticklish question to decide what proportion of the total of representatives should be Mohammedans. The United Provinces were adamant in refusing separate representation to the Muslims, but after a heated debate a separate electorate was accepted, though only as a special measure and under special circumstances. But nobody was prepared to accept the Mohammedan demand for half the total representation. Finally Tilak prevailed upon Pandit Madan Mohan Malaviya and Jinnah, the leaders of the opposing groups, to come to an understanding rather than wreck the scheme on the question of details. He argued that it would be disgraceful for educated Indians not to be able to arrive at a settlement at a time when it was admitted by all that the demand for self-government should be made with one voice. His appeal did not fall on deaf ears, and the Hindu and Muslim leaders agreed to submit to his wisdom and judgment.

It is rightly claimed by Tilak's followers and admirers that the Hindu-Muslim unity which he achieved at Lucknow was the crowning event of his career. It is true that he displeased a few Hindu leaders, but certainly he captured the hearts of the Mohammedans, and this became evident when on December 31st he attended the session of the Muslim League, where he was accorded the warmest reception and the grandest ovation. The great Muslim leader, Dr. Ansari, who became Mahatma Gandhi's right-hand man in later years and was present at the Lucknow Congress, writes: "During the course of conversations between the Congress leaders, chief amongst whom were Amvika Charan Mazumdar, the Congress President, Surendranath Bannerjee, Madan Mohan Malaviya, Mrs. Annie Besant and Lokamanya Tilak, and the leaders of the Muslim League, consisting of Mohamed Ali Jinnah, President of the League, Mazarul Haq and the Rajah of Mahmudabad, Tilak's part was always notable for the liberality and magnanimity towards the Muslims. It may be asserted without any doubt that his generous gesture was a great factor in winning over the Mussulmans and in inducing them to accept the proposals which form the Lucknow Pact. The introductory portion of his speech, when proposing the resolution embodying the pact in the open session of the Congress—It has been said by some that we Hindus have yielded too much to our Mohammedan brothers. I am sure I express the feelings of the Hindu community all over India when I say that we could not have yielded too much"—breathed the only spirit in which a majority can win the complete confidence of a minority.

His vision was not of Hindu domination, as some people have wrongly asserted, but of a united India marching forward to attain its freedom."

Though Tilak appeared to yield too much to the Mohammedans, he had infact won the case for the Hindus. The Mohammedans were in a numerical majority in Bengal and Punjab and demanded a majority of the seats for those provinces, which would have given them a statutory majority in the councils. Tilak rightly urged—and carried his point—that their proportion of seats should be based not on population but on the number of voters. In accordance with this principle Bengal Muslims were allotted only forty per cent and Punjab Muslims fifty per cent of the seats in the general electorate. But there was to be no such allotment in the special constituencies (the universities, Chambers of Commerce, and some other special electorates).

One more feature of the electoral arrangements was altered by Tilak's settlement to the advantage of the Hindus. By the Morley-Minto reforms the Muslims had two doors open to them for election. Not only were they allotted separate constituencies in which no non-Mohammdedan could oppose them, but they were also free to contest any of the other seats. This was plainly unfair to the Hindu, and so under the Lucknow Pact the Mohammedans agreed not to contest these other seats. Thus, though apparently conceding too much, Tilak took care to see that nowhere would the Mohammedans gain a statutory majority.

The Lucknow Congress finally buried the hatchet between Hindus and Muslims and between the Moderates and the Nationalists and, above all, gave birth to a demand for *Swaraj,* Home Rule, on a truly national scale. It is for this reason that the Lucknow session of the Congress has been regarded as a turning point in India's political evolution. Tilak himself regarded the Congress achievements at Lucknow as something in the nature of a miracle. Writing on the subject, his newspaper *Kesari* says, "Friday 29th December, 1916 is a day in Indo-British relations worthy to the written with golden letters. On tha day, on the banks of the sacred river *Gomati* the flag of Indian *Swaraj* was unfurled. The resolution of *Swaraj* passed on that day was an act of historic importance; the aspirations of India were crowned on that day, so to speak, and all her subjects came there to pay their homage to Mother India. Caste distinctions, differences of opinion, personal jealousies and everything that was gross and went to destroy the unity of the nation was finally drowned in the waters of the *Gomati*, and India assumed a new and scacred form. It is true that the country took thirty to forty years to give concrete shape to its aspirations and to give adequate expression to them but on that Friday the whole nation with one voice declared to the entire world what it wants and what it stands for. It is impossible for India ever to forget that resolution and her every effort in future will be to attain that declaration.

"The Government used to pity the advocates of *Swaraj*, pointing to the differences in the political camps of India, but now time has taken revenge on them and it will be the Government who will be pitied from now on. Since the inception of the Congress the Muslims were successfully divided from the Hindus; in the last ten years the bureaucracy had succeeded in dividing even the Hindus by rallying the Moderates, but now everything stood changed. In less than four years, not only the Moderates and the Extremists had come together but even the Hindus and Muslims had forgotten their differences. What is the magic wand that brought about this metamorphosis? Surely it is the growing national consciousness, whose glow melted and destroyed all those anti-national and anti-social differences. We have no hesitation in issuing a warning to the bureaucracy that its days are numbered now that the united voice of India has given it the final notice to quit."

It is interesting to note what the Government thought about the Lucknow Congress. In its yearly publication *India* for 1917-18 it described the Congress in these words "When the Congress met it was plain that the Left Wing of the Nationalist party, commonly called the Extremists, as represented by the followers of Mrs. Besant and Mr. Tilak, was in a distinct majority." This was a tacit admission that henceforward the government would be obliged to take note of the Congress demand and that Nationalist leaders like Tilak would have to be listened to, not ignored as they had been till then.

It is true that the war (Worldwar I) did not originate the demand for home rule but it certainly did give it a new meaning and a new urgency; and what is perhaps more important in the context of world events at the time, it gave it an air of reality which it had never possessed before. Indians had grown accustomed to foreign rule; in fact, many leaders like Sir Pherozeshah Mehta, Pandit Madan Mohan Malviya, Sir Surendranath Bannerjee and Mudholkar, were much more conscious of the benefits of English rule than of its harmful effects. It was the war that brought home to them the humiliations of foreign conquest and the real meaning and value of *Swaraj*. What would happen if Germany conquered England was a question often asked in India. And the picture which British statesmen usually painted in reply was so terrible that no sacrifice was considered too great to prevent such a calamity. Furthermore, British statesmen, in order to arouse sympathy and support for the Allied cause, labelled the war as "a war to make the world safe for democracy". They gave an assurance that every nation, large or small, was henceforth to have the right of self-determination; and no nation, however small or weak it might be, was to be forced to live under a form of government of which it did not approve.

Tilak took these declarations at their face value and used them to press forward the cause of Indian freedom. Under the leadership of Mrs. Besant in the Madras Presidency and Tilak in the Bombay Presidency intensive propaganda for home rule was carried on with great enthusiasm and consummate skill. Both these leaders were anxious to give all possible help in the prosecution of the war but they believed that the war offered India a heaven-sent opportunity to win freedom, and they must on no account allow it to be lost. Whenever Tilak or his followers were invited to war conferences they raised the issue of *Swaraj* and equality of status and linked it with the question of war aid. They boldly declared that it was not right to ask the people to fight if they were to be treated as mere hewers of wood and drawers of water. Indians must be given an equal position with the British in the Army, Defence Forces and Reserve Forces. They must be allowed to hold the King's commissions and occupy high service and civilian appointments; most important of all, they must receive a clear assurance that at the end of the war they would return to a free country.

The year 1917 began with unparalleled political activity all over the country. Although frail and weak in body, Tilak carried his message of *Swaraj* from one part of the country to the other, addressing mammoth meetings in Cawnpore, Calcutta, Amraoti, Nagpur, Yavatamal, Karanja and many other places. As the tempo of the campaign rose, he widened the scope of India's political demands. At Cawnpore, for instance, he said, "We will remain in the Empire only as equals. We will not live in the Empire merely as servants and load-carriers. India has now realized her true strength and character just as the proverbial tiger cub, raised in a flock of sheep, realized his true nature on seeing his reflection in the water. The Indian people are now fully awakened to their true status and destiny. If the Japanese, who are Asians like the Indians, can enjoy the liberties and responsibilities of *Swaraj*, why cannot we?"

In May 1917, Tilak went to Nasik to attend the first annual meeting of the Home Rule League. The report which the secretaries presented is an eloquent testimony to his drive and powers of organization. In twelve months the League had registered 14,218 members and collected Rs. 9,000 from subscriptions and Rs. 6,000 from donations. The head office had sent out 5,000 letters and had received as many. The League had published six Marathi and two English books explaining the demand for *Swaraj*. Seventy-five thousand copies of Tilak's speeches were issued and they were also published in Gujarathi and Kanarese.

In his address to the Nasik meeting Tilak said, "The resolution on *Swaraj* was passed at Lucknow because a large number of the members of the Home Rule League attended the session and supported the resolution. In the Congress organization there is still some weakness in that it has not yet evolved a functional machinery to carry out the work from day to day, and from year to year. However, so long as it looks upon the Home Rule League work with approval and appreciation we should regard our work as the Congress work. We must make every effort to enrol 50,000 members and collect Rs. 50,000 in the coming year. We have to do a great deal of work in England, for which plenty of funds will be required. We must maintain permanently one or two able men in England to educate the English people, which will cost a lot of money, but we must not grudge the expenses. Home Rule League workers must from now onward devote themselves to propagating the idea of Swaraj fearlessly and ceaselessly."

The Home Rule League campaigns in Bombay and Madras alarmed the Governments of the two presidencies which therefore tried to suppress the new movement indirectly by placing restrictions on the liberties of its two leaders—Tilak and Mrs. Besant.

A circular was issued forbidding pupils of schools and colleges to attent Home Rule meetings. The provincial governors delivered speeches denouncing the propaganda for Home Rule and warning the leaders of the movement. The Government of Madras went further and issued internment orders against Mrs. Besant and her two associates, Wadia and Arundale. They also helped the *non-Brahmins* to start an anti-Home Rule campaign, thus encouraging them to fan the flames of communalism in the presidency of Madras. The internment of Mrs. Besant created a storm of opposition and indignation from one end of the country to the other. Protest meetings were held all over India and prominent men like Surendranath Bannerjee and Mohammed Ali Jinnah, who had refrained from joining till then, enlisted in a body as members of the Home Rule League and accepted responsible offices.

At the July meeting of the all-India Congress committee Tilak raised the question of starting passive resistance as a reply to the Government's repression, but he did not press its immediate acceptance as some of the Moderate leaders wanted the matter referred to the provincial Congress committee for opinion. However, he strongly pressed upon the Committees his proposal to elect Mrs. Besant as President of the next Congress session, irrespective of whether she was released or not, as a mark of their appreciation of her great services to the Indian cause. Although many of the Moderates did not like the proposal, the various Provincial Congress committees took up Tilak's suggestion and recommended Mrs. Besant for the Presidency of the 1917

Congress. The acceptance of Tilak's proposal marked the triumph of his party over the Moderates who still spoke the language of Surat—"Do not openly flout the Government; for then the Government will quickly throttle our movement." Mrs. Besant's election meant that India had once and for all given up the policy of going with cap in hand to ask for favours. She now realized the respect she owed herself and had made up her mind to fight for her independence. This was indeed a bold challenge. It dared the Government to do its worst and to measure its powers of repression against the determination of the Indian people to win their freedom. The political situation in India thus became so grave that it arrested the attention of the British Government.

Tilak was the most representative type of the Indian lot, and in being so, he had no intention of hurting the feelings of his Muslim countrymen, but he added that "the Hindus must never forget that friendship and good relations can exist only between people of equal strength." And from then on, he devoted himself to organising the Hindus and making them strong enough to live in peace with the Muslims on a footing of equality. One of the occasions he used to bind together and strengthen the Hindu community was the annual celebration of the Ganapati and the Shivaji festival.

Being an embodiment of India's aspirations and ideals, he trusted the people, and the people trusted him and followed him implicitly. In his person, India found a new force and also its expression, a phenomenon which the British administrators of the day failed not only to appreciate, but even to understand. The bureaucrats branded him as an agitator and a rebel. What they failed to realise was that he was no ordinary malcontent but a constructive revolutionary, one of those men who give form and force to what would otherwise begin and end in futile unrest.

In his speeches on Shivaji, Tilak made it clear that the festival was meant to provide a focus for the national spirit and had no anti-Muslim idea behind it. Indeed, far from himself being anti-Muslim, he had come to the help of Muslims in difficulties in times of plague and famine. Patriotic Muslims understood Tilak's high ideals and devotion to the cause of Indian rejuvenation, and many individual Muslims were among his staunchest supporters. In later years, Tilak disproved the contention of his enemies that he was anti-Muslim by bringing the two communities together in a solemn pact, signed by the most prominent leaders of Hindus and Muslims, among whom was the late Mohammed Ali Jinnah, the founder of Pakistan.

A number of British authorities were particularly responsible for circulating the mischievious story that Tilak was anti-Muslim. The most prominent among these mischief-makers was Sir Valentine Chirol, who was sent out to India by *'The Times'* as its special correspondent. In his book *'Indian Unrest'* he wrote: "In 1893, some riots in Bombay of a more severe character than usual gave Tilak an opportunity of broadening the new movement by enlisting in its support the old anti-Mohammedan feeling of the people. He not only convoked... meetings in which his fiery eloquence denounced the Mohammedans as the sworn foes of Hinduism, but he started an organization known as the "Anti-Cow-Killing Society", which was intended and regarded as a direct provocation to the Mohammedans, who, like ourselves, think it no sacrilege to eat beef."

Even before the serious Hindu-Muslim riots of 1893-94, Tilak had foreseen the widening gulf between the two communities and had deplored the unrealistic and aggressive attitude of the Muslims which he put down to their lack of education and to a false pride in their having once been rulers of India. The Anglo-Indian Press continued to misrepresent Tilak as a bigoted Hindu leader dreaming of the Mahratta Empire; newspapers like the *Times of India*, Bombay, and the *Pioneer* of Allahabad were his worst calumniators and carried their vendetta against him to absurd and indecent lengths. This was bound to have some effect on half-educated Muslim youths and even on some of the so-called constitutional leaders among the Hindus. But the thinking Muslims were not, fortunately, taken in by this dishonest propaganda. They showed an awareness of the situation and some of them acted towards Tilak in a spirit of understanding.

On many occasions, Tilak was the complete democrat, who wished to take the politics of the Congress to the humble villager; on other occasions he appeared to be an advocate of Brahamanical supremacy. It was part of Tilak's charisma that most of his followers did not see such remarks as inconsistent, and each group tended to appropriate the sayings which appealed to it. Even by his biographers, Tilak has been referred to variously as the defender of tradition, as a centrist and as a social revolutionary. Even Tilak's desire to launch a new party was based on a combination of thwarted political ambitions and a desire to provide an alternative to mendicancy, with the issue of social reform and religion providing the means of attaining political power.

By the year 1890 or so, Tilak's opinions on religion were well-crystallized. He had read the articles of Max Muller, praising Hinduism. He was already impressed by Theosophy and had noted with very great admiration the success achieved by and the acclamation accorded to Swami Vivekananda in America. Right from the beginning, Tilak had noted the break-up of the old order, and time and again, had lamented the feeling of rootlessness shown by the English-educated generation in matters of religion. As the editor of *Kesari*. Tilak announced indifference to religion, because *Kesari* was started not for religious or ethical propaganda but for pure secular and worldly matters. However, in his personal life, Tilak followed all the orthodox practices and showed himself to be a conservative. In college, he was inclined towards agnosticism by a reading of Mill Spencer, though he never gave up his orthodox practices.[40] Tilak's ethical philosophy has also been compared with Kant's ethical ideal, as the ethical philosophy of both Kant and Tilak was based on the assumption of the double nature of man, as consisting of irrational and rational parts. The goodness or the badness of an act depends entirely on the quality of will and not on consequences. Duty must be done because it is duty—a feature imbibed in *Karmayoga*.[41]

On the other hand, in political ideology, Tilak initially stuck to the liberal principles, but gradually differences between him and the liberals had become more and more marked on matters of strategy. He wished to concentrate all his energies on the political front, and thus he threw himself heart and soul in the political activity, as outline by the Congress. By 1893, when the Congress had already survived a major crisis, Tilak realised that the liberal leadership of the Congress was against any widespread agitation. This was clearly demonstrated in the threatened split between the liberals and the extremists at the time of the Hume circular. Tilak had also parted company with Agarkar on the question of social reforms, and Tilak was in search of a more resolute and realistic stand.

Politically, therefore, Tilak realised the necessity of taking the message of the Congress to the hearths and homes of the masses. He also felt that there was no point of contact between the leaders and the masses, who drifted in their own traditional ways, unconcerned about their past, present and future. Tilak's mind worked in the direction of giving a deep-rooted cultural basis to the political movement by breaking through the routine of the somewhat academical nature of the Congress movement, and he strove to bridge the gulf between the present and the past and to restore continuity to the political life of the nation. He wanted to develop, in the words of Aurobindo Ghouse, "a language and a spirit, and he used methods which Indianised the movement and brought into it the masses."[42]

Tilak became the idol of the people mainly because he identified himself with the poor. He understood them as no other Indian leader did. It is true to say that everything that happened to India seemed to happen to him. He felt the sufferings and the sorrows of the Indian masses as if they were his own. He worked for the masses. Their wretched condition, their thin and under-nourished bodies, their disease-ridden hovels, their joyless existence haunted him day and night. He was never tired of telling the educated middle-class youth to "go to the villages, mix with the peasants and try to improve their condition."

Tilak's single-minded devotion to the cause of the Indian masses was the source, both of his strength and his weakness. By temperament and circumstances, he was a rebel and a revolutionary; he fought against political injustice and tyranny all through his life. His political actions and struggles, whether against his own countrymen—like the moderate leaders—or the alien power, have a ring of sincerity and consistency which leaves no room to doubt his motives.

Tilak tried to use the religious fervour of the people for political purposes by reviving the Ganapati festival, which was celebrated on a large scale in Maharashtra at the time of the Peshwas, but with the advent of the English rule this festival had lost its national importance. The ingenuity of Tilak lay in giving the festival a community aspect and making it an effective means of creating national enthusiasm, religious consciousness and social solidarity. He organised the Ganesh festival as a vast community celebration which lasted for ten days, and Tilak's followers took advantage of these gatherings and spoke on religious subjects to the assembled people.

Tilak found in the Ganesh festival a "Powerful engine for imparting instructions to the masses" which were; he said, "Our ultimate court of appeal". He advised his countrymen to reorganize the festival of Ganesh, the Elephant God. From times immemorial, Hindus have worshipped this god with display and ceremony, but the festivities were mostly confined to the household. Friends and relatives dined together and exchanged gifts of sweets with each other, but no public celebrations were held. The ingenuity of Tilak lay in giving the festival a community aspect and making it an effective means of creating national enthusiasm, religious consciousness, and social solidarity.

He organized the Ganesh festival as a vast community celebration which lasted for ten days. Under his guidance, big cities and small villages made the worship of Ganesh a public function to be celebrated with great splendour and with much enthusiasm. People gathered together every evening to see the artistic displays and listened to the music played before the god. Tilak, who was a profound scholar of Hindu scriptures and mythology, drew liberally on the ancient epics of the Hindus—the Ramayan and the Mahabharat—to illustrate his themes, which were often a slender and thin disguise to the political and economic problems of the day. This religious movement caught the imagination of the people and in less than two years spread to every province of India.

In a recent analysis of Asian nationalism, an American writer, William Holland observed that religion played an important role in India where the nationalist movement was characterised by a strain of Hindu revivalism. Like all empires, the British suppressed political meetings but they observed a hands-off policy with regard to religion. This provided a loophole which nationalists like Tilak exploited to the full for their own purposes, and the revival of the Ganapati festival is an outstanding example.[43]

Tilak seemed to have had two general aims in view, in trying to establish this as a national festival. Victor Barnouw, writing in the American Anthropologist Journal of February, 1954 says, "First of all, he (Tilak) thought that a public ten-day festival would provide a good occasion for lectures and anti-British propaganda. Second, Tilak hoped that a public Ganapati festival would bring the Hindu community together vis-a-vis the Muslim and provide a sense of Hindu solidarity." Barnouw goes on to say that Tilak's second aim might have been the less significant of the two. Be this as it may, the building of Hindu solidarity seems to have been the immediate reason for the organization of the Ganapati festival. The Hindu-Muslim riots of 1893 in Bombay and Poona, gave Tilak every reason to believe that the British Government was favouring the Muslims and directly or indirectly encouraging them to take up an aggressive attitude. He rightly argued, therefore, that the Hindus must take a firm stand against Muslim provocation, not because they were Muslims, but because they were allowing themselves to be used as agents of foreign rulers. His stand was against the power behind the Muslims rather than against the Muslim community itself.

Until this time, Hindus had always taken part in the annual Muslim festival of Moharram. Local Muslim organizations used to take a collection every year to pay for the public entertainments—singing and dancing, and for a procession—to which the Hindus liberally contributed. Almost all Hindu communities used to join in the celebrations. But after the riots, Tilak urged the Hindus not to contribute to or take part in these Moharram festivities. Instead, they should organize their own celebrations on similar lines around the Ganesh idol. The following year, the number of community Ganapatis grew, and in 1896, there were more than fifty centres in Poona itself celebrating the festival on public lines. There was no doubt that the movement had become a tremendous success. Tilak wrote articles in *Kesari* calling on the intellectuals of India to take part in the festival, and not to stand aside and scoff as some members of the "social reform" movement had been doing. He exhorted them to seize the opportunity to go out among the people and spread the message of *Swaraj*.

One interesting question is often asked is: Why did Tilak select the Ganesh festival in preference to so many other possible festivals in the Hindu calendar? There are many likely answers, and each of them may have had a share in his decision. The climax of this festival is the immersion of the god in the local river or pond, which resembles the immersion of the *tabuts* (decorative structures representing the tombs at Kerbela) which takes place at the end of the Muslim festival of Muharram, and may easily have been modelled on it. The report of the Sedition Committee (1918-19) suggested that the Hindu procession and immersion of Ganapati, which are such a close parallel to the Muslim ceremony, were intended by Tilak as a deliberate insult to the Muslims. But it should also be observed that many Hindu festivals, such as those of Durga and Saraswati Pooja, end in a similar way with a procession and immersion.

The Report of the Sedition Committee, presided over by Rowlatt, stressed the anti-Muslim character of the festival. It said: "Public Ganapati festivals appear to have arisen out of an anti-Mohammedan movement started after riot which broke out in the city of Bombay, in 1893, between Hindus and Mohammedans. Agitators who were interested in widening the breach between these two communities encouraged the holding of these celebrations in honour of Ganapati, the elephant-headed God of wisdom and success, on a much larger scale than in previous years. The idea appears to have been to make the procession in which the God is carried to his final resting place in the water, as offensive as possible to Mohammedans by framing them upon the same lines as the procession at Muharram festival."[44] Sir Valentine Chirol also expressed the same views.

Nonetheless, the version of Chirol and the Report of the Rowlatt Committee carried their own refutation with them. Prejudices had engulfed them to such an extent that they never cared to differentiate between anti-Moslemism and Hindu solidarity. A more reliable and authentic interpretation of the Ganapati festival was given by Bipin Chandra Pal. He compared the word 'fGana' to the Greek word 'demos'. The Ganapati festival had a democratic implication to the extent that all sections of the population, from the *Brahmins* to the *Sudras* could participate in it. Every community could bring its own Ganapati to the procession, and thus it became an experiment in democracy.[45]

The reorganisation of the Ganapati festival was a mixed success. Although it proved a means of politicizing the masses in general and the *Brahmans* in particular, it is questionable whether it added many *non-Brahmans* to the Congress ranks. But measured by the standards of the time, it enhanced Tilak's stature and reputation as a leader. He acquired the support of the orthodox faction, together with some of the young college graduates of Poona. He became a force not only in Poona, but in the Congress as well. Tilak was aware that appearances were as important as the realities of power. It was difficult for any of his moderate critics to counter the myths propagated in Tilak's journals and to prove that Tilak was not doing what he claimed! It was Tilak, rather than Ganapati, who benefitted most from the reorganised festival.

Having successfully launched the Ganapati festival, which was mainly directed to revive the religious enthusiasm of the Hindu community, Tilak turned his attention to organising the enthusiasm of the people in secular matters. Like Thomas Carlyle and Emerson, he believed that the "heroes" of the world are the creators of history. It is their great work which inspires the ordinary man, gives him ideals to aim at, and raises his moral stature. He believed that a community can only continue to live and prosper if it can produce an unbroken chain of great men to serve and inspire it. When it no longer throws up great men, the community declines and dies. This reasoning led him to the conclusion that the people must be given a hero to worship who would help them to rediscover their self-esteem and self-respect, without which they could never hope to make the supreme effort in self-sacrifice for their political liberation.

Fortunately, he found in Shivaji, the founder of the Mahratta Empire, a hero who was revered and worshipped all over Maharashtra. To the millions he was the ideal man, the ideal king, valiant in war and wise in council; pure, just and compassionate. Villagers sang his praises in traditional ballads, and poets wrote new songs every year to commemorate his great achievements. Tilak decided to organize an annual festival round the personality of the hero Shivaji, and thus create a new movement to gather into a single stream the forces of nationalism and patriotism. Shivaji was not a hero of the *Brahmin* community only; he was claimed as their own by the vast *non-Brahmin* populace of Maharashtra. Shrewdly, Tilak calculated that Shivaji would be an acceptable figure to *Brahmins* and non-Brahmins alike, and the agitation for *Swaraj* would reach the masses more quickly than by any other means. The Mahratta hero was hailed as the symbol and embodiment of Hindu courage, sacrifice and chivalry. In Maharashtra, Shivaji and *Swarajya* are the two sides of the same coip. By founding the Shivaji festival, Tilak reached the hearts of the people and roused the patriotic instinct of the Mahratta youth. Whereas Ganapati was a quasi-political figure, Shivaji was a direct symbol of political action, the epitome of the *Kshatriya* tradition of Maharashtra. To recapture the martial spirit of the Maratha hero was a means of stimulating a resurgent Maratha nationalism. By honouring the person of the *non-Brahman,* Shivaji, Tilak selected a popular symbol which, directly appealed to communities outside the Congress sphere, for Shivaji was the one cause on "Whom all the different castes of Maharashtra could focus their loyalty.[46]

Moreover, Tilak felt that festivals like these proved an incentive to the legitimate ambitions of a people with a great historic past. They served to impart courage, such courage as an appreciation of heroes securing their salvation against odds, could give.

In 1895, Tilak organised a public meeting in Poona and resolved to raise a Memorial Fund to build Shivaji's Tomb at Raigarh, which was then in a very dilapidated condition. The movement was an instant success, with thousands attending the festival. And, by contrast with the glorious past, everyone at the festival was made sharply aware of the degrading conditions under which they were living. In the address which followed, Tilak suggested that the object of the festival was to bring Maharashtrians together and to foster a feeling of confidence "which would be conducive to the maintenance of their religion and institutions."

However, the character of the celebration suggests that Tilak was more concerned, in the Shivaji festival, with symbols which would enunciate the ideology of his party and establish its legitimacy than with direct politicization of the *non-Brahmans*. Whereas there was some direct attempt in the Ganapati festival to involve the *non-Brahmans* in a *Brahman*-sponsored movement, the main purpose of the Shivaji festival was to enunciate a symbol for popular mobilization.[47]

The Shivaji festival, like its predecessor, the Ganesh festival, soon became an annual event. Even in Bengal, a province which was supposed to have suffered at the hands of the Mahrattas, the people responded very enthusiastically and Calcutta celebrated it with as much enthusiasm as Poona. To a Bengali audience Tilak said in 1907: "Our political aspirations need all the strength which the worship of a *Swadeshi* (native) hero is likely to inspire in our minds. For this purpose, what greater hero than Shivaji could be found in Indian history. He was born at a time when the whole national required relief from misrule; and by his self-sacrifice, courage and heroic deeds he proved to the world that India was not a country forsaken by providence. It is true that the Mohammedans and the Hindus were then divided; and Shivaji, who respected the religious scruples of the Mohammedans, had to fight against the Mughal rule that had become unbearable to the people." Tilak exhorted his Muslim listeners to pay no attention to the Anglo-Indian writers who were making a bogey of the Shivaji festival and telling the people that the Mahratta hero was anti-Muslim. He asked them to accept Shivaji as one who "in his own days took a bold stand against the tyranny of his time". Shivaji's fight, Tilak suggested, was not against the Mughals because they were Muslim but because they were oppressive, tyrannical and despotic rulers.

Tilak did not expect the people to copy every incident in Shivaji's life, as the times had radically changed. It was the spirit which actuated Shivaji in his exploits, not the exploits themselves, that was held up as model and an example to the rising generation. Tilak was well aware that the British Press in India was trying to make mischief by labelling the festival as a deliberate attempt on his part to stir up the Hindus against the Muslims. He warned his Muslim countrymen not to fall into the Anglo-Indian trap. "The Shivaji festival," he declared, "is not celebrated to alienate or even to irritate the Mohammedans. Times have changed and the Mohammedans and the Hindus are in the same boat as far as the present political condition of the people is concerned." The people understood and followed him implicitly. The political movement of the towns had begun to reach the villages.

It is important to note that some Muslims, at least in the beginning of the festival, joined in the celebrations together with the Hindus, which gives the direct lie to men like Sir Valentine Chirol, who asserted that Tilak had inaugurated the Shivaji cult as an anti-Muslim movement.

By 1906 this festival had travelled far beyond the country of the Mahrattas. It was being regularly celebrated in Benares, Calcutta, Karachi and Madras, so embracing the four corners of the country. Tilak's warm sympathy for Bengal over the partition of the Province, his support for the political programme which the Bengalis had proposed to make their protests effective, and his vast popularity as a militant leader were drawing the Bengali leaders to him with growing affection and confidence. Millions had heard his name; now they wanted to see him in person.

In response to an invitation from the organizers of the Shivaji festival committee, Tilak went to Calcutta and delivered a series of lectures on the life and mission of the

Mahratta hero. The European community was quite unable to understand how a Mahratta leader like Tilak could be so enthusiastically received and heard with such rapt attention on his favourite theme of Shivaji, by Bengali audiences, sometimes numbering tens of thousands.

In the late eighteenth century Raghuji Bhonsle of Nagpur had actually invaded Bengal, since when the people of the province came to dread the very name Mahratta. The Bengali mothers used to frighten their children by invoking the *borgi*, meaning the "Mahratta freebooter". Shivaji was the bogey-man of Bengal, yet the magic of Tilak's name, and his superbly logical way of explaining the life work of Shivaji, changed the old prejudice into warm affection and respect for the Mahratta hero. Bengalis accepted Shivaji as their own national hero and drew new inspiration from him. Ever since those days bands of sympathy and affection have bound together Maharashtra in the West and Bengal in the East— a unique phenomenon in Indian politics. These two provinces stuck together throughout the national struggle from 1905-1947 and a unity of purpose and ideals was established which led to a union of minds. Bengal and Maharashtra, after this Calcutta visit of Tilak, began to think and act alike, whether it was over the programme of the New Party, the terrorist movement of secret societies, or organized opposition to Mahatma Gandhi's programme of non-cooperation. As the Sedition Committee said in its report, "Any cult started in Maharashtra has its echoes at once in Bengal."

These festivals were the scene of Tilak's earlier work and popularity. They cover the period of his political career from 1893 to 1905, a time during which he is seen to be directing all his energies to re-awakening in the people of Maharashtra a sense of their past greatness and so preparing them for a sustained fight against British rule.

The Congress was fulfilling the function of making the people politically conscious; but its message could only reach the fringe of the educated few. And the Congress leadership itself had not yet fully realized the importance of developing the organization into a mass movement. Some of the arm-chair politicians were frankly contemptuous of any contact with the masses, and called Tilak " a leader of oilmen and betel-nut sellers", meaning the common man of India, the worker and the peasant. But in the Ganapati and Shivaji festivals Tilak could claim to have brought the rich and the poor together in a common struggle to reach the goal of Indian liberation.

It is important to remember here that the first case for sedition against Tilak also arose out of a speech that he delivered in one of the Shivaji festivals.[48] This speech was the presidential address delivered by Tilak, but some of the words were alleged to have a direct bearing on the contemporary political situation, and Tilak was charged with giving incitement to violence. Two great convulsions of the period had aroused popular indignation against the Government and Tilak, who had taken up the people's cause with his usual fiery ardour, was looked upon as a trouble-maker by the Government. These two convulsions were a result of the twin calamities of the great famine of 1896 and the plague.

Tilak's work during the famine and plague had given a solid foundation to his popularity and leadership. He was a rising star in politics whose activities had begun to catch the imagination of the people and his appeal to their self-respect and patriotism was making a strong impression, especially on the educated classes of Maharashtra. All this profoundly disturbed the British bureaucracy. The officials knew that the people were poor and half-starved; that they were dying of plague and cholera; and that malaria was taking a heavy toll every year. But their knowledge of these dreadful conditions was largely derived from the paper reports which they received from subordinate officers in the villages. And indeed what other means had they of knowing the condition of Indians? Very few of the British members of the Indian Civil Service took pains to learn the language of the people who were in their charge and as a result were unable to have free intercourse with them. Moreover, in London, before they left for India, they were officially advised not to fraternize with the natives.

It is not surprising then, that the average British administrator failed at first to realize and appreciate the extent and depth of Tilak's work and his influence over the people. He sincerely believed that it was God's will that the Indians should be under beneficent British rule and it should therefore be accepted without question or complaint. As this was the psychology of the average Britisher in India at the end of the last century, he could not understand a man like Tilak who dared to denounce and condemn the bureaucracy's indifference to the public interest. The rest is familiar history, till Tilak's untimely death in 1920, with his growing experience of politics. He devoted his inexhaustible energies to the task of influencing public opinion in the light of the ideas crystallised in his mind after a long process of thought, feeling and action. The ideas did not remain with Tilak as abstractions, but were given a concrete shape through programmes which touched the hearts of people and made them active participants, rather than passive onlookers.

Tilak was the first to realise the limitations of the social and political institutions which were mostly imitative in character. He realised the need of securing a wider basis for the political ideals and he felt that participation of the people in the newly started movements was possible after creating in them a feeling of confidence and after making the pattern of the new movements conform to the traditional ways, so as to make people feel perfectly at home in them. It was a psychological transformation—the revival and use of religious fervour for the political mobilization of the masses. Tilak believed that the new ideals must be grafted- and not transplanted on the life of the people, by creating in them a pride in the glorious past, which was an assurance of the glorious future in spite of the dismal present.

In spite of their popular form, these revival movements would have grown stale and fizzled out, but Tilak knew that service, and not advice, was the right medium for getting an access to people's mind. The qualities of a leader are tested in times of crisis and Tilak's superb abilities as a leader were testified by the work he did during the famine and the plague.

The success of Tilak was due to his ability both to understand the traditions of his society and to epitomize them. He was the heroic leader cast in the mould of Shivaji who, by his reorganisation of the Ganpati festival, linked himself with the popular religious tradition of Maharashtra. In his writings and speeches, he drew upon his familiarity with mass culture to introduce humour, sarcasm, and various dramatic techniques by reinterpreting and disseminating vedic knowledge he established a connection with the high Sanskrit tradition. He was a unique individual who symbolised the range of Maharashtrian experience.

Tilak was also not blind to social evils and injustices. But he was convinced that the emancipation of the country must have the first priority in his national programme, for without it social reform could make no real headway. And to prepare the masses for a sustained fight against a powerful government, he considered it vital for the people's party to remain absolutely free from any suspicion of being in collusion with leaders who played the courtier in Indian politics. Thus, it was quite natural for Tilak to keep away from the social reformers, and concentrate on his programme of organising and consolidating the people for their political independence. Tilak's aggressive nationalism could not search for support from social reformers alone. One must also admit that Tilak never felt the same religious and moral fervour and enthusiasm for social reforms which he felt for the cause of political independence.

Tilak's opposition to social reforms, at least in the early part of his public career, presents a difficult problem. One dare not suggest that Tilak—endowed with a keen intellect and sensitive mind which could react instantly to the slightest political injustice done to the Indian people—could remain insensitive and apathetic to the many social injustices and inhuman customs which bedevilled Hindu society. It would be equally preposterous to doubt his courage to face the people's opposition if he had decided to join hands with Agarkar and Ranade in their crusade for social reform. There is no doubt that the Social Reform Party was keenly disappointed in Tilak's attitude. They were fully conscious of the extraordinary hold he had on the masses; one word from him would have changed popular hostility to reform into friendly cooperation. But Tilak did not say the word. The irony of the situation is that he was at heart no less ardent a reformer than Ranade and his followers. His opponents accused him of hypocrisy and chicanery, but the charge falls to the ground when a study is made of the socio-political set-up of the time.

K.V. Godbole has pointed out that Tilak's opposition to social reform was more apparent than real. He was not blind to social evils and injustices and would never have tolerated them in a free India. But he was convinced that the emancipation of the country must have the first priority in his national programme, for without it social reform could make no real headway.[49]

The Bhandarkars and Ranade would probably have profited from Tilak's support for their social programme, but in all probability, in return, they would not have given their support to Tilak's aggressive nationalism and made common cause with him in his fight for political freedom.

Nationalism, for Tilak, was essentially a psychological and spiritual conception—the presence of a psychological unity fostered by the heritage of historical tradition and religious beliefs. He wanted to create a solid nationalistic following in Maharashtra by symbolizing the permanent religious and historical traditions of the people. Few critics opine that in the immature stage of Indian nationalism. Tilak tried to exploit obsolete semi-religious symbols, entities and slogans as ideological superstructure for his political game, but such an exotic interpellation fails to gauge the department of experience to which religion appeals in the Indian cultural context.

A survey of the political and social forces which were shaping the future of some of the modern states of Europe and Asia from about 1880 to 1920—the period of Tilak's active political career—brings out a striking contrast between the ideals and methods of Tilak in India and of men like Bismarck, Cavour and Ito in Germany, Italy and Japan. By means of ruthless discipline and astute intrigue Bismarck raised Germany to a powerful nation and organized the Federal Union. Within a few years Germany became a dangerous competitor to England and France in trade and commerce. But Bismarck achieved this remarkable success with the help of the Princes of Bavaria, Silesia and Prussia, big landlords, and powerful industrialists (like Krupp). The roots of his strength were in the upper stratum of German society which gathered round the House of Hohenzollern. The moment the Hohenzollerns fell, the German power collapsed and Bismarck's dream of a strong and prosperous Germany came to naught.

In Italy, Mazzini had a fundamental understanding of the democratic forces but, revolutionary idealist that he was, proved incapable of organizing them into a powerful movement. It was under the leadership of Count Cavour that Italy regained her national independence. But the peculiar circumstances then prevailing in the country forced him to co-operate with Victor Emmanuel, King of Sardinia. The aristocracy also joined in the national struggle, and so Italy gained political independence after centuries of division and foreign domination. A democratic regime of a sort was set up, but it lacked a firm foundation in the common man's consciousness of his democratic rights and responsibilities. Soon the experiment in Italy, too, failed and the power slipped back into the hands of princes, aristocrats and monopoly capitalists.

In Japan, the social and political revolution was brought about, as it were, by a miracle. Overnight, by an imperial decree the old divisions of the Japanese society were abolished; the aristocrats and the Samurai became, by a stroke of the pen, one nation, casteless and classless. Ability and not birth became the criterion for appointment in the Emperior's service. It appeared likely that a democratic and almost classless society would emerge in the land of the Rising Sun. But it soon became only too evident that social inequality cannot be abolished by a mere act of parliament or by an imperial edict, and that such acts and edicts are powerless before age-old practices and prejudices. Japanese society remained classless on paper, but in reality power began to concentrate once more in the hands of the small number of families which had dominated the country in the past. The workers and peasants remained as inarticulate and unrepresented as before.

Tilak, on the other hand, did not seek the help of the princes, aristocrats and landlords to regain the lost independence of India; he wooed the masses and by so doing laid the foundation of a truly democratic state. Whatever of democracy and freedom India is able to enjoy today is the fruit of Lokamanya Tilak's profound vision and dynamic action.

In his well-informed essay on *Indian Democracy* Dr. P.G. Sahasrabudhe has ably shown how every page of *Kesari* bears witness to Tilak's great concern for workers, peasants, artisans, weavers, gardeners, aborigines—all the vast numbers of the toiling masses who are the majority of the Indian people. "India means these workers and peasants," was the one theme to which Tilak returned again and again. As early as in the first year of *Kesari,* 1881, Tilak wrote, "Whether a country is rich or poor, conquered or free, the majority of its inhabitants as a rule, earns its livelihood by manual labour. It cannot be said therefore that a particular country has, economically speaking, improved so long as the conditions of the toiling majority in that country have not improved."

Tilak became the idol of the people mainly because he identified himself with the poor. He understood them as no other Indian leader did. He loved the poor and helpless and was always ready to make any sacrifice for them. It is true to say that everything that happened to India seemed to happen to him. He felt the sufferings and the sorrows of the Indian masses as if they were his own.

He worked for these masses. Their wretched condition, their thin, undernourished bodies, their disease-ridden hovels, their joyless existence haunted him day and night. He was never tired of telling the educated middle-class youth to "go to the villages, mix with the peasants and try to improve their condition". In a stirring message to the social workers he wrote in 1896, "There is no greater folly than the assumption of the educated classes that they are a separate class from the mass of the people. They must realize that they are part and parcel of the whole—the Indian masses. Their own salvation depends on the salvation of the people".

Here is Tilak's creed and testament in his own words: "I regard India as my Motherland and my Goddess, the people in India my kith and kin, and loyal and steadfast work for their political and social emancipation my highest religion and duty."

This single-minded devotion to the cause of the Indian masses was the source both of his strength and of his weakness. By temperament and circumstance he was a rebel and a revolutionary; he fought against political injustice and tyranny all through his life. His political actions and struggles, whether against his own countrymen—like the Moderate leaders—or the alien power, have a ring of sincerity and consistency which leaves no room to doubt his motives. But his opposition to social reforms, at least in the early part of his public career, presents a difficult problem. One dare not suggest that Tilak—endowed with a keen intellect and sensitive mind which could react instantly to the slightest political injustice done to the Indian people—could remain insensitive and apathetic to the many social injustices and inhuman customs which bedevilled Hindu society. It would be equally preposterous to doubt his courage to face the people's opposition if he had decided to join hands with Agarkar and Ranade in their crusade for social reform. There is no doubt that the Social Reform Party was keenly disappointed in Tilak's attitude. They were fully conscious of the extraordinary hold he had on the masses; one word from him would have changed popular hostility to reform into friendly co-operation. But Tilak did not say the word. The irony of the situation is that he was at heart no less ardent a reformer than Ranade and his followers. His opponents accused him of hypocrisy and chicanery but the charge falls to the ground when a study is made of the socio-political set-up of the time.

K.V. Godbole has pointed out that Tilak's opposition to social reforms was more apparent than real. He was not blind to social evils and injustices and would never have tolerated them in a free India. But he was convinced that the emancipation of the country must have the first priority in his national programme, for without it social reforms could make no real headway. And to prepare the masses for a sustained fight against a powerful government he considered it vital for the people's party to remain absolutely free from any suspicion of being in collusion with leaders who could be described as "King's men". In reality, were not leaders like Bhandarkar, Ranade and Gokhale playing the courtier in Indian politics. Had not their feeble behaviour and their faith in British rule as God-given cut them off from the masses. Did not Gokhale tender an abject apology to the Government for some remarks of his in England about the Plague administration, although some of his friends were ready to stand by him and produce evidence to support every single one of his statements? Tilak's support of the Social Reform Party would have been construed by the people as support for men like Gokhale who had forfeited the people's confidence and trust. Was it unnatural then for Tilak to keep away from the social reformers and concentrate on his own programme of organizing and consolidating the people for their political independence? True, the Bhandarkars and Ranades would probably have profited from Tilak's support for their social programme, but could they in return have given their support to Tilak's aggressive nationalism and made common cause with him in his fight for political freedom? Even their best friends would not care to say they would. In the circumstances who can blame Tilak if he thought it best not to become entangled with the Reform Party and so run the risk of dividing the popular forces and dissipating the nation's strength?

This is a perfectly legitimate defence of Tilak's attitude to social reform and one must accept it, particularly as it related to the peculiar social and political conditions that prevailed up to Tilak's transportation and long exile in 1908. But this defence begins to wear thin after his release and return from Mandalay. We cannot ignore the fact that his sacrifices and sufferings in the service of his country gave him such a high position and authority after 1915 that there was no danger of the people misunderstanding his actions, if he had cared to come out more openly in support of social reforms. Indeed, in the last two or three years before his death Tilak did speak for social reform and particularly for the removal of untouchability, when he declared that he would refuse to acknowledge God if he thought that He sanctioned the vile practice of treating a section of the community as sub-human. But one is forced to admit that he never felt the same moral fervour and enthusiasm for social reform which he felt for the cause of political independence. This was perhaps partly due, as some critics have claimed, to the narrow religious influences which prevailed in and around Poona, Tilak's main centre of activity. Believing that the division of energies means the dissipation of energies, he made his choice—to the exclusion of every other consideration—of working for the political emancipation of the country. It is unfair therefore to judge the value of his service to India by what he did not do. He made the liberation of his Motherland his life's mission and staked everything—his fortune, his personal comfort, his family life, his scholarship, his health, time and energy. He lived only to give to Mother India whatever he possessed;

no sacrifice was too great for him and no suffering too heavy. If ever there was a man who lived a dedicated life it was Lokamanya Tilak.

Who can deny that Tilak's personality has made an indelible mark on the modern political thought and development of India? It is his work stretching over forty years which made it possible for Mahatma Gandhi to push on the task of nation-building and to crown it with the attainment of independence. He did not live to see the *Swaraj* of his dream materialize, but is it possible to think of India's independence without recalling the stupendous pioneering efforts to Tilak? Mahatma Gandhi and Pandit Jawaharlal Nehru were able to rear the grand edifice of *Swaraj* in the sure knowledge that the foundation was well and truly laid in the sweat and blood of Lokamanya Tilak.

Tilak's untimely death coincided with Gandhi's inauguration of the non-cooperation movement. From the 'Father of Nationalism' to the 'Father of the Nation', the national movement changed its connotations from local and sectional to national and secular. Yet, who can deny that Tilak's personality made an indelible mark on the modern political thought and development of India. The Indians called him an "Avatar", an incarnation of God's spirit; in contrast his Anglo-Indian critics called him a genius of destruction. In his lifetime, Tilak was at once the object of unlimited veneration and unreasoning hatred, a man worshipped by the millions and detested by not a few. The key to his power over the masses was to be found in his realisation of the central and vital teachings of the ancient philosophy of India; the complete absence of an anti-thesis between the ideal and the real. Tilak discovered the need for bringing a spiritual element to the politics of the country by infusing into them a religious fervour, for he realised that no nation could hope to build a great and powerful movement without giving it a secure foundation in the spiritual life of the people.

Not only did Tilak's work bring India's freedom nearer by many years, but it also made a powerful impact on Asian psychology. It was his work stretching over forty years which made it possible for Gandhi to push on the task of nation-building and to crown it with the attainment of independence. Although Gandhi regarded Gokhale as his political 'guru', it is believed that it was the Lokamanya's mantle that fell on him.

Tilak did not live to see the Swaraj of his dream materialise, but is it possible to think of India's independence without recalling the stupendous pioneering efforts of Tilak? It was Tilak who conceived the possibility of enlisting the masses in the Indian struggle for liberation, and used mass action in the form of passive resistance. He galvanized the masses with a new spirit, and organised them in a national movement where they contributed to the final outcome—the end of the British Raj in India and of imperialism in Asia.

And where Tilak as the Lokamanya perished, Gandhi as the Mahatma emerged. For one thing, long before Gandhi preached his gospel of Non-cooperation, Tilak had set before the nation whole programme of Non-cooperation

REFERENCES

1. Stanley A. Wolpert, *Tilak and Gokhale: Revolution and Reform in the Making of Modern India,* Delhi: Surjeet Publications, 1982, p. 62.
2. T.L. Shay, *The Legacy of the Lokamanya,* Bombay: Oxford University Press, 1956, p. 44.
3. A.R. Desai, *Social Background of Indian Nationalism,* Bombay: Popular Prakashan, 1984, pp. 318-19.
4. U.S. Srivastava, *The Evolution of the Concept of Swaraj (1885-1906),* Bisheshwar Prasad (ed.), *Ideas in History,* London: Asia Publishing House, 1968, p. 298.
5. *Ibid.*

6. Hal W. French and Arvind Sharma, *Religious Ferment in Modern India*, New Delhi: Heritage Publishers, 1981, p. 104.
7. Mahatma Gandhi regarded Gokhale as his Political Guru.
8. Hal W. French and Arvind Sharma, *supra n. 6*, p. 104.
9. A.R. Desai, *supra n.* 3, p. 328.
10. D.V. Tahmankar, *Lokamanya Tilak: Father of Indian Unrest and Maker of Modern India*, London: John Murray Publishers Ltd. 1956, Foreword by Vijaya Lakshmi Pandit, p. ix.
11. *Ibid.*
12. Richard I. Cashman, *The Myth of the Lokamanya: Tilak and Mass Politics in Maharashtra*, Berkeley: University of California Press, 1975, Introduction, p. 2.
13. S.L. Karandikar.
14. Stanlay A. Wolpert.
15. Richard I. Cashman, *supra n.* 12, p. 3-4.
16. Daniel Argov, *Moderates and Extremists in Indian National Movement*, Bombay; Asia Publishing House, 1967, Foreword by Hugh Tinker, p. 7.
17. P.K. Jose, *Gandhi and Tilak: Values in Conflict*, Verinder Grover (ed.), *Political Thinkers of Modern India*, New Delhi: Deep and Deep Publications, 1990, Vol. 4, pp. 383-84.
18. *Ibid.*, p. 385.
19. Chapekar was executed in 1897, following the assassination in Poona of two British Plague Commissioners. This was further exacerbated by the subsequent hanging of Chapekar's younger brother and his accomplice named Vasudev who had avenged Chapekar's betrayer. The martyrdom of the two Chapekar brothers marked a turning-point in the history of the Indian freedom movement, and it proved to be the harbinger of a tumultuous revolutionary period.
20. T.L. Shay, *supra n.* 2, p. 52.
21. *Kesari* (Poona), 1 June, 1897.
22. D.V. Tahmankar, *supra n.* 10, pp. 23-24.
23. *Ibid.*, p. 25
24. Nihar Nandan Singh, *Lokamanya Bal Gangadhar Tilak*, New Delhi: Congress Centenary (1985) Celebration Committee, 1985, p. 11.
25. *Ibid.*, p. 12.

26. D.V. Tahmankar, *supra n.* 10, p. 27.
27. I.M. Reisner and N.M. Goldberg (ed.), *Tilak and the Struggle for Indian Freedom*, New Delhi: People's Publishing House, 1966, p. 38.
28. Robert W. Stevenson, *"Tilak and the Bhagavadgita's Doctrine of Karmayoga,"* Robert N. Minor (ed.), *Modern Indian Interpreters of the Bhagavad Gita.* Albany: State University of New York Press, 1986, p. 45.
29. B.G. Tilak, *The Arctic Home in the Vedas*, Poona: Tilak Bros., 1971, Preface, p. v.
30. Stanley A. Wolpert, *supra n.* 1, p. 64.
31. B.G. Tilak, *His Writings and Speeches*, Madras: Ganesh & Co., Appreciation by Aurobindo Ghose, p. xvi.
32. D.V. Tahmankar, *supra n. 10*, p. 320.
33. B.G. Tilak, *supra n.* 31, p. 258.

    It is an extract from the summary of the speech of Tilak delivered at Amraoti in 1917.
34. *Ibid.*, pp. 258-59.
35. Tilak wrote Srimad Bhagavad Gita Rahasya in Mandalay jail during the winter months of 1910-11. At the time, he was serving a sentence of six years' deportation imposed by the British colonial government in India for sedition.
36. *Ibid.*, 261.
37. Robert W. Stevenson, "Tilak and the Bhagavad Gita's Doctrine of Karmayoga", Robert N. Minor (ed.), *supra n. 28*, p. 52.
38. *Ibid.*, p. 54.
39. Richard I. Cashman, *supra n.* 12, pp. 55-56..
40. G.P. Pradhan and A.K. Bhagwat, *Lokamanya Tilak: A Biography*, Bombay: Jaico Publishing House, 1959, p. 81.
41. B.R. Kulkarni, "Lokmanya Tilak's Metaphysic of Morals" *Lokamanya Tilak Memorial Lectures*, Poona: University of Poona, 1973, pp. 4-5.
42. B.G. Tilak, *supra n. 31*, Appreciation by Aurobindo Ghose, p. xv.
43. D.V. Tahmankar, *supra n.* 10, pp. 61-62.
44. V.P. Varma, *The Life and Philosophy of Lokamanya Tilak*, Agra: Lakshmi Narain Agarwal, 1978, p. 65.
45. *Ibid.*, p. 66.

46. *Kesari* (Poona), 28 April, 1896.
47. Richard I. Cashman, *supra n.* 12, pp. 108-09.
48. Report in *Kesari* (Poona), 15 June, 1897.
49. D.V. Tahmankar, *supra n.* 10, p. 321.

CHAPTER 3

GANDHI: MORALITY AND SECULARISIM

Gandhian parameters of the study and use of religion for mass-mobilization have been markedly different from all the traditional and modern typologies. Gandhi, with his traditional bearings envisioned a moral order in a world shattered by man's selfishness, and intolerance, where poverty reigned supreme with injustice inflicting all nooks and corners of humanity. Gandhi's prescriptions of love, truth and non-violence have been of great relevance and his supremacy lays embedded in his advocacy of democratic decentralisation, people's participation and planning at the grass-roots.

For Gandhi, the state was not an instrument of domination or power. He was unique in defining politics not as a game of power or a system of reconciliation of conflicting interests, but viewed politics as an activity motivated by social service. Inspired by whatever is noble and ethical in religion, Gandhi reacted against the western industrial civilisation. Baffled by the biblical predicament, "What shall it avail a man if he gains the world and loses his soul", Gandhi's spiritual orientation drawn from Indian experience posed a formidable challenge to the Western life of material comfort and stark individualism.

In his biography, 'Mahatma Gandhi', Romain Rolland wrote, "If Tilak had lived, Gandhi would no doubt have remained the religious leader of the movement. How magnificently the people of India could have marched on such a double leadership. They would have been irresistible, for Tilak was a master of action, just as Gandhi is a master of spiritual power. But fate decided otherwise."[1]

Unlike Gokhale and Tilak, whose lives ran on parallel lines for nearly thirty years, Tilak and Gandhi worked simultaneously only for five and a half years, during thirteen months of which the former was away in England for the Chirol case. Even in these four and a half years, they came together only at the Congress sessions at Lucknow (1916), Calcutta (1917) and Amritsar (1919), and on a few other platforms. Both could not attend the Delhi Congress (1918). Tilak was the dominating figure at the Lucknow Congress and he went out of his way to find a seat for Gandhi on the subjects committee. At the Calcutta and Amritsar sessions, too, Tilak was the most prominent in the public eye, but the cry of Mahatma Gandhi Ki Jai had begun to ring the welkin at the latter place.

It was not through the Congress organisation, however, that Gandhi emerged on the Indian political scene. What led him there were the victories he scored successively at Viramgam, Champaran, Kheda and Ahmedabad by the new weapon of *Satyagraha*. It was the amazing response to his call for hartal to protest against the Rowlatt Act that projected him into national leadership. Here was a messiah, talking, in strange accents of truth, love, non-violence, voluntary suffering and soul-force, writing to the Viceroy as to an equal, chastising the people for their misdemeanour, confessing to "Himalayan blunders" and getting away with it all. Nothing like this was heard and seen in Indian politics before.

And while Gandhi was thus engaged in his first non-violent skirmishes with the British Government, he was simultaneously acting as its recruiting sergeant. He wrote to the Viceroy, Lord Chelmsford, in May 1918, after the Delhi war conference, to which Tilak was not invited: "If I could make my countrymen retrace their steps, I would make them withdraw all the Congress resolutions and not whisper 'Home Rule' or 'Responsible Government' during the pendency of the war. I would make India offer all Her able-bodied sons as a sacrifice to the British Empire at its critical moment. I write this because I love the English nation and I wish to evoke in every Indian the loyalty of Englishmen.'[2]

This gush of loyalty must have flabbergasted Tilak who, too, had offered to help the recruiting campaign but strictly on a 'quid pro quo' basis. He was familiar with similar professions of Moderates but Gandhi's letter had a new ring, a compelling earnestness whose significance could not be denied. For, in that very letter, Gandhi wrote: "You have appealed to us to sink domestic differences. If this appeal involves the toleration of tyranny and wrong-doing on the part of officials, I am powerless to respond. I shall resist organised tyranny to the uttermost. The appeal must be to the officials that they do not ill-treat a single soul and that they consult and respect popular opinion as never before."[3]

Tilak discovered that here was emerging into prominence a kindred spirit which was irrespressible and deserved all possible support. He found the policy and the strategy followed by Gandhi to be extraordinarily simple and straight, and that here was a man of resolve who had the humility, fearlessness and self-confidence that had something of the Divine touch. Tilak had understood the efficacy of the method of the passive resistance but he had not come to the conclusion that it was the only method, the only effective method, the only just, legitimate and powerful method to convert and win over the human mind, and therefore he had not practised it and tested its efficacy. His appreciation of it was more or less intellectual. Its conception was more akin to retaliation and reprisal, not presumably free from a spirit of vindictiveness.

That Tilak had thought of passive resistance as a legitimate method is evident from the replies he had given during his cross-examination in the Chirol case. The case was based on certain sweeping statements derogatory to Tilak made by Sir Valentine Chirol in his book *'Indian Unrest'*, published in 1910. Tilak was unable to take action against the author when the book was first published as he was then serving the sentence of six years in Mandalay.

Sir Valentine, as director of the Imperial and Foreign Department of *'The Times'* newspaper, visited India in 1910 to study the growth of unrest. He collected material for a series of articles which he wrote for *The Times* and later published in book form under the title *Indian Unrest.*

At the outset of his inquiry Chirol noted "a lull in the storm of unrest" which had lately "swept over India". But what he asked himself was, Does the lull indicate "a gradual and steady return to more normal and peaceful conditions? Or, as in other cyclonic disturbances in tropical climes, does it merely presage fiercer outbursts yet to come? Has the blended policy of repression and concession adopted by Lord Morley and Lord Minto really cowed the forces of criminal disorder and rallied the representatives of moderate opinion to the cause of sober and constitutional progress? Or has it come too late either permanently to arrest the former or to restore confidence and courage to the latter?" After long and laborious work Chirol produced his book, whose main conclusion was that there was not very great unrest in India and what there was, was confined to a few districts in Maharashtra, the Central Provinces, Bengal, and the Punjab. These conclusions were based mainly on the files of the Extremist newspapers and the C.I.D. reports against Tilak and other Nationalist Party leaders. The Provincial Governments placed their secret and confidential files at the disposal of Chirol, who looked upon his work as a valuable vindication of their policy of repression. He says as much: "In writing my book *Indian Unrest* in 1910 I relied largely in regard to Tilak on information from official sources placed at my disposal by Sir George Clarke.....He was of opinion that I was rendering a public service in seeking to enlighten English readers as to the political methods and aims of a man who had misused his great capabilities for the purpose of discrediting and undermining British rule, and that it was therefore in the public interest that I should receive a considerable measure of assistance." The assistance did not end there; it continued throughout the preparation of his defence and the subsequent trial. We shall see presently that although it was Chirol that Tilak had sued, the Government of India fought the case with all the resources of a State at its command, just as though it was itself on trial.

Suffice it to say that after consulting the best advice available in Bombay and London. Tilak filed the suit for libel and for an injunction to restrain Sir Valentine Chirol and his publishers from publishing the matter complained of. After nearly three years of delay, partly due to the war, the case came up for hearing in the King's Bench Division in London before Mr. Justice Darling and a special jury. Sir, John Simon, K.C. and Mr. E.F. Spence appeared as Counsel for the Plaintiff, and Sir Edward Carson, K.C., M.P., Sir Ellis Hume-Williams, K.C., M.P., and Mr. Eustace Hills appeared as counsel for the Defendants.

Tilak's contention was that Chirol had libelled him in *Indian Unrest* in six different ways. Though Tilak had never formed or subscribed to any societies for protecting cows, he was accused by Chirol of having started them in order to provoke the Mohammedans. Though Tilak had never organized gymnastic societies, Chirol charged him with having done so with the object of developing the war-like instincts of the people so that force could be used against the British rule. These gymnastic societies were also described by Chirol as "juvenile bands of dacoits to swell the coffers of *Swaraj*".

Most damaging of all were Chirol's libels about the Rand-Ayerst and the Jackson murders: "What Tilak could do by secret agitation and by a rabid campaign in the Press to raise popular resentment to white-heat he did... The inevitable consequences ensued. On June 22nd, 1897...Mr. Rand and Lieutenant Ayerst...were shot down by a young Chitpavan Brahmin. No direct connection had been established between the crime and Tilak." (*Indian Unrest*, p. 48.)

"In reply to the Magistrate who asked him why he committed the murder, Kanhere said, 'I read of many instances of oppression in the *Kesari*, the *Rashtra Mata* and the *Kal* and other newspapers. I think that by killing Sahibs we people can get justice. I never got injustice myself, nor did anyone I know of. I now regret killing Mr. Jackson. I killed a good man causelessly.'

"Can anything be more eloquent and convincing than the terrible pathos of this confession? The three papers named by Kanhere were Tilak's organs. It was no personal experience or knowledge of his that had driven Kanhere to his frenzied deed, but the slow, persistent poison dropped into his ear by the Tilak Press. Though it was Kanhere's hand that struck down 'a good man causelessly', was not Tilak, rather than Kanhere, the real author of the murder? It was merely the story of the Poona murders of 1897 over again." (*Indian Unrest*, p. 62.) These were the passages Tilak's counsel claimed were libels.

Tilak had justified adoption of passive resistance as legitimate though it involved breach of laws and had to be followed by suffering on the part of the breaker. If such suffering was borne in a religious and selfless spirit, it produced the necessary effect on the wrongdoer. But much more convincing and direct support to Gandhi's method has luckily been recorded in Tilak's own words in the preface he wrote on March 16, 1918 to the biography of Gandhi written by Mrs. Avantika Gokhale who had joined Gandhi as a volunteer in Champaran. It reveals not only genuine appreciation but also a penetrating insight by Tilak, "Gandhiji's life is such a life and I heartily recommend that it should be studied from this point of view to build one's moral strength and spiritual power."[4]

As a result of his confrontation with the British Raj in India, Gandhi emerged as a political leader who openly questioned the pretensions to limitlessness of that power. The history of the struggle for freedom ushered in a new chapter that finally closed in 1947. In that chapter Gandhi unquestionably remained the most dominant figure. Gandhi's style claimed a new status in politics, a style which could not be ignored but which was difficult to comprehend. He transformed the freedom movement and gave it a new content. Gandhian confrontation with the British Raj was unprecedented in historical importance and global significance. Gandhi mobilized the masses without having been always understood by them.

Although Gandhi's campaign lacked the glamour of the battlefield yet it had a halo of its own unparalleled in human history. It reflected the bravery of the soul. It depended on the strength of self-suffering and triumph of the human spirit. Gandhi realized that it was his duty to disobey iniquitous laws and also make the people disobey them. Disobedience became the first duty. He understood that internal discord and moral degradation had condemned the Indians to political subjection which had also led to their moral degradation and exploitation. He felt that in order to uplift the people it was necessary to infuse in them a spirit of self-respect and self-reliance which could be done only by encouraging them to carry on a non-violent struggle for their social, economic and political rights. He undertook the cause of social justice alongwith political freedom.

Gandhi sought to redeem his people from the cultural domination of the West. It was clear to him that he did not seek to isolate the Indians from the world community. He stated, 'I do not want my house to be walled in on all sides and my windows to be stuffed. The humiliation to which Gandhi was subjected in South Africa simply because he was an Indian was felt by him as an outrage on human freedom and dignity. On his coming to India, he gave wide publicity to the treatment meted out to the people of Indian origin in South Africa. This infuriated the Whites in South Africa and some of them manhandled him on his return to Durban. Gandhi worked for the emancipation of man in the total sense. By this supreme creative and imaginative genius, he found an answer to the question as to what the humblest Indian could do to help his country. His techniques were closely related to the sanctity of human freedom and dignity.

Between 1915 and 1918, Gandhi frequently protested against the government and expressed his deep concern over some of its decisions. His techniques were developed in India. Now the dimensions were also bigger because those who participated in the movements led by him were fighting for the cause of nation. This had tremendous potentiality of a struggle for national liberation.

The Kaira *satyagraha* was undertaken by Gandhi for getting the revenue assessment for the year suspended due to crop failure. The Bardoli *satyagraha,* a model of intensive organization and thorough planning, was undertaken by 88,000 peasants under the leadership of Vallabhbhai Patel to protest against the arbitrary and unwarranted enhancement of land revenue.

The government with all its mighty resources and inspite of a frightful reign of terror failed to crush the no-tax campaign and had to yield to practically all the demands of the *satyagrahis*. The government had also to restore the forfeited lands of the *satyagrahis* which had been sold out and to reinstate the village officials who had resigned in protest.

As regards the oppressed raiyats in Champaran are concerned, their cause was considered to be outside the normal fold of politics of nationalism of that time. Champaran became the seedbed of many of Gandhian firsts, such as his concern for the masses, his genius for compromise, his utter emphasis on the means as also on the ends, and finally, the Gandhian technique of non-violent struggle–a completely revolutionary idea in the second decade of the 20th century.

In essence, Champaran pointed to the Gandhian way—the expression of an inflexible commitment, Gandhi's indomitable will and devotion to what he considered to be his duty in the cause of the people. His style certainly exemplified the style of a man who had freed himself first. The tools and techniques devised by him were used for the first time on Indian soil. He offered unique rewards, self-suffering, going to jail and a life of discipline voluntarily accepted without external pressure. It would be rather trite to say that Gandhi won a victory over the government at

Champaran. He innovatively introduced a new style, a new way and a new technique of resolving conflicts.

Gandhi's involvement with the cause of the raiyats against the Europeans and the planters who had become landlords in Champaran almost fortuitously, led to his entry into Indian politics in 1917.

Champaran is of immense significance in Gandhi's life and work in India. Gandhi's first *satyagraha* on Indian soil bore fruit. The Champaran Agrarian Act of 1918 was passed. The miseries of the raiyats were attended to legally. Whether they were substantially reduced has remained a controversial subject.

But in the Gandhian way there was no victory or defeat. There is always a solution to a problem. Champaran partially resolved the conflict by getting a more equitable law passed by the government. Champaran drew the attention of the well-to-do Indians to the utter misery of the raiyats. Champaran brought social welfare work in the village through the volunteers who responded to Gandhi's appeal for such help. Champaran also gave some hope to the fear-stricken people of the villages.

As for the economic sphere, non-violence and the related principle of non-possession rule out exploitation under capitalism and the *zamindari* system. Land should belong to the actual cultivator and no cultivator should have more land than is necessary to support his family on a fair standard of living. Production should be on the basis of cottage industries, carried on by individual or cooperative efforts for the equal benefit of all concerned. The indispensable large-scale production should be nationalized and should be managed jointly by the state and the representatives of workers. But this goal could not be reached in a day. Capitalism, landlordism and exploitation are hard realities of modern economic life. Gandhi was opposed to them all but was against violent revolutionary changes on Marxian lines.

Gandhi's approach to economic conflicts was not the class struggle for the extermination of the haves by the have-nots but class collaboration and class co-ordination as the first step towards the classless society in which every one will perform some form of productive physical labour and there will be no exploiters and the exploited. He did not consider class struggle to be inevitable and was against the extermination of the capitalists and *zamindars* because no human being is so perfect as to warrant his destroying those he wrongly considers to be wholly evil.

Champaran stands out as an event of far-reaching historical significance. Gandhi came to grips with the people's problems in India. He gained deep knowledge and received personal experience of the agriculturists' problems, their sorrow, the injustice and indignity they had to undergo because they were unlettered, under-privileged and economically at the lowest rung. They were always used and exploited not only by the government but also by the landlords and the planters. Gandhi became more and more convinced that work among the masses would bring Home Rule.

Gandhi also became convinced that 'where the cause was non-political one damaged it by giving it a political aspect, a lesson he well remembered throughout his career in India. He also declined to appeal for funds, a much needed resource for helping him conduct the enquiry, lest this should give a political complexion to the Champaran matters. He even declined an offer of Rs. 15,000 from friends in Bombay.

Through Champaran, Gandhi built up a lasting and deep relationship between the people of Bihar and himself. Gandhi found Bihar as one of his most important bases for political and social actions. This was of great historical significance because Bihar was considered to be a backward province. Surprisingly the people of this backward area grasped Gandhi's new style of public behaviour towards an alien government and foreign planters. Importantly, the masses responded affirmatively.

The government took cognisance of this fact and began to weigh up the points for or against having Gandhi with them or against them. Gandhi's leadership as seen in Champaran was rooted in tradition. The tradition of Bihar, being the land of King Janaka of the Ramayana, was important for him. By fulfilling traditional expectations, he could go beyond them.

The people were ready for a leader who would suggest solutions, a leader who was creative and courageous. Gandhi provided that kind of leadership. His vision was revolutionary, tracking from repression and turning the unutilized potential of the people in a new direction. In this, he was more revolutionary than charismatic.

The government was forced to recognize Gandhi's large following in Bihar. After Champaran he began to get recognition in other parts of India–a reputation of extreme moral rectitude.

The Ahmedabad labour satyagraha lasted for a month in February-March, 1918. Gandhi launched it against a personal friend, Ambalal Sarabhai, who was one of the mill owners. The dispute arose over the amount of dearness allowance to be paid to the mill workers as the cost of living had gone up. When in January, 1918, the mill owners made known their intention of withdrawing one specific bonus, the workers made an appeal for a 'cost of living' allowance because of the rise in prices. In the beginning, Gandhi was requested by the mill owners to intervene in the situation on their behalf.

Gandhi concluded after his investigation that a 35 per cent increase was a just demand by the workers of the mills. He advised the workers to ask for no less but no more than the 35 per cent increase. When the mill owners rejected this demand, conflict followed. Gandhi became the leader of the workers who, he became convinced, were the aggrieved party. He introduced *satyagraha* as the mode of action in order to seek a constructive solution. For the sake of truth and resolution of conflict, Gandhi was not deterred from changing his position from one of a conciliator sought out by the mill owners to that of a leader of the workers who were deprived of justice and right wages.

In Kaira in 1917, the district land revenue assessment authority totally disregarded the wishes and welfare of the peasants. Therefore Gandhi informed the government of his intention to launch a *satyagraha,* which ultimately compelled it to come to terms acceptable to the cultivators there. The Kaira and later the Bardoli *satyagraha* campaigns were cases of seeking justice for the farmers and cultivators in Gujarat who suffered from arbitrary enhancement and assessment of land revenue. The Kaira campaign took place in 1918 and the Bardoli campaign from February to August, 1928.

The immediate objectives in both cases were to persuade the government to start an impartial inquiry into the merits of the enhanced assessment. But in essence, these *satyagraha* campaigns were against injustice betrayed by the political power.

Besides these campaigns. Gandhi led and participated in several other *satyagraha* movements as an individual not only challenging the British government but also the princely states which perpetuated discrimination and inequity in this social, economic and religious fields. Gandhi reaffirmed his principles that one need not consider the other as enemy because there was disagreement. His objective always remained to create possibilities and formulate fruitful means of communications to resolve conflicts and establish harmony.

Durga Das thus described Gandhi at the time of Rowlatt Bills: 'I first saw Gandhi from a distance when he sat in the public gallery of the imperial Legislative Council during the debate on the Rowlatt Bills in the 1918-19 Winter Session in Delhi. He wore a long loose coat and turban awkwardly tied. The debate on the Bills left an indelible mark on Gandhi's mind and gave an idea of the issue on which he could build a nation-wide agitation'.

In 1920, referring to the viceroy's speech in the legislature, Gandhi wrote, "The remarks on the Punjab meant a flat refusal to grant redress... The immediate future is to compel repentence on the part of the government on the Punjab matter." Later he added, 'I have therefore, ventured to suggest the remedy of non-co-operation...which, if it is unattended by violence and undertaken in an ordered manner, must compel it (the Government) to retrace its steps and undo the wrongs committed'.

Gandhi wrote to the press on 28th February, 1919 regarding his decision to launch *satyagraha* against the Bill. Gandhi addressed several meetings at Allahabad (11th March, 1919), Bombay (14th March), Madras (18th and 20th March), Tanjore (24th March) Trichinapoly (25th March), Tuticorin (28th March) and Nagapatnam (29th March). He published his message for *Satyagraha* Day at Madras on 23rd March. He also published several articles informing the people about the grave injustice and insult that was done to the nation.

Gandhi recognized the helplessness of the people. He described the Bills as the determination of the British government to retain its grip on our necks. He was convinced of the Bills being evil, being against the people were affecting their rights, dignity and honour. The disease lay with the ruler but the people of India had to bear the brunt of it. The situation needed a drastic remedy as he said in his speech at Allahabad on 11 March, 1919. Gandhi was determined to oppose this evil and organize the people's opposition.

Gandhi expressed his anguish thus: 'For my work in South Africa I was given by Lord Hardinge a Kaiser-i-Hind Gold Medal. When War broke out in 1914... I raised a volunteer ambulance corps in London...chiefly students...Lately in India when a special appeal was made at the War Conference in Delhi in 1917 by Lord Chelmsford for recruits, I struggled at the cost of my health to raise a corps in Kheda.....the first shock came in the shape of the Rowlatt Act, a law designed to rob the people of all freedom. I felt called upon to lead an intensive agitation against it.'

He wrote, 'Rowlatt Bills are unjust, a subversive of the principle of liberty and justice and destructive of the elementary rights of individuals on which the safety of the community as a whole and the State itself is based; we solemnly affirm that, in the event of these Bills becoming Law and until they are withdrawn, we shall refuse to obey these laws...and we further affirm that in this struggle we will faithfully follow truth and refrain from violence to life, person or property. The press was full of reports of protest meetings, articles on the movement and letters opposing the Bills during the whole of March 1919.

The obvious choice of the means toward this end would be to launch a *satyagraha* on an all India basis. Gandhi was consistent in his understanding of the dimensions of the problem and its effect on the people. *Satyagraha* was the only legitimate weapon in the hands of the people. To him, *satyagraha* against any evil, was absolutely legitimate. He wanted to restore moral force to its rightful position, i.e., a government dependent on the will of the people and not on armed force or repressive laws.

Already in Champaran in 1917 and during Ahmedabad labour *satyagraha* in 1918, Gandhi had shown the effectiveness of *satyagraha*. By 1919, *satyagraha* had become a part of the Gandhian way of dealing with injustice. According to Gandhi, 'Moral force never fails.' Therefore, he said, 'I shall resist organized tyranny to the uttermost.'

Gandhi like a true *satyagrahi*, informed the viceroy of his plan of action and the 'pledge' draft. He said that he would be inviting people to become *satyagrahis* if the viceroy did not reconsider his position. He hoped that if satyagraha ultimately took place, it would purify the atmosphere. Gandhi made an appeal to the viceroy at a citizens' meeting in Madras on 20th March, 1919 asking him to withhold his consent to the Rowlatt Bills.

In February 1919, the first phase of the Rowlatt *satyagraha* had begun. The immediate objective was, of course, to protest against the injustice of the government and against its assumption of violent powers. Gandhi believed, that the *satyagrahis* by their determination to undergo every form of suffering, would make an irresistible appeal to the government towards whom they bore no ill will.

Gandhi's ultimate objective was to intensify political awareness among the people in the country by mobilizing popular support, a continuous process in the Gandhian struggle for *Swaraj*. Gandhi's Rowlatt *satyagraha* was a part of the continuing nationalist struggle. The nationalist movement was being transformed into a mass movement.

The actual invitation to people to join the *satyagraha* was given by Gandhi at Madras: 'After much prayerful considerations and after very careful examination of the

Government's standpoint, I pledge myself to offer *satygraha* against the Bills and invite all men and women who think and feel with me to do likewise.'

Two days later he again said, quoting President Wilson's speech at the time of introducing the League of Nations Covenant, 'Armed force is in the background in this programme... if the moral force of the world will not suffice, physical force of the world shall'. Rejecting President Wilson's contention, Gandhi said, 'The message of the West which the Government of India, I presume, represent, is succinctly put here by President Wilson. We hope to reverse the process... that physical force never fails. If we could but restore that faith in the supremacy of moral force, we shall have made a priceless contribution to the British Empire. The viceroy's response was: 'I think he (Gandhi) is trying to frighten us, and I propose to call his "bluff"... I am quite happy defending my position.'

Gandhi proposed that the second Sunday after the publication of the viceregal consent to the Rowlatt Bills, that is, 6th April, 1919, be observed as a national day of humiliation and prayer. The people should fast and pray on that day as acts of self-purification. This should be combined with public meetings. All work except for public interest should be suspended for the day. Markets and business places should be closed. Those who worked on Sundays should take leave before suspending work. He asked the various *satyagrahi* associations to organize the day. Hartal observed in many parts of the country was non-violent on the whole. Even the police reports conceded that it was a strategic success for Gandhi. Srinivasa Sastri commented that the *satyagraha* movement here at Madras registered a moral miracle. In Delhi, owning to a confusion in communication, hartal was observed on 30th March, 1919. Some shops closed; some, such as sweet-shops at Delhi station, were kept open and were forced by a crowd to close down. The police opened fire; army was summoned. There was loss of life. But Gandhi was not sure that the government version was true. However, he made it abundantly clear that violence if any, was inconsistent with the *satyagraha* pledge.

Later, Swami Shradhananda was requested to investigate the matter. He denied the allegations of violence at Delhi station, stoppage of trams or of stone throwing. He condemned police firing on innocent people.

Gandhi communicated this to the people through the press. He further advised that no one should be pressurized to become a *satyagrahi*. Speeches should be free of passion, sufferings must be accepted, there should be self-restraint and absolute adherence to truth. He hoped Delhi would help *satyagrahis* steel their hearts and help them go on with *satyagraha* in the true spirit.

The hartal was a way of popularizing Gandhi's campaign against the injustice of the government. It did spread political awareness in the Gandhian way. But Gandhi later learnt that the extent of hartal varied from region to region. Bengal and Bihar had hartals in towns; so did U.P. and the Punjab. However, Gandhi wanted to intensify the movement throughout India.

The *Satyagraha Sabha* reviewed the movement and the pledge under Gandhi's leadership and advised *satyagrahis* to disobey selected laws, e.g., laws regarding prohibited literature and registration of newspapers. He advised that *satyagrahis* should receive prohibited literature for distribution but they must write their names and addresses as sellers so that they could be traced easily when wanted by the government for prosecution. The stress seemed to have been on individual *satyagraha* with more responsibility. It may be recalled that before the October Revolution in

Russia, a lot of prohibited literature was distributed to educate and arouse the masses.

Also, the move would be constructive because newspapers and literature would be educative. The books banned by the Bombay government in 1910 were *Hind Swaraj*, *Sarvodaya* (translation of Ruskin's *Unto This Last*), *The Story of A Satyagrahi* (Defence and the Death of Socrates), etc.

Gandhi advised 'distribution of prohibited literature. On 7th April, 1919 Gandhi started an unregistered news-sheet and called *Satyagrahi* urging satyagrahis and readers to copy and circulate it widely. He sent a copy of the *Satyagrahi* to Griffiths from Mani Bhawan on 7th April, 1919.

The government instructed now that Gandhi should be arrested if he was guilty of breach of law in any province. There was popular excitement in Delhi and Amritsar because the Punjab government was beginning to adopt repressive laws. When Gandhi was invited by the local leaders of the Punjab, he was removed from the train at Palwal and sent back to Bombay where he was set free.

Chelmsford's letter to the secretary of state makes interesting reading: 'Gandhi is incapable of hurting a fly and is as honest as the day, but he enters quite light-heartedly on a course of action which is the negation of all government...'

Gandhi was served with an order not to enter the Punjab and the district of Delhi. He was to restrict himself to Bombay presidency. Gandhi disobeyed the order, saying: 'I was bound in virtue by my pledge to disregard it which I have done. And I shall presently find myself a freeman, my body being taken by them in their custody. It was galling for me to remain free while the Rowlatt legislation disfigured the Statute Book. My arrest makes me free.'

Before being arrested on 10th April, Gandhi asked that there should be no action tainted with violence and untruth. He urged Hindu-Muslim unity to be continued which had become a feature of the movement, reminding Hindus that being in the majority they had greater responsibility toward maintaining this unity. He expected women to share the responsibility as *satyagrahis* and as workers for Hindu-Muslim unity.

Gandhi's arrest was very brief. He was set free the next day at Bombay. But the news of his arrest led to unrest and violence in Ahmedabad. The mill-hands had heard that Anasuya Sarabhai had also been arrested along with Gandhi on 9th April.

There were killings. The jail, the collector's office and the telegraph office were burnt. Hunter's Report states: 'Two officers were killed, twenty-eight rioters were killed and 123 were wounded. Probably, there were other casualties... nine lakhs worth property was destroyed.' Gandhi was greatly distressed. On 11th April, Gandhi said in a message, 'It is not *satyagraha*. It is worse than *duragraha*. *Satyagrahi* is responsible for the results that follow from the movement....my responsibilities will be million times heavier. I have embarked upon the struggle with a due sense of responsibility. He warned, 'Time may come for me to offer *satyagraha* against ourselves. What followed was historically important in the Gandhian technique.

In a speech at Sabarmati *Ashram* on 14th April Gandhi listed the evils done by the people: 'burning of buildings, capture of weapons, extortion of money, stopping trains, cutting of telegraphic wires, plundering of shops, and attacking private houses.' He expressed his distress by saying that if such deeds could save him from the scaffold, he would not like to be saved. Gandhi strongly condemned evil and stood by those who had suffered during violence, in this case, government and the English in India who were themselves the wrongdoers in the first place. He did not hesitate to take responsibility upon himself for all the violence that broke out.

Gandhi certainly realized the importance of this first all India movement which he had chosen to lead. He recognized its shortcomings and was ready to rectify them in his own way. He highly deplored the fact that the situation was so bad that the English in Ahmedabad had to leave their homes and seek shelter in Shahibag: 'This is a matter of humiliation for us all.' said Gandhi.

He had decided to court arrest after his release on 12th April. He was planning to go to Delhi to seek rearrest as he believed that this move would strengthen the *satyagraha* movement. But 'now instead of going to Delhi it remains to me to offer *satyagraha* against our own people for the violence that has occurred. He asked the people of Ahmedabad to surrender all weapons and take a firm resolve to desist from violence. As a 'penance' Gandhi suggested that they contribute eight annas each towards helping families whose members had been killed in the outbreak of violence. He suggested private individual fasting for retrospection. Since he felt that his own responsibility was million times greater, he decided to fast for 72 hours.

The final phase of the *satyagraha* was affected by Gandhi's reaction to the April violence. In a speech at Bombay, he advised temporary suspension of *satyagraha* on 18th April. He said on that occasion, 'I would be untrue to *satyagraha* if I allowed it by any action of mine to be used as an occasion for feeding violence, for embittering relations between the English and the Indians.' Rather, remaining true to the principles of *satyagraha,* Gandhi suggested that *satyagrahis* should help the authorities restore order, curb lawlessness and gain adherence of the masses to the fundamental principles of *satyagraha*.

Yet Gandhi's attitude towards the Rowlatt legislation remained the same, as he reiterated, 'Indeed, I do feel that the Rowlatt legislation is one of the many causes of the present unrest. But in a surcharged atmosphere I must refrain from examining these causes.' He publicly declared that his had been a 'Himalayan miscalculation' in offering *satyagraha* when he did because people were insufficiently prepared by the discipline of *satygraha* to be able to practise it.

Gandhi did not hesitate to write to J.L. Maffey, private secretary to the viceroy: 'It is a matter of deepest humiliation and regret for me. I see that I overcalculated the measure of permeation of *satyagraha* amongst the people. I underrated the power of hatred and ill will. My faith in *satyagraha* remains undiminished....I am correcting the error....untill I feel convinced that my co-workers can regulate and restrain crowds and keep them peaceful, I propose to refrain from seeking to enter Delhi or other parts of the Punjab.' He admitted that he overcalculated the measure of 'permeation of *satyagraha* amongst the people'.

Gandhi also realized that many *satyagrah*is were really 'joiners' as his words describe: 'I am sorry when embarked upon a mass-movement, I underrated the forces of evil and I must now pause and consider how best to meet the situation.' Although Gandhi suspended the *satyagraha* movement in the political field yet he did not suspend his work for *satyagraha*. True to his words, he began educating the reading public in the first instance by means of *satyagraha* leaflets published by Shankarlal Banker. He also acquired *Young India* and *Navajivan,* the former in English and the latter in Gujarati, which he used as important media for educating the public in *satyagraha* principles.

The outburst of violence at Chauri Chaura (5th February, 1919) which had been preceded by violent scenes at Bombay, Madras and other places, led to the suspension of mass civil disobedience. The sudden suspension disappointed the country. The government intensified its repression. Gandhi and other leaders were sent to jail and the movement got slackened.

Gandhi ordered temporary suspension of the movement when he saw that people were not able to conform to his high standards. By his withdrawal, he exposed himself to the derision of his opponents. Gandhi said, 'Let the opponent glory in our humiliation and so-called defeat. It is better to be charged with cowardice than to be guilty of denial of our oath and sin against God. It is a million times better that I should be the laughing stock of the world than that I should act insincerely towards myself....I know that the drastic reversal of practically the whole of the aggregate programme may be politically unsound and unwise but there is no doubt that it is religiously sound. 'What is morally wrong cannot be politically right.'

To Gandhi, it seemed so unbecoming, so degrading to the self-respect of an individual or a nation to submit to such means, to go through the mire. How can one escape being sullied by it? How can we march ahead swiftly and with dignity if we stoop or crawl. We were angry when we learnt of this stoppage of our struggle at a time when we seemed to be consolidating our position and advancing on all fronts. Gandhi advised. 'We must fearlessly spread the doctrine of *satya* and *ahimsa* and then and not till then shall we be able to undertake satyagraha.'

Gandhi accepted that in an atmosphere of excitement disobedience to law found ready acceptance but truth and *ahimsa* commanded little respect. He emphasized that *satyagrahis* must restrain the crowds and themselves keep peaceful. This vital condition of any *satyagraha* movement must be accepted unconditionally by every *satyagrahi*. Few in power could realize that the natural leaders of people and not bayonets could restrain masses.

Gandhi called a meeting of his co-workers. A conference was held on 21st May, 1919 where Gandhi placed before the members a new issue, the issue of the Punjab. He said there should be a commission of enquiry into the violence and disturbance accompanying martial law, especially in the age of the inhuman happenings of the Jallianwala Bagh. If this was not done, there should be individual *satyagraha* to be offered by the *satyagrahis*.

On 12th June Gandhi asked the *Satyagraha Sabha* to consider renewal of *satyagraha*. He said that the people knew what was expected of them. The government was also fully prepared to face all emergent situations. He believed that the *satyagraha* movement was designed to work as a moral revolution to attain reforms. As a precaution against misuse of *satyagraha*, he suggested that he should be allowed to determine the time, place and the nature of participation.

However, Gandhi did not resume *satyagraha* because of an interview with the governor of Bombay on 12th July. He took this decision on the hope that the Rowlatt Act might be withdrawn. But he told the press that *satyagraha* could not be avoided permanently if the Rowlatt Act was not repealed.

Although the last word rested with him, Gandhi called another meeting at his *ashram*. The following attended, which shows how broad-based the movement was going to be: Vallabhbhai Patel, Anasuya Sarabhai, K. Thakoor, Jamnadas Dwarkadas, Sarojini Naidu, B.G. Horniman and Chandulal Desai. There were members of the Home Rule League, labour leaders, the editor of *Bombay Chronicle* and *ashram* followers. Out of this meeting a *Satyagraha Sabha* emerged. The *Sabha* issued a statement which became the *satyagraha* pledge for its members. Once again the pledge shows how it directly affected the life of the Indian people.

The leader cannot afford to allow a gap between himself and the people. People's failure was in a sense the leader's failure. By withdrawing the *satyagraha,* Gandhi underlined this important fact at a time when people's movement had not crystallized anywhere in Asia. His introduction of individual *satyagraha* from 7th April also stresses this aspect. He had said then (after Delhi disturbances), 'When we have acquired habits of discipline, self-control, qualities of leadership and obedience, we shall be better able to offer civil disobedience.'

The Rowlatt *satyagraha* has been called a failure. It did not obtain the objective, namely, the repeal of the Rowlatt Act. The *satyagraha* movement launched for moving the government by moral force of non-violence had erupted into violence. Thus, the immediate objective of *satyagraha* suspended once could not be easily resumed. However, the Second Rowlatt Bill was brought before the Imperial Legislative Council for enactment and the Rowlatt Act which had been enacted was never invoked.

Historically, it is important to note one very significant happening after the Rowlatt *satyagraha.* The masses had participated in this movement for the first time, however imperfectly. Gandhi's appeal for action struck a chord in the hearts of the people, specially the common people, because he drew inspiration from the stories of India's epics and ancient books (e.g., the story of Prahlad) known to almost every household.

The Bombay inspector-general's report of 1919 mentioned that Gandhi had a hold on the imagination of the masses, specially in Gujarat. Gandhi had been able to generate loyalty which was deep in Gujarat and held potential for his future leadership. Undeniably, the Gandhian phase in the national movement had been inaugurated.

The forces of nationalism were strengthened. Gandhi was able to begin the process of transforming social group into a cohesive and articulate political community. A wide range of classes, sections and religious groups participated in the movement. The strength of participation differed from region to region. For example, the movement was stronger in Bombay, Gujarat and Madras than in Bengal, North-West Frontier and Jammu and Kashmir. But the administration had to admit in reference to the North-West Frontier that 'most educated Indian here, both the Hindus and Mohammadans, evidently feel strongly in favour of Mr. Gandhi.'

Gandhi himself used the experience of the Rowlatt *satyagraha* and continued his experiments with truth. The regions covered by the movement were widespread although distance made communication a little difficult.

The Khilafat issue, arising out of the imposition on Turkey of the iniquitous Treaty of Sevres (10th August, 1920), occupied great importance during the resumed non-cooperation movement. Gandhi gave the Khilafat issue a spontaneous and consistent support. He commented, 'It is an inalienable right of the people thus to withhold co-operation...In a great cause like the Khilafat, we could not do otherwise than non-cooperate with Government in case of a betrayal.

The address presented by Gandhi and the Ali Brothers reflecting the wishes of the Indian Muslims regarding Khilafat included Muslim control over the whole Jazirat-ul-Arab, Khilafat's wardenship of the Holy places and integrity of the Ottoman empire. The Arabs and the turks, by removing their mutual differences, and preserving as far as possible their national aspiration, should act in the interest of Islam and the great Muslim fraternity.

Gandhi said, 'Even apart from the religious issues involved in the Khilafat, the Muslims are still on the path of justice. The Allies had accepted, and so had President Wilson, the principle that the boundaries of different countries as they existed when the war started should remain intact, and that no country should be made to suffer by way of punishment. The Muslims want them to abide by this principle. The demand that the territories held by Turkey in August, 1914 be restored to her, that Arabia and the holy places of Islam remain under the control of the Khalifa, and they say that they would not mind the Sultan being asked to furnish reasonable guarantees for the protection of his Christian and Jewish subjects, consistent with his dignity. The Arabs must remain free. I find none of these demands unreasonable. Hence I feel that, if we wish to do our duty by our neighbours, it is incumbent on us to help our Muslim brethren.'

'If twenty-two crores of Hindus intelligently plead for the Muslims on the Khilafat issue, I believe that they would for ever win the vote of the eight crores of Muslims...The Khilafat issue was a splendid opportunity as much as a grave problem before the people of India. It was a splendid opportunity, because if the Muslims used wisdom in solving the problem, their moral power would increase and India would come to enjoy a moral empire; Hindu-Muslim unity would increase, both Hindus and Muslims would grow stronger, their moral level would rise and the English would stop looking down upon us as an inferior race....Friendship is possible only between equals. The English do not regard us as their equals; even we consider ourselves as their inferiors. And therefore, we Hindus and Muslims, should solve this problem and ensure that the three become equals.'

The two events that stood out most prominent among others were the inauguration of swadeshi and the laying of the foundation of genuine Hindu-Muslim unity. Gandhi appealed to the Hindus to sympathize with and support their Muslim brethren. Muslim hearts were sore as they had never before been sore over the threatened dismemberment of the Turkish empire and over the question of Khilafat. If the Hindus failed to sympathize with the Muslims on that occasion, the great opportunity of cementing the unity would go, never perhaps to recur. He addressed 50,000 people in Madras on 12th August, 1920. He asked the Hindus to support the Muslims because he felt that the cause of the Indian Muslims was just. He had read the report of what had happened at the interview between the prime minister and the Khilafat deputation, and he found there was no demand urged by the deputation that was not just.

To the Muslims, *swaraj* meant, in Gandhi's view, India's ability to deal effectively with the Khilafat question. Gandhi spoke of '*Swaraj* in one year'. He wrote, 'Much laughter has been indulged in at my expenses for having told the Congress audience at Calcutta that if there was sufficient response to my programme of non-co-operation, *Swaraj* would be achieved in one year.' The attainment of *Swaraj* was the quickest method of righting the Khilafat wrong. To Gandhi, the solution of the Khilafat question was attainment of *Swaraj* and vice versa. Gandhi moved a comprehensive resolution in a meeting of the citizens of Bombay reaffirming the resolution of the Congress Working Committee which was passed on 5th October, 1921.

Maulvi Ahmed Said favoured the idea of boycotting English goods and recommended the use of *swadeshi* goods. He offered his services and wealth to any of the workers who was wiling to go to jail or bear death if need be in the cause of Islam.

On 17th October, 1920, Khilafat Day was observed throughout India and a movement was started to boycott the peace celebrations of December, 1920. The Khilafat Committee met in Delhi on 23-24 October. It was attended by Gandhi and other prominent leaders. It passed 'violent' resolutions advocating total abstention from the peace celebrations, the gradual boycott of British goods and abandonment of cooperation with government. The Committee recommended:

- surrender of honorary offices.
- refusal to attend government *darbars,*
- gradual withdrawal of children
- gradual boycott of British courts
- refusal to serve in Mesopotamia
- refusal to offer as candidate for election
- boycott of foreign goods.

Inspite of the joint Hindu-Muslim front over the Khilafat question and the resumption of non-cooperation over this issue, the movement continued for about two years with varying intensity in different provinces. Ultimately the Indian Muslim community and Gandhi were overtaken by external events, notably the resumption of war by Turkey and the conclusion of the resultant peace treaty of Sevres. Under the Lausanne Settlement of 24th July, 1923, the questions of the fulfilment of Indian Muslims demands in connection with the Khilafat and the Ottoman empire were effectively scotched.

In the period after the non-cooperation and Khilafat movements, there was a lull in the political movement. There were Hindu-Muslim discords which expressed themselves in communal riots in Delhi, Gulbarga, Nagpur, Lucknow, Shahjahanpur, Allahabad, Jalalpur, Kohat and Calcutta in 1924-25.

In thinking of Gandhi's understanding of religion, it should be remebered that he did not claim to have framed any consistent formulation of his outlook. It is not surprising that religion so ruled his thought and action. As Dr. S. Radhakrishnan says: "The spiritual motive dominates life in India."[5] Religion, in the Indian context, covers both the complex structures of consciousness and their behavioural manifestations. Gandhi's own religious life was not mainly shaped by philosophical texts, even by scriptural authorities, but by a host of other factors. Gandhi did not feel that religion acts in a separate sphere. He felt that 'mere religious knowledge' was futile. Religion, for him, was not really what is grasped by the brain, but a heart grasp.

When Gandhi assumed the leadership of the Congress in 1920, he had already developed his moral and social philosophy, but it was not until 1930 that he had perfected his political techniques for a successful all-India *satyagraha*. Gandhi's philosophy was moulded in South Africa, and was influenced by such diverse factors as the Jain and Vaishnava environment of his youth, the example of Christ, and the philosophic teachings of Tolstoy,[6] Ruskin[7] and Thoreau. These factors combined in his complex and hypersensitive personality (partially resulting from his feeling of rejection by the orthodoxy of his homeland and the world of the Western European) to produce neither a western nor a traditionalist philosophic system. The Moderates turned to European Liberalism; Tilak turned to Hindu traditionalism; Gandhi synthesized a system from the aberrant philosophies of both West and East.

Gandhi received an early but limited religious education from his mother, but as a youth was excommunicate from caste and thus from his religious community. A careful study of Gandhi's life and thought reveals that both were deeply rooted in the Hindu tradition. Gandhi himself openly acknowledged his indebtedness to the past when he said, "I have presented no new principles, but have tried to restate old principles."[8] Gandhi accepted Hinduism not as a dogma but as a working hypothesis of human conduct adapted to different stages of spiritual development and different conditions of life. Simply speaking, the ancient Indian spirit takes on a new form without ceasing to be itself, in every age. However, questioning the morality of the method, Gandhi asserted that, "Every formula of every religion has, in this age of reason, to submit to the acid test of reason and universal justice if it is to ask for universal assent. Error can claim no exemption if it can be supported by the scriptures of the world.[9]

What attracted Gandhi to Hinduism was not its religious prescriptions of the rituals or the mysticism of the legends, but its propensity to accommodate the positives and eliminate the negatives of different religious persuasions. While spiritualism and renunciation are supposed to be the core of Hindu religion, Gandhi did not undermine the importance of these concepts, but he emphasised more on its ethical components. For Gandhi, rather than being one cohesive religion, Hinduism was the melting pot of various religions, and not Hindu religion alone. Gandhi was convinced that Hinduism emerged stronger and richer with the historical interactions with the alien religions, like Islam, Buddhism and Christianity. For Gandhi, the Indian civilisation was hospitable to criticism and reform. It imbibed the quintescence of all religions to the extent that it exercise tremendous influence in the shaping of his philosophy and action.

The interpretation of life, at once, idealistic and existentialist, was obviously inspired by his deep religious sense and belief. Indeed it is this basic religious outlook and concern that enabled him to see life as a whole and to see it steadily so, through the three score years of involvement in public affairs. To this was added a strong strain of asceticism (a part of the idealist vision) which he practised with a unique thoroughness, especially so far he had chosen the path of involvement, rather than of withdrawal. Equally unique was his courage to practice what he preached—the courage to live, nay die, for his convictions.![10]

Among the books that Gandhi studied carefully were Butler's *'Analogy'* and Henry Drummond's *The Natural Law in the Spiritual World*. In 1928, he compared Drummond's classification of natural laws to the exposition in the fourteenth chapter of the *Gita* on sattva, rajas and tamas, the three-fold division of the qualities of nature, affecting the "ascent of man" through three stages to the position of the Perfect Man, *Purushottama*. In 1934, Gandhi also indicated that he was influenced by Adam Smith's discussion in *The Wealth of Nations,* and in 1944 he condemned Marx's *'Das Kapital'*.[11] Gandhi never claimed to be a well-trained intellectual but his reading, especially on morals and politics, was greater and wider than is usually realised, though less systematic than that of the other leading Indian intellectuals of his generation. Yet, no other Indian intellectual was as steeped as Gandhi was in the religious and philosophical texts of the classical Indian tradition as well as in the writings of daring Western moralists of the nineteenth century like Emerson and Carlyle.

It is also significant to note in Islam the semblance of Gandhian thinking, particularly his creed to truth, non-violence, non-acquisition, prohibition and religious tolerance. His insistence on conscience and soul-force is derived from the *Quran* more than from elsewhere, for in no other religious texts are moral disciplines so explicitly and clearly prescribed. For Gandhi, Islam did not stand for separation or for forcible conversion but for tolerance and fellow-feeling.

During the first part of his stay in South Africa, Gandhi was in very close contact with ardent Christians who tried their best to win him over to their beliefs. The resultant interchange raised in Gandhi's mind a large number of questions around scriptural authority, specifically of the *Bible* and of the *Vedas*. He found a lot of arguments to counter his Evangelical friends in the books of Edward Maitland, founder of the Esoteric Christian Union, which presented allegorical interpretations of the Gospels and proclaimed the fundamental identity of all great religions. In his difficulties and doubts he turned to his friend and mentor, Rajchandra Rajivbhai, with some of his questions, and later he recalled that a long letter from his friend had eased his mind. The anxious doubts about scriptural authority seem to have receded because he no longer considered Christianity a personal challenge that threatened his adherence to Hinduism. It was only after his final return to India that questions about the nature of scriptural authority started to return to the fore; this time they were prompted by Hindus who disagreed with his doctrines, with his interpretations of scripture, or with what they saw as his rejection of clear shastric injunctions. These new pressures made Gandhi formulate and clarify his own ideas.

The basis of Gandhi's interpretation of the authority of the *shastras* was his conviction of their historical character— that no scriptures are eternal in themselves, but that they are all the limited products of a particular time: "*Vedas, Upanishads, Smritis, Puranas* and *Itihasas*... do not enunciate anew the eternal truths, but show how these were practised at the time to which the books belong." Consequently, he believed, it was not surprising that they abound in contradictions, and, even worse, that "there is hardly an immoral practice for which it would be difficult to find Shastric sanction". Moreover, there is such a profusion of books called *'shastras'*, that even listing them would seem an impossible task. Even if one accepted, as Gandhi did, that some works, such as the *Samhita,* are of primary importance, these works too suffered from what he called "a process of double distillation": "First they come through a human prophet, and then through the commentaries of interpreters. None of them comes from God directly" Elsewhere he stressed the same idea in the context of a discussion about the Gospels: "Only God is changeless and as His message is received through the imperfect human medium, it is always liable to suffer distortion in proportion as the medium is pure or otherwise."

On the one hand, therefore, Gandhi accepted that the *shastras* suffered from severe historical limitations, but on the other he stood by their authority, which he repeatedly affirmed: "I do accept the *Shastras* as authoritative", "the sum total of these books is certainly inspired", "I believe in the *Puranas* as sacred books..." But what exactly was that authoritative core of truth, and how did one proceed to peel off the misleading layers of historicity? In this respect he indicated the broad criteria for rejecting shastric statements thus: "That which is opposed to trained reason, cannot be claimed as *Shastra,* no matter how ancient it may be." Gandhi mentioned the test of reason, but questions of 'rationality' did not often preoccupy him, except for the occasional affirmation of his disbelief in miracles, and his objection to logical inconsistencies. This is not surprising given the fact that Gandhi had no interest whatsoever in the 'dogmatic' or 'theological' superstructures of religion. He expressed that attitude very forcefully as follows: "It is a misuse of our intellectual energy and a waste of time to go on reading what we cannot put into practice."

The crucial, final test of the validity of a scriptural text lies elsewhere: "From my youth upwards, I learnt the art of estimating the value of scriptures on the basis of their ethical teachings. Here we touch the control nerve of the Gandhian approach: religion is about action, and "what cannot be followed in day-to-day practice cannot be called religion". No wonder that morality was for Gandhi the infallible touchstone of the truth of the *shastras*. He affirmed this conviction over and over again: "Nothing that is inconsistent with the universally accepted first principles of morality has for me the authority of the *Shastras*" and "... any conduct that is contrary to truth and *ahimsa* is to be eschewed and any book that violates these principles is not a *shastra*", etc. Gandhi referred to difficulties he experienced in coming to grips with the most sacred and ancient of Hindu scriptures, the *Samhita*; these difficulties were not problems of intellectual grasp of their meaning, but difficulties "in applying them to daily conduct." The crucial acid test of ethics made him "refuse to accept the authority of a *shastra* which supports untouchability." He most emphatically affirmed that supremacy of ethics when he stated.

> If I discovered that those scriptures, which are known as *Vedas, Upanishads, Bhagavad Gita, Smritis,* etc., clearly showed that they claimed divine authority for untouchability..., then nothing on this earth would hold me to Hinduism."

If it is through that supreme test of ethics that one is enabled to peel away the unacceptable and historic layers from the essential core of the *shastras,* then it must follow that the essential truth of the *shastras* consists of an ethical message:

> Learned men may please themselves and draw seemingly profound meanings from the *Shastras,* but

what they offer is not the real sense of these. Only those who have experience in the practice of their truths can explain the real meaning of the *Shastras.*

The *Gita* itself, in stanza 16.23, says "Let the Shastra be thy authority". Gandhi's interpretation is of considerable interest when he explains the meaning of the *Gita's* injunction: "We should be quided by the authority of the Shastras. That Shastra means shistachara, that is we should follow the example of those forefathers of ours who were holy and fearless". According to him that is what scriptures are about, right conduct, and that is where the scripture speaks with authority—the authority of the saints of yore who have successfully put the ethical principles they proclaim into practice in their own lives. It is successful practice, no passive reception of "revealed" truths, that lends authority to their precepts.

The book, which became Gandhi's strongest bond with Hinduism as well as the greatest influence on him and which he called his "spiritual dictionary", was the *Bhagwad Gita,* to whom he was introduced by the Theosophists. While he never claimed to be well-versed in the scriptures, he preferred to rely upon reason and, his own moral sense when the scriptures conflicted with his own philosophy.

From the multitude of available texts, Gandhi chose the *Gita* as his personal guide, and as the touchstone of all shastras: "nothing that is inconsistent with the main theme of the *Gita* is *Shastra,* no matter where it is found printed." This firm assertion is often repeated in different words: The Gita is "the essence of dharma," "a synthesis of the Hindu religion" and "the key to a knowledge of the *Shastras.*" He stated: "whatever is contrary to its main theme I reject as un-Hindu," and "if all the other scriptures were reduced to ashes, the seven hundred verses of this imperishable booklet are quite enough to tell me what Hinduism is and how one can live up to it."

One of the reasons for this pre-eminence of the *Gita* is its pan-Hindu universality: "It is accepted by all Hindu sects as authoritative." As such it is distinct from the many sectarian scriptures that find favour with only a section of Hindus. Although other texts, and in particualr the *Samhitas,* do have that same pan-Hindu quality, what makes the *Gita* more effectively universal is that it is an easy text, cast in "incredibly simple Sanskrit," and accessible in the original to anyone with even arudementary knowledge of that language. The difficult language of the *Vedas,* for example puts them out of reach of all except a few specialists. The *Gita* differs from many other texts in yet another way: according to Gandhi it is free from dogma, and as such is accessible, acceptable and applicable to everybody, because, it "excludes no Faith and no teacher."

However, these reasons for the pre-eminent place of the *Gita* were only peripheral to Gandhi; the cardinal reason was that "in a short compass it gives a complete reasoned moral code," and it provides "in a nutshell the secret art of living." In other Hindu texts the ethical core is dispersed and hidden in an abundance of embellishments, obscurities, dogmatic elaborations, mythical cycles, and ritualistic discourses; it requires scholarship, effort and endless time to sift the pure religious discourse without any embellishment. It simply describes the progress of the pilgrim soul towards the Supreme Goal. Therefore, there is no question of selection." The Gita is supreme among the *shastras* because, in a clear, direct and succinct fashion, "it enunciates the principles on which all conduct must be based."

Since for Gandhi the essence of religion lay in ethical action, it is quite logical that for him the *Gita* occupied the highest place among the *shastras*. Moreover, he did not look upon the *Gita* as being just a book of theory, a handbook with rules for religious living; to him the knowledge it contained was "the fruit of experience." The author of the *Gita* was not just an inspired theoretician: he summarized the basic principles of perfect living after having put them into practice, and the knowledge that resulted was the fruit of that test. Gandhi heard the echo of that truth reverberate in the very text: "I have felt that the *Gita* teaches that what cannot be followed out in day-to-day practice cannot be called religion."

There is no doubt that much of the text of the *Gita* deals with principles of action. However, it also contains, especially in later chapters, a significant number of statements of a different kind, dealing with questions of a theoretical and theological nature. To Gandhi these were of a secondary significance, and he made this quite clear by unequivocally indicating what he considered to be the "core" of the *Gita:* "the theme of the *Gita* is contained in the second chapter", "From the last verse of Chapter II, it would seem that Sri Krishna had nothing further to add", and, "with Chapter II the Gita ends. It need not have been followed by anything more." In fact, Gandhi was prepared to go even further, and he repeatedly declared that the last nineteen stanzas of Chapter II constituted the essence of the *Gita* and that all the rest was no more than an explanation and elaboration of that basic message. "These stanzas are the key to the understanding of the *Gita*. I would even go so far as to advise people to reject statements in the poem which bear a meaning contrary to that of these nineteen stanzas". These assertions by Gandhi about the crucial importance of the second chapter are confirmed by his writings on the *Gita;* nearly half of his commentary, (120 pages), is devoted to chapters two, three, and four. The remaining thirteen chapters get very short shrift; they average less than ten pages each. A rough count of Gandhi's quotations from the Gita confirms that pattern: about two-thirds of his quotations (approximately 110) come from chapters two and three (as opposed to upto only ten, or none at all, found in each of the remaining chapters).

The *Mahabharata*, the epic of which the *Gita* forms a part, has been a part of Hindu heritage for at least 2500 years. Gandhi put forward the view that the epic was an allegorical and not a historical work. He attempted to employ traditional terms to communicate his own philosophy and wrote a commentary on the *Gita* which, however, was so controversial that he was widely attacked by the orthodox scholars.

Gandhi did not accept the traditional interpretation of the *Gita* as the poetic presentation of Lord Krishna's exhortation to Arjun, the warrior, to go forward and meet his cousins in combat. The battlefield of Kurukshetra was only a symbol of the battle between good and evil which rages in every human heart. To those who insisted on taking the story of *Mahabharata* literally, Gandhi pointed out that even if the story was taken at its face value, the *Mahabharata* had demonstrated the futility of violence: the sinful war had ended in universal devastation in which the victors had been no better off than the vanquished.[12]

This proposition put forward by Gandhi cannot be necessarily accepted. In the Indian legendary literature, war has been considered necessary for the destraction of evil forces. It seems odd to interpret the *Mahabharata* as a counsel against war. War for heroic purposes, and for preserving and extending an eternal way of life is a must. It is a means for justifiable moral ends.

Gandhi, thus, attempted to hint as to the right way to understand religious or spiritual texts. He alleged that as contrasted with books about the objective world whose truth can be easily ascertained by checking them with outer fact, religious or spiritual texts, which are concerned with experience that is in the main subjective, cannot be similarly understood. Were the *Gita* a mere narrative of objective facts, its truth could be easily checked by an external verification; but insofar as a good deal of what it says relates to the life of the spirit, a quite different approach is needed here.[13]

Gandhi's Marxist critics had a shrewd suspicion that he deliberately underplayed the quietistic and esoteric elements in Hinduism because of the harm which excessive preoccupation with them had done to the Hindu society, and that he sought confirmation in the *Gita* for his own framework of values: *ahimsa* (non-violence), *varnashrama* based on division of labour rather than of birth, manual work and *brahmacharya*.[14] However, it will be safe to say that Gandhi was one of the greatest innovators in the history of Hinduism. He re-shaped and re-defined time-honoured concepts. Gandhi placed no special emphasis on the spirit of Hindu history though he admired various historical figures, such as Gautam Buddha.

It was during his South African period that he first gave serious thought to the meaning of the scriptures and the essence of religion. This reflection was stimulated by close Christian contacts whose claims about Christianity—raised doubts in his mind about Hinduism. He wrote to Edward Maitland, founder of the Esoteric Christian Union, who sent him two of this books, which Gandhi "greatly liked." In fact, he became a propagandist of Esoteric Christian Union Literature, and mentioned the organization on his letterhead. He corresponded regularly with Maitland till his (Maitland's) death in 1897, ordered multiple copies of his books, and defended the author in the *'Natal Advertiser'*. The connection, therefore, was not simply a casual one, and it is worthwhile to investigate what ideas on scripture Maitland pro-pounded.

The Christians who tried to convert Gandhi to Christianity were mostly Evangelicals, who believed that humanity had fallen into sin and that only the atonement of Christ could save; faith in Christ was the door to heaven. They held that proof of their beliefs lay in the unique and final revelation of the *Bible,* which they interpreted in a fundamentalist way. Many of Maitland's ideas provided Gandhi with an answer to the questions and anxieties he experienced when assailed by the arguments of profoundly convinced Christians whom he admired and loved. First of all he believed in the universality of revelation: specific sacred books were only the constant re-revealing of a universal revelation Second, Maitland rejected historic and fundamentalist interpretations. To him the Gospel narrative does not deal primarily "with material things or persons, but with spiritual significance" and its purpose is "to exhibit and illustrate processes and principles which are purely spiritual." It is most interesting to note the way in which Maitland interpreted the figure of Christ: "Christ Jesus, then, is no other than the hidden and true man of the Spirit, the Perfect Humanity, the Express Image of the Divine Glory." In fact, "between the man who becomes a Christ, and other men, there is no difference whatever in kind. The difference... consists in difference of unfoldment of the spiritual nature possessed by all in virtue of their common derivation."

Maitland's ideas must have helped Gandhi cope with the claims of some Christian friends, but he remained unclear about the position and validity of Hinduism and its scriptures. In 1894, he wrote to his Jain friend, Rajchandra Rajivbhai, whom he called Raychand, listing a number of pertinent questions. Raychand's answers "pacified" him. It is in these answers that we find fundamental ideas that are very similar to those we found to be the basic principles of Gandhi's concept of scripture and religion, and of *Gita*-interpretation.

In answer to questions about *Atman* and *Moksha*, Raychand offered the following ideas. The *Atman* is fundamentally different from all else that exists, and is the author *(karta)* of its own *Moksha*. In the state of bondage, the *Atman* commits deeds of anger, love, attachment, greed, etc. *Moksha* is freedom from such attachment, from all bondage of passions and the body; it is the state of self-realization in which the spirit fully realizes its own pure nature and its freedom from all connections with matter. The word God, or *Isvara*, does not signify a unique being of great power, or a creator of the universe; it is the perfect state of the *Atman* in *Moksha*.

Raychand made it quite clear that in his opinion scriptures, and specifically the *Vedas* and the *Gita*, were historical works composed by human beings. To say that they were "revealed by God" really meant that they were composed by persons who had attained the illumination of *Moksha*. In answer to the question as to how one should go about assessing the claim of superiority by any particular religion, Raychand pointed to the "test of proof" that religion alone is best and truly strong which is most helpful in destroying the bondage of worldly life and can establish us in the state which is our essence." In other words, the real test of the validity of a religion and its scriptures consists in the practical application of its precepts. Raychand reaffirmed this when he wrote about the *Puranas* that he thought that Brahma, Vishnu and Shiva had to be understood "allegorically," and that it would be better" to try to profit from the instruction they (the Puranas) contain, rather than attempt in vain to ascertain the principles embodied in the personification of Brahma, and so on."

In answer to Gandhi's questions about Christ and Krishna, Raychand asserted that "incarnations" or avatars were logically impossible. Calling Krishna "God" only meant expressing the belief that Krishna's *Atman* had attained *Moksha,* interestingly, Gandhi also asked explicit questions about *bhakti:* "Can an illiterate person attain *Moksha* through *bhakti* alone?" and "Can we attain salvation through faith in them (Krishna and Rama as avtars)?" Raychand's answers were revealing: *bhakti* has the power of purifying knowledge, but knowledge is the cause of *Moksha,* whereas *bhakti* only plays a subsidiary role. Faith in Krishna and devotional worship cannot cause *Moksha* but they can help us to gain the means for attaining *Moksha,* if they help us follow Krishna's teaching and example and thus free ourselves from all forms of attachment.

The parallelism between Raychand's ideas as expressed in that letter of 1894 and those of Gandhi were so persistent and striking that one has to conclude that Raychand's influence on Gandhi's ideas was decisive. Gandhi's admiration for his friend has been conclusively shown, but it is of interest to draw attention to the exact terms in which Gandhi expressed his praise:

> "His writings are the quintessence of his experiences...One rare feature of his writings is that he always set down what he had felt in his own experience... He was a man of self-control, ... the state of freedom from attachment was spontaneous to him,...his devotion to dharma was evident in every action of his."

Gandhi admired Raychand because of his self-control and his freedom from attachment: he was like the *sthitaprajna* of the *Gita.* He admired his writings on religion because of their pragmatic and experimental nature.

Raychand obviously was a man very much after Gandhi's own heart.

While Raychand undoubtedly had great influence on Gandhi during a crucial period of his personal development, this seed did not fall on virgin soil. From his youth Gandhi had been disenchanted with ritualism and myth, and was irritated by the exclusive and contradictory claims of various religions. Moreover, by temperament and inclination, he had always been a moral practitioner and a stubborn individualist; during his South African period he was constantly experimenting with various forms of self-control. Raychand's general principles struck a chord in him. They provided a logical framework that not only supported his moralistic and individualistic approach to religion, but also allowed him to judge other religions and accept their positive aspects without having to reject Hinduism. That framework in the final instance determined most aspects of Gandhi's interpretation of the *Gita*.

This does not mean that Gandhi inherited Jainism from Raychand; he always considered himself thoroughly a Hindu. However, one should remember that for Gandhi all religions were in essence the same. When he was very pointedly asked the question "What is the difference between the *Gita's* theism and the Jain doctrine that there is no God?" he answered, "I have never seen any difference between the Jain doctrine and the general Vedic doctrine. The difference is only one of point of view." He then went on to explain how the point of view was different. The *Gita*, he wrote, "is a poem," and "the conversation between Lord Krishna and Arjuna is imaginary"; this imaginative way of writing was not "inappropriate or untruthful," however. Jainism, on the other hand" stated the truth logically and unpoetically" in declaring there was no God. When one went to the root of things, Jainism and the *Gita* both expressed the same truth, that religion was the individual's effort to achieve freedom from attachment; only the medium for expressing that truth was different.

Gandhi's approach to the *Gita* differs markedly from the method of many traditional interpreters who expend great effort on textual interpretation and on establishing the internal logic of the various theoretical statements and practical directives of the text. But in one important way Gandhi's approach is in close conformity with a major traditional rule of interpretation. He identifies the central, the key passage in the text; the *mahavakya*. "the great statement" that gives the central message, in terms of which all the rest of the text must be explained. For Gandhi the last twenty stanzas of chapter two constitute the *Gita's mahavakya* in the description of the *sthitaprajna*. This passage in fact expresses most succinctly, without any mythical, ritual, or dogmatic paraphernalia, without "imagination," the essence of religion as he saw it. His concept of the nature of the scripture was largely inherited from Raychandra. Jainism, moreover, gave Gandhi the basic theoretical structure that best fitted his own deepest nature, that of a "religious activist," with its dualism of *jiva-ajiva*, spirit and matter, its inexorable law of *Karma*, and its conception of the gradual purification of the *Atman* necessary on the highroad to self-realization.

Gandhi professed a form of Hinduism, no doubt, but deviated so far from orthodoxy as to equate God and Truth, as rationally perceived, and to emphasize the validity of all religious beliefs on the basis of their moral worth. Truth was the supreme value not only for Gandhi, but has been a key concept in the Indian traditional ethico-religious thought. However, Gandhi accepted Truth not merely as a concept, but sought to realise it in practice as the 'sovereign principle' of life and conduct, and as a reality. And since

God is also thought of as being the only Eternal Reality, He is, for Gandhi, the same as Truth. The two have been essentially equated, for Gandhi found in Truth the quickest and the easiest way to realise God. Gandhi made truth paramount.[15] Nonetheless, in his search for Absolute Truth, he was fully aware that the absolute cannot be known by the yet unfulfilled human mind.

In Gandhian philosophy, closely connected with the ultimate or absolute end was the problem of means. Gandhi laid surpassing emphasis on the use of right means for achieving objectives. For him, means and ends were convertible terms. The two were inseparable and should be equally pure. As Gandhi himself said: "The means may be likened to a seed, the end to a tree; and there is just the same inviolable connection between the means and the end as there is between the seed and the tree."[16] Specifically speaking thus, non-violence as a means became the supreme value for Gandhi. Not only this, but Gandhi's interpretation of *ahimsa* (non-violence) is also striking for its unparalleled richness of significance because, for Gandhi, it did not stand for pacifism, but as an inspiration for the individual and the nation to achieve complete harmony with all the impulses of human nature. However, the impression that one gets is that Gandhi believed in non-violence as a creed, as an eternal virtue and as a supreme way of life to which even the freedom of the country could be subordinated. But still, a more careful analysis of his activities would betray a tendency on Gandhi's part to equate expediency with principle. The pains that he took to emphasize the extreme intimacy of the inter-relation between truth and non-violence is a remarkable feature of Gandhi.

Another clear contribution of Gandhi is the way he practised and understood fasting—as a heightened moment in the practice of *ahimsa*. He used it, on the hand, to achieve social objectives and, on the other, for the realisation of his essential, identically with others. In fact, he illustrated how fasting is being very close to God.[17]

Gandhi also found a needful and continual self-expansion of every concept in the setting of practice in his knitwork, of vows, namely,

(i) Brahmacharya: This is not isolated control of sex, but simultaneous control of all the senses. And in the practice of *brahmacharya,* Gandhi stressed the role of will, as against mere insinctual thoughts. It ought to be observed in thought, word and deed.

(ii) Asvada: Though it is not merely bodily in significance, *brahmacharya* vitally depends on the control of the palate. Gandhi, therefore, turned asvada into a distinctive vow, thus enriching the Hindu ethical tradition.

(iii) Asteya: Though *asteya* literally means not to commit theft, Gandhi interpreted it in a far subtler way. He described the essence of non-stealing as stealth (or the tendency to conceal) and not mere abstention from theft of others' property. Like *asvada, asteya* has a positive significance. It calls for definite effort to abstain from conditions which bar the manifestation of truth.

(iv) Aparigraha: Though the literal meaning of *aparigraha* is not to possess property; it has (like *asvada* and *asteya*) a distinct positive significance in Gandhian thought. Gandhi's treatment of this vow is the idea that *aparigraha* requires one to be non-attached even to the body which too is a kind of possession. Gandhi believed that if one looks upon the body merely as an instrument of service, one can attain real happiness and the beatific vision in the fulness of time.

(v) Abhaya: Following the *Gita,* Gandhi gave the place of pre-eminence to the observance of *abhaya* or fearlessness. He regarded this vow as indispensable for the growth of

other noble qualities. Nonetheless, instead of extolling fearlessness categorically, Gandhi cared to say that one does not need to fear the inner foes.

(vi) Apart from the above vows, Gandhi also insisted on the four distinctive vows of Removal of Untouchability, Principle of Bread-labour (fruits of labour accure only to him who has worked for it), *Sarvadharma Samabhava* (equal respect for all religions) and *Swadeshi.*

Ethical religion brought about a distinctiveness in Gandhi. Gandhi did not accept the orthodox interpretation of religion though he employed the concept to convey his own philosophy, but like the Buddhists, he taught a universalised religion on *ahimsa*. He also interpreted religion or *dharma,* as selfless service of others, mastery over passions fearlessness and most important of all, devotion. Accordingly, dharma, for Gandhi, became an embodiment of the content that was shaped by one's own special gifts, the discipline a man voluntarily undertakes, and a moral insight which leads a man beyond the performance of his customary duties.

In his description of *dharma,* one of the main things Gandhi emphasized was that caste had nothing to do with religion. It was a later excrescence on what had originally been basically the principle of labour and of duties. What remained was an outstanding feature of the Hindu social system, but this should in no way be confused with religion, with *dharma,* with the life it was good and reasonable for men to lead.[18] Gandhi realised that the caste system was opposed both to his principle of universal *ahimsa* and his programme to abolish untouchability. He demanded the abolition of caste as unjust and immoral, and the substitution of a non-religiously-sanctioned occupational, but hereditary class structure.

Gandhi turned the tables on Swami Vivekananda's formula that all men should be *brahmins*, by saying that all should be *sudras*. *Sudras* are those who serve, and nothing more was needed than service, whether in Indian society or elsewhere. Gandhi thus, attempted to incorporate the duties of scavenging and bread labour in the concept of *dharma*. He tried working out his ideas in a society where dirty work was the lot of the untouchables, the outcastes of the Hindu society, and where manual work was considered inferior to the work of the scholar, lawyer and teacher. Thus, Tolstoy's therapeutic value of manual work and Ruskin's views on the equal value of different kinds of work to society became the basis of Gandhi's thought that trusted for the good of society.[19]

Gandhi interpreted his own life as being guided by the *dharmas* of social service, poverty, harmlessness, vegetarianism and celibacy, whose practical applications were, for him, no more than mere experiments with truth. As he himself said: "The instruments for the quest of truth are as simple as they are difficult. They may appear quite impossible to an arrogant person, and quite impossible to an innocent child. The seeker after truth should be humbler than the dust. The world crushes the dust under its feet, but the seeker after truth should be so humble himself that even the dust could crush him. Only then, and not till then, will he have a glimpse of truth."[20] However, what has been unique in Gandhi's experiments with Truth was that they were carried out not in the seclusion of an *ashrama*, but in the arena of life. And when the scene shifted to the political front, religion became a means of mass-mobilization.

Gandhi considered his own philosophical system superior to the Hindu art of politics. He endeavoured to develop a sense of unity by employing traditional terms, but was far more successful in communicating to the masses through his personality and ways of life, appearing as he did as a modern *sanyasi,* and this traditional appearance especially influenced the Indian women, chiefly devotees of *Bhakti* worship.

Like Tilak, Gandhi realised that effective political action demanded that the Congress become a mass organisation, and as such, he and Sardar Patel provided it with a well-disciplined authoritarian structure. He also tended to follow the heretical attitude, which forms a sub-strata of the Hindu tradition, emphasizing world and life-negation, renunciation, self-sacrifice, and suffering for a moral purpose. And above all, Gandhi abhorred the use of force, but utilised the political techniques of Tilak, not because they were the only expedient techniques but because he could justify them in terms of his own moral philosophy by emphasizing non-violence, the "constructive programme" and a return to the spinning wheel and the simple life.

The combination of religion with politics or religious politics is the very essence of Gandhism, and on its legitimacy or otherwise depends the whole significance of the fact of Gandhi. Gandhi himself asserted: "Yes, I still hold the view that I cannot conceive politics as divorced from religion. Indeed religion should pervade every one of our actions. For me there is no politics without religion not the religion of the superstitious and the blind, religion that hates and fights, but the universal religion of toleration. Politics without morality is a thing to be avoided."[21] Here Gandhi claimed to be in stark contrast of Machiavelli's concept of complete separation of religion and politics.

That, Gandhi was opposed to Machiavellian approach to politics seems plausible. His exhortations with regard to the restoration of moral values in political practice might appear utopian in the present context when politics has gone downhill. But for him, it was a practical proposition.

His periodic reference to conscience in dealing with decision-making in day-to-day functioning was an indication of his faith in the corrigibility of man. That is why, Gandhi was disturbed by the emergence of religious intolerance, communal frenzy and the like, which marred peace and harmony in society.

Gandhi repeatedly asserted the oneness of life. It was one continuous whole and could not properly be conceived as compartmental. Therefore, it was not a matter of "mixing" religion and politics, for they were already rightfully one. However, there is a probability that Gandhi himself experienced a dichotomy between his religious pursuits and political endeavours, which was never completely resolved. But in spite of such a tension, he succeeded in evolving a well-integrated personality, especially religiously-oriented.

Gandhi felt that spiritual values has no relevance unless they were put into social practice by those who professed them. As such, it was not very difficult for a semi-clad contemplative *sanyasi* to become a *karma-yogi* in the field of politics. Gandhi's actions may also be justified in the sense that in the Hindu tradition, religion is such an integrative force that there is bound to be a close relationship between religion and politics. It can also be said that historically, culture, politics and religion have been synonymous with Hinduism. One may recall that both Gautama Buddha and Mahavira, founders respectively of Buddhism and Jainism, were of the ruling or warrior caste. Part of the *shastras* are political texts, such as the *Arthasastra* attributed to Kautilya and parts of the Laws of Manu. Nevertheless, tension was not entirely absent between religion and politics, for the latter often took a ruthless turn and, thereby stimulated transcendental speculation in Indian religious life.

Gandhi's religious quest helped him to mould not only his personality, but the political technique with which he confronted racialism in South Africa and colonialism in India. Gandhi inherited *Swaraj* as the political objective of the Congress; however, he felt compelled to find a moral issue upon which to base his campaigns of political agitation, and he finally succeeded in being able to rationalise that, while *Swaraj* was not a self justifying objective in the traditionalist sense, the immortality of the British Raj made Indian *Swaraj* a morally justifiable goal.

Gandhi felt that, in India, the masses had no political consciousness. Their politics was confined to bread and salt and to communal adjustments. Therefore, he wanted that the politicians must represent the masses in opposition to government. "But if we begin to use them before they are ready we shall cease to represent them."[22] And for this, he stressed the necessity of using the imagination when making moral decisions. To be capable of moral judgement and moral conduct on a significant scale, one has necessarily to put oneself in the place of other people and imagine sympathetically how they feel. Gandhi recognised no God except the God that is found in the hearts of the "dumb millions". Anything that millions can do together is, he believed, charged with a unique power, the magical potency of collective tapes or moral fervour, the cumulative strength of generally shared sacrifices.[23]

Gandhi was concerned with the integrity of the Indian tradition as well as the needs of a vast, revolutionary movement. He rejected the borrowed conception of terrorism as a legitimate instrument of a revolutionary programme, and, at the same time, he discarded the prevailing notion of the spiritual life as a matter for monks in monasteries or peripatetic pilgrims and recluses. He believed that the moral or religious approach to politics had an enobling effect upon those who adopted it and as well as upon those against whom it is exercised. Politics, he asserted, could thus be transformed. The crude of political power be softened by the practice of diverse technique of moral coercion.

The Marxists contend that the social ostracism practised by the Hindus played a very important role in keeping the Muslims away from the national struggle led by the Congress. The Muslims resented the Hindu orthodox snobbery but when it was defended by persons like Gandhi, they felt bitter.[24]

However, the other aspect of the issue holds the contention that the emergence of Gandhi on the Indian political scence ushered in a new era in the history of the problem of communal unity. With his universalist religious philosophy, he refused to accept that the religious differences of the Hindus and the Muslims made them two separate nations which could not be united on issues vital to their socio-political life in India. He believed that unity between the Hindus and the Muslims was imperative not only from the religious point of view but also from the political point of view. Gandhi looked at the communal problem in the capacity of a socio-religious reformer as well as a shrewd politician. That is why he emphasized the need of Hindu-Muslims unity on religious as well as political grounds."[25] Gandhi's belief in the absolute oneness of God led him to advocate the fellowship of faiths and human brotherhood. And he held that religious distinctions should not come in the way of their common destiny. Specially on Hindu-Muslim unity he said "that the two communities were wedded to India; they are neighbours, sons of the soil. They are destined to die here as they are born here."[26]

From the very beginning, the Indian National Movement launched by the Indian National Congress was characterised by the absence of Muslim participation. Barring a few prominent Muslims of the time, the Indian National Congress failed to attract Muslims towards itself. They were more drawn towards the leadership of Sir Syed Ahmed Khan and his successors. The events that followed the death of Sir Syed led his successors to think in terms of organising Muslims on a political plane. Consequently, in the year 1906, the All India Muslim League came into existence with the demand for a separate electorate to safeguard the Muslim interest. This was granted by the British in 1909 and ratified by the Congress in 1916 when the Lucknow Pact was signed. The Lucknow Pact was a sort of recognition that Muslims were a separate political unit in India.

Gandhi did not approve of Muslim separatism. To him, it amounted to the negation of national unity. And he considered it a hurdle in the way of achieving India's independence from the British rule. He was convinced that Hindu-Muslim unity in India was necessary. To Gandhi, unity is strength, "a rule of life, is in no case so clearly illustrated as in the problem of Hindu-Muslim unity. Divided we must fall—unity not only between Hindus and Mussalmans but between all those who believe India to be their home, no matter to what faith they are".[27]

Gandhi's approach to the problem of Hindu-Muslim relations in India was based on the view that it is a phenomenon of recent origin. He did not believe that ever since the advent of Islam in India as a political force the relations between the Hindus and the Muslims have remained strained and they were always at war with each other. He rejected the idea that an ingrained and ineradicable animosity exists between the two communities.

As a part of the demonstration of theory on practical grounds, Gandhi took up the Khilafat issue alongside his non-cooperation Movement. Alongwith Tilak, he viewed the Khilafat agitation as a golden opportunity for cementing Hindu-Muslim unity and bringing the Muslim masses into the national movement. Actually, the ground for common political action by Hindus and Muslims had already been prepared by the Lucknow Pact, and also that the nationalist agitation against the Rowlatt Act had touched all the Indian people alike and brought Hindus and Muslims together in political agitation.

The Khilafat agitation made an important contribution to the Non-cooperation Movement. It had brought urban Muslims into the nationalist movement and had, thus been responsible in part for the feeling of nationalist enthusiasm and exhilaration that prevailed in the country in those days. Some historians have condemned this display on the grounds that religious consciousness spread to politics, and in the long run, the forces of communalism strengthened. The nationalist leadership failed, to some extent, in raising the religious political consciousness of the Muslims to the higher plane of secular political consciousness.

However, Gandhi's efforts for the blending of the two communities made him popular with the Muslims overnight. Mohibbhul Hassan observes: "No Muslim leader, not even Maulana Mohammad Ali or Jinnah, ever received the adulation of the Indian Muslims as Mahatma Gandhi did during the Khilafat and non-cooperation days from 1919-1922. He was the idol of the Muslim masses and there was hardly a prominent Muslim, with the exception of Jinnah, who did not accept his leadership." [28]

At the same time, it should also be kept in view that the Khilafat agitation represented much wider feelings of the Muslims than their concern for the Caliph. On the other hand, even though the Non-cooperation had ended in apparent failure, the national movement had been strengthened, for it resulted in the politicisation and mobilization of the mass of the people.

Nonetheless, Gandhi's call for communal understanding was based on a liberal interpretation of Hinduism. Though this is much to be appreciated as providing a religious sanction for the secular or political programme of Hindu-Muslim unity, the Muslims consciously or unconsciously suspected that it was a tactical move which used one religion to overshadow another. The unity of religions was sought to be achieved from a basically Hindu standpoint according to the Muslims and therefore, they were aloof and alienated. But what Gandhi desired at heart was that people of different religions should forget their differences and make a common cause to achieve the independence of the country. And therefore, he emphasized more on Hindu-Muslim unity and said that there is no question more important and pressing than this one. However, it must be remebered that differences of religious opinion will persist to the end of time; toleration is the only thing that will enable persons belonging to different religions to live as good friends and neighbours.

Gandhi thought that the Hindu-Muslim problem in India was essentially religious and unity in the country should come through religion. This led him to adopt the religious and humanitarian approach to the resolution of Hindu-Muslim conflict. He was well aware that religious issues of both the Hindus and the Muslims, such as cow-slaughter, music or other disturbances before mosques and Shuddhi and Tabligh movement have always been a constant source of communal riots in the country. Gandhi believed that these religious issues ought to be resolved peacefully the awakening the true spirit of religion in the two communities.

The period 1922-37 is important in the annals of Indian history when certain developments took place which shaped the future course of events. Various attempts were made to forge unity between the two communities through Unity Conferences, Round Table conferences, correspondence and talks between the representatives of the Congress and the League. But these proved futile and the mutual distrust and differences kept multiplying to the extent that Jinnah, who was once considered an ambassador of Hindu-Muslim unity, became an advocate of the two-nation theory which posed a serious challenge to Gandhi's view of religion. For, it was hardly conceivable to him that religion could stand as a permanent barrier between the two communities and a change in religion could alter nationality. He clung fast to his faith that religion was not a divisive force as all religions were different roads converging on the same point. He, therefore, viewed it as an untruth and sought to resist it till his death.

However, he was not opposed to the realisation of cultural and economic aspirations of the Muslim masses, nor was he against the fulfilment of genuine political demands of the Muslim elite. He was aware that at the root of Muslim separatism was the fear among the Muslim elite that they could not hope to get their due share of power in a Hindu dominated political system. For Gandhi, such apprehensions were the result of ignorance, a sort of illusion. But for the Muslim elite, they were real and so could not be dispelled simply by words. Only some concrete steps ensuring cultural identity and due share of political power to the Muslims in independent India alone could remove such fears. He, therefore, went a long way in meeting the political aspirations of the Muslim elite, especially when freedom appeared to be in sight. He offered to the Muslims the right of self-determination provided it was confined only to meeting their genuine political, economic and cultural aspirations. This did not signify, from his point of view, any erosion of his concept of nationalism which rested in the principle of unity in diversity and democracy. This outlook was at the root of his own formula which he offered at the end of his talks with Jinnah in 1944 and his identification with C. Rajagopalachari formula or his blessings to Sapru Committee proposals and Desai-Liaquat Pact.

But Jinnah's own political compulsions such as the threat to his leadership from the leaders of his own party or from non-League political parties, especially in the Muslim majority areas, the mass hysteria that he had raised round the goal or slogan of Pakistan and the sympathies of a section of the British bureaucracy with his demands, hardened his attitude that made all efforts of Gandhi towards compromise futile.

However, Gandhi never thought that partition based on Jinnah's two-nation theory was inevitable. He, therefore, made every possible move to avert it. But the innumerable difficulties confronting him transcended his powers and resources. His own life style, his commitment to non-violence and purity of means not only restricted his moves but also left enough room for an astute politician like Jinnah to take advantage of his position. Following his principle of non-violence, he could rely only on persuasion for carrying the Muslims with him. He summed up his position in the following words:

> I know of no non-violent method of compelling the obedience of eight crores of Muslims to the will of the rest of India, however powerful a majority the rest may represent. The Muslims must have the same right to self-determination that the rest of India has. We are at present a joint family. Any member may claim a division...

The Congress, under his leadership, was thus left only with one course to avert partition and that was to negotiate with Jinnah.

However, mere appeals to the League leadership were not sufficient to bring them round to the Congress point of view for an amicable settlement. For, the demand for partition was a political move and its edges could be blunted only by a clever handling of the political situation, though not necessarily by surrendering the principles of non-violence and purity of means. Had the Congress abandoned its ideological stances and made the Muslims, especially those of the Muslim minority provinces realise the difficulties that they would face as a result of partition, the Muslim leadership might have given a second thought before lending their support to Jinnah. Azad did think of a move in this direction when he bluntly told the Cabinet Delegation that the creation of Pakistan on the basis of two-nation theory would relegate the Muslims in India to the position of aliens. But due to lack of support from the Congress leadership, it could not yield the desired results.

It was all the more important because prior to 1946, Jinnah did not have the wholehearted support of the Muslim leadership even in some of the Muslim majority areas. Sikander, in the Punjab, and Fazl-ul-Huq, in Bengal, could have posed a challenge to Jinnah's leadership had the Congress taken care to bring them into their fold. It was important because Sikander, the Premier of the Punjab, and after his death in 1942, Khizr Hayat Khan, who headed the ruling Unionist Party, did not subscribe to Jinnah's conception of Pakistan. But Sikander's alignment with the British bureaucracy in the Punjab, which he could ignore only at the risk of losing power, stood in the way of the Congress-Unionist rapprochement. The Punjab Congress leadership could be instrumental in building up a bridge between Sikander and the all-India Congress leadership but they failed to do so, though a limited understanding between the two was not impossible as the Unionist Party and the Congress did form a coalition ministry after the election of 1945-46. But it was too late as the League by that time had acquired tremendous influence over the Muslim voters in the Punjab. Besides, there were several other Muslim political parties and groups in the Punjab such as the Ahrars and the Khaksars who would not toe the line of Jinnah over the issue of Pakistan. Similarly in Bengal, the Congress did not lend its support to Fazl-ul-Huq which ultimately alienated the latter. Thus, it is possible that if the Congress had more time and more astute leaders, especially in the Muslim majority provinces, the forces against Pakistan amongst the Muslims could be consolidated compelling the League to arrive at some kind of understanding with Gandhi and the Congress.

Again, Gandhi's limited manoeuvrability was to be applied on a much larger plane as he was to carry with him all sections of Hindu society, both inside and outside the Congress, and a vast section of the Muslims, both Leaguers and non-Leaguers. Further, Gandhi was fighting at two fronts. One, against the League's demand for the partition of the country and the other, against the British for the freedom of the country. This situation provided ample opportunities to the League leader to seek the support of the British for the attainment of his goal.

It is true that the British were not in favour of partition on the basis of Jinnah's two-nation theory. But on the commencement of World War II, they were left with no choice but to humour Jinnah in order to build him up as a counterpoise to the Congress which had refused to cooperate with them in their war efforts. This gave opportunity to Jinnah to consolidate his position among the Muslim masses as the field was clear for him on account of the imprisonment of the Congress leaders following their direct clash with the British. As a result, Jinnah had a landslide victory in the 1945-46 elections. The Muslim League formed ministries in Bengal and Sind and came out as the single largest party in the Punjab. It won all the Muslim seats in Assam and considerably improved its position in North-West Frontier Province. This was a feather in Jinnah's cap who emerged an unquestioned leader of the Muslims and the League gained the position of being their (Muslims) sole representative. The election results contributed a great deal towards the realisation of Jinnah's goal.

An additional opportunity was provided by Prime Minister Attlee's Statement of February 20, 1947. Jinnah interpreted it as the acceptance of Pakistan in principle. The League leader, of course, was not wrong in drawing such conclusions, for, the British authorities were thinking in similar terms, George Edmund Abell, Private Secretary to the Viceroy, wrote to Ronald Montague Harris, Private Secretary to the Secretary of state:

> "It would appear that HMG still fight shy of saying clear things clearly. They might as well have stated categorically that agreements would be entered into with the Congress for the Hindu majority areas and with the Muslim League for the Muslim majority areas. If paragraph 13* has any meaning this is the only manner in which agreement for the transfer of power can be successfully negotiated."

The letter of Instructions to Lord Mountbatten, reinforced Jinnah's contention and he resorted to 'Direct

* Paragraph 13: His Majesty's Government will negotiate agreements in regard to matters arising out of the transfer of power with the representatives of those to whom they propose to transfer power. (Nicholas Mansergh, op.cit., Vol. IX, p. 775).

Action' which unnerved the Hindus, the Muslims and British alike and almost clinched the issue of the partition of the country.

The British Government was divided over the question of grant of independence to India. The unfavourable attitude of the Conservative Party towards it is amply evidenced by the acts and uterrances of Linlithgow, Amery, Wavell and Churchill. Though the British approach underwent a considerable change after the installation of the Labour Government in England, it was perhaps too late for them to undo the damage done by their predecessors. The recognition of Jinnah's intransigence which wrecked the Simla Conference proved a hurdle in arriving at an amicable settlement of the communal problem. The British, in fact, did not show firmness in their opposition to Pakistan. This offered enough encouragement or leeway to British officers in India holding sympathies with the League to extend their help and cooperation to it in the creation of Pakistan. The continuous presence of the British, therefore, was a source of strength to the Muslims. Consequently, they relied more on the British for the fulfilment of their demands than on the Congress leaders for any political settlement. Gandhi thus, was driven to the conclusion that the presence of the third party was an obstacle in the way of any communal settlement. He was sure that the elimination of the British from the Indian politics would pave the way for an amicable settlement between the two communities.

With this end in view, he impressed upon Jinnah to arrive at a mutually agreed solution without the help of the British. He had unlimited faith in the inherent goodness of man and power of persuasion for a just cause. The League leader, however, being an astute statesman with rock-like determination remained steadfast to the condition of acceptance of the principle of Pakistan as a prerequisite to any offer for the communal settlement.

Jinnah had a strict control over the League and was its sole dictator and spokesman. On the other hand, Gandhi's hold over the Congress varied from time to time as all Congress leaders did not have full faith in his principles of non-violence and truth and his technique of *Satyagraha*. Consequently, his position in the Congress, at times, was reduced to that of merely an adviser. It is true that he occasionally emerged as the strongest man in the organisation and appeared more or less its dictator, particularly so, when the Congress leadership were placed in direct confrontation with the Government and needed him to start a mass movement. But when the British showed readiness to arrive at a settlement with the Congress in 1945, his influence over its leadership started sliding downhill with accelerated pace. Consequently, he moved to the periphery of the decision-making bodies of the Congress at the most crucial period of India's destiny when the issue of partition was to be decided once for all. It seems that he was left with no choice but to accept the *fait accompli*. Its rejection would have worsened the communal relations in India and might have forced the British to give a second thought to their decision of handing over power to the Indians.

The partition of the country, however, was not the end of the journey for Gandhi. He still nurtured the hope of bringing the two communities which had become two nations on the withdrawal of the British from the Indian subcontinent, closer. When the leaders of the two communities were rejoicing at the fulfilment of their cherished goals, Gandhi was engaged in healing the wounds caused by the partition of the country. He had before him the more arduous tasks of building bridges between the two communities as the division of the country had raised more problems instead of solving the communal question. The presence of two antagonistic neighbours posed the problem of safeguarding the international border between the two countries for which they had to divert a substantial amount of their resources—an amount that could well have been utilized for development purposes.

All this could have been avoided if the League had accepted division on the basis of Gandhi's formula envisaging division between two brothers which significantly differed from Jinnah's concept of division on the basis of two-nation theory. K.B. Sayeed has rightly pointed out:

> If one started from Gandhi's point of view that India was a sort of joint family, some of whose members were breaking away from the family, then one would think in terms of a confederal or federal arrangement under which the separated members would still come together by a treaty or some other arrangement to 'provide for the efficient and satisfactory administration of foreign affairs, defence, internal communications, customs, commerce and the like, which must necessarily continue to be the matter of common interest between the contracting parties.'

Though the partition was not inevitable, it had become unavoidable because of the acts of omission and commission of the leadership of the League and the Congress as well as of British statesmen and bureaucrats.

But peace was not there to be preserved, when the climax of the independence struggle seemed to end on the platform of anti-climax where it moved from unity to parity. The demand for autonomous and sovereign states for the Muslim majority provinces in the East and in the West brought to an end all the fond hopes and false expectations of Hindu-Muslim unity. Jinnah, the Muslim leader, did not want any plebiscite in the Muslim majority provinces. And above all, he got the religious and moral leader committed to the principle of the division of India. Gandhi wrote to Jinnah: "If the vote is in favour of separation, it shall be agreed that those areas shall form a separate state as soon as India is free from foreign domination and can therefore be constituted into two sovereign independent States."[29]

Gandhi had declared on several occasions that Pakistan was a sin, a denial of God and an untruth. He had asked the protagonists of Pakistan to vivisect him before they vivisected India. The Mahatma stooped to conquer but his methods failed against the shrewdness of Jinnah. On May 30, 1947, Gandhi told his prayer audience that if the Pakistan of Jinnah's conception was a reasonable proposition, he should have no difficulty in convincing India to accept it![30] As such, August 15, 1947 undoubtedly was a great day in the history of the world as it saw a great liberating force released in Asia in the form of Indian independence, and the birth of the biggest Muslim state under the sun. The idea of Hindu-Muslim unity which Gandhi had put forward when he took up the Khilafat issue on entering active politics came to an end the moment Pakistan was established. The concept of religion for politics tragically ended in the politics of religion. As if that was not all, Gandhi's politico-communal assassination at the hands of a Hindu fanatic re-asserted the necessity to re-examine the dichotomy between religion and politics.

Gandhi's techniques, grounded in *dharma,* may have been flawless, but they failed to realise the inconsistancy of human nature. This was due to his inability to trace the socio-historical genesis of that antagonism. He discovered its origin not in the material life processes of the Indian society, but in the weak ethical structure of the people.

Gandhi, thus, symbolised a peculiar blend of bold advances followed by sudden and capricious halts. Living in the society, how could he remain untouched by its pitfalls.

Yet Gandhi had a strongly rational and sceptical streak which enabled him to fashion for himself a religious philosophy which, though grounded in Hinduism, acquired a deeply humanist and cosmopolitan complexion. Gandhi's religious thinking was stamped not only by his own confessional character, but it also shot through with a splendid vision which he believed could be a beacon light for all men everywhere. Gandhi's personal experience of living in a society, where the distinction between sacred and profane was a somewhat unnatural one, shared the Hindu hope of *Ramarajya* which he used interchageably with the kingdom of God. He once went so far as to say: "*Swaraj* is synonymous with *Ram Raj*—the establishment of the Kingdom of Righteousness on earth."[31] However, this was utopian to say the least. In any event, on the eve of India's independence, he had apparently given up any hope that particular *Swaraj* would be *Ramarajya*.[32]

In essence, *Ramarajya,* notwithstanding its religious tenor and antiquated reference, stands for an egalitarian, non-violent democratic order, with moral values forming the base of such an order. Gandhi was not a revivalist embarking on bringing back the ancient *Ramarajya* into the present framework of reality, he was only conceptualising an ideal state for the future with a vision transcending the present ills of society and polity. Gandhi's political philosophy was merely the application of moral truths to the facts of social life. Gandhi's politics was only formally concerned with power and government, and fundamentally with the moral development of human beings also see Appendix-II.

REFERENCES

1. Romain Rolland, *Mahatma Gandhi: The Man Who Became One with the Universal Being,* New York: The Century Company, 1924, pp. 29-30.
2. N.G. Jog, *Builders of Modern India: Lokamanya Bal Gangadhar Tilak,* Government of India, Publications Division, Ministry of Information and Broadcasting, 1962, p. 188.
3. *Ibid.*
4. T.V. Parvate *B.G. Tilak,* Ahmedabad: Navajivan Publishing House, 1958, pp. 516-19.
5. S. Radhakrishnan, *Indian Philosophy,* London: George Allen and Unwin Ltd., 1929, Vol. I, p. 25.
6. Tolstoy's book *The Kingdom of God is Within You* which was published in 1893, had an abiding influence on Gandhi. With Tolstoy, he shared his belief in the therapeutic value of manual work.
7. Ruskin's views on the equal value of different kinds of work to society confirmed Gandhi in his belief that all hold their talents in trust for the good of society..
8. *Young India,* (Ahmedabad), 2nd December, 1926, p. 419.
9. *Ibid.,* 26 February, 1925, p. 74.
10. Frank Thakur Das, *"Gandhi on Religion and Politics"*, Verinder Grover (ed.), *Gandhi and Politics in India,* New Delhi: Deep and Deep Publications, 1987, pp. 83-84.
11. Raghavan N. Iyer, *The Moral and Political Thought of Mahatma Gandhi,* New York: Oxford University Press, 1973, pp. 16-17.
12. B.R. Nanda, "Gandhi and Religion", *Gandhi Marg,* New Delhi: Gandhi Peace Foundation, April-June, 1990, Vol. XII, No.1, p. 8.
13. Suman Khanna, *Gandhi and the Good Life,* New Delhi: Gandhi Peace Foundation, 1985, p. 14.
14. Agehananda Bharati, *"Gandhi's Interpretation of the Gita"*, Sibnarayan Ray (ed.), *Gandhi-India and the World,* Bombay: Nachiketa Publications Ltd., 1970, pp. 61-63.
15. Suman Khanna, *supra n.* 13, pp. 18-19.
16. M.K. Gandhi, *Hind Swaraj or Indian Home Rule,* Madras: G.A. Natesan and Company, 1908, p. 60.
17. Suman Khanna, *supra n.* 13, pp. 55-58.

18. Margaret Chatterjee, *Gandhi's Religious Thought,* London: the MacMillan Press Ltd., 1983, p. 19.

19. *Ibid.*, p. 20.

20. *M.K. Gandhi, An Autobiography or the Story of My Experiments With Truth,* Translated from Gujarati by Mahadev Desai, Ahmdabad: Navajivan Publishing House, 1927, pp. xi-xii.

21. *M. K. Gandhi, In Search of the Supreme,* Compiled and edited by V.B. Kher, Ahmedabad: Navajivan Publishing House, 1961, Vol. II, p. 308.

22. *Young India, supra n.* 8, September, 1924.

23. Raghavan N. Iyer, *supra n.* 11, p. 144.

24. Satya M. Rai, *Gandhi and the Communal Politics in India,* Verinder Grover, *supra n.* 10, p. 187.

25. Mohammad A. Khan, *Gandhian Approach to Communal Harmony,* Delhi: Ajanta Publications, 1986, p. 8.

26. *Ibid.*, p. 11.

27. *Ibid.*, p. 10-11.

28. Madhuri Wadhwa, *Gandhi Between Tradition and Modernity,* New Delhi: Deep and Deep Publications, 1991, p. 23.

29. Dhananjay Keer. *Mahatma Gandhi: Political Saint and Unarmed Prophet,* Bombay: Popular Prakashan, 1973, p. 727.

30. *Hindustan Time* (New Delhi) 1 June, 1947.

31. *Young India, supra n. B.* 4, May 1921, p. 143.

32. *Harijan* (Ahmedabad), 13 July, 1947, p. 235.

CHAPTER 4

LOKAMANYA AND MAHATMA

The use of religion for political mobilization by Tilak and Gandhi may be regarded as Hindu responses to an alien culture and regime, since the British took several decades to consolidate their rule over India and followed different policies in different parts of the country and with respect to its different communities, Indian responses to their rule were diverse, articulated at various levels and showed considerable regional and communal variations. They provided the basic conceptual framework within which Gandhi formulated his own response. At one level he represented the culmination of, and at another a radical departure from, his nineteenth century Hindu predecessors. Second, the Hindus were the first to take an early and keen interest in their new rulers, socially interacting with them, offering their services to and engaging in a critical dialogue with them and, in the process, developing a rich tradition of discourse unmatched by any other Indian community.

From the very beginning, the Hindu discourse displayed an unusual feature not to be found in that of other communities and relatively rare even in the history of anti-colonial struggles. Rather than concentrate on the colonial rule and ask whether to ignore, welcome or fight against it, as the Muslims were to do later, Hindu leaders, almost to a man, located and discussed it in the wider context of their social regeneration. The British, who had never seriously encountered the Hindus before, were puzzled by them as a people and bewildered, at times even offended, by some of their beliefs and practices. Even in the allegedly halcyon days of Warren Hastings, they could not easily place the Hindus who were neither like them nor like the 'noble' or ignoble African 'savages' whose descriptions were then beginning to circulate in Europe. They, therefore asked questions, some very sharp and critical, which the Hindus could not ignore. More importantly, the British could not govern India without defining the Hindus and reducing them to manageable categories largely derived from their own ways of thought. The Hindus did not like their essentialist and inevitably biassed definition, and had no other way to counter it save by providing an alternative self-definition. It is therefore hardly surprising that the writings of almost all the Hindus writers from Ram Mohan Roy onwards were taken up not only with social reforms but also with the prior and deeper question of self-definition. They could not define themselves and specify the content of their collective identity without conceptualising themselves as a single, distinct and homogenous community, something they had never done before except to a rather limited extent under Muslim rule. The hitherto diffused and vague Hindu self-consciousness thus began to acquire, for the first time in its history, a corporate articulation during British rule. The fact that the Hindu social self-consciousness of colonial rule, each shaping and in turn being shaped by the other, meant that Hindus could not define and make sense of themselves without defining and making sense of the colonial rule and vice versa. The two modes of consciousness were not separate but interdependent dimensions of a single process of self-consciousness. The colonial rule was not an independent and external phenomenon brought about by the British, but an expression of the inner processes occurring within the Hindu society. It thus not only provided the context in which the Hindu collectively defined both what and who they were, but also a mirror in which they caught glimpses of themselves, of their character, strengths and especially their weaknesses.

Since Hindu leaders discussed colonial rule in the wider context of the health of their society and civilisation, their responses to it were inseparable from and varied according to their analyses of the latter. Some saw little wrong with their society, and consequently either took no interest in British rule or dismissed it as inconsequential. Most, however, were deeply disturbed by the state of their society and wondered if and how the new rule could help them regenerate it. For the modernists, the Hindu society was beyond hope and their salvation lay in radically restructuring it along modern or European lines. The critical modernists or syncretists pleaded for a creative synthesis of the two civilisations, whereas the critical traditionalists preferred to mobilise their own indigenous resources, borrowing from Europe whatever was likey to supplement and enrich them.

The traditionalists were content to glory in the greatness of their civilisation. They were convinced that it was in good health, and either put up fierce defences of even such offensive practices as *sati*, female infanticide and child marriages, or argued that these were 'aberrations', inevitable in an old civilisation long under foreign rule and which they intended to eradicate. They did not think much of their ruler's 'materialistic' 'irreligious', individualist, selfish, violent and greed based civilisation. The Europeans had roamed the world as if they were its masters and enslaved, brutally assaulted and even eliminated large groups of people in their unscrupulous pursuit of wealth and power.

The fact that Britain had conquered India did not signify the moral superiority of her civilisation. Might did not imply right. The British had conquered India by means of force, duplicity, mendacity, intrigue and corruption, and that hardly reflected favourably either on their national character or on the civilisation which sanctioned such means. All uncivilised people loved war and excelled at it. The important Spartans defeated the wise Athenians, the illiterate Macedonians humbled Greece, and the uncivilised barbarian tribes destroyed the Roman empire. Their victories proved pyrrhic, as their culturally superior victims eventually triumphed over them. The British conquest only showed that Indians were a gentle and peace-loving people ill-versed in the barbaric art of waging wars. India had survived many such conquests and would survive the present one as well. The traditionalists considered the colonial rule morally and politically inconsequential and advised their countrymen to hold on to the traditional order. They were far more exorcised about the impatient Hindu reformers than about their British rulers. And some of them were even prepared to collaborate with the latter if they agreed not to yield to the reformist pressure.

Though the traditionalist response was limited to only a few Hindus, as a mood it was shared by many more. Its self-confidence and spirit of defiance were a source of great moral and psychological strength in a confrontationist colonial context and sustained the self-esteem and cultural pride of even those better disposed to European civilisation. Ram Mohan Roy had thanked Providence for sending the British to India, arguing that it had much to learn from them in the fields of politics, science, literature and religion. When, a few years, later, a missionary rebuked him for daring to make even a minor criticism of Christianity which had brought his 'ignorant' and 'effeminate' people 'rays of intelligence', the Raja shot back saying that the 'world was indebted to our ancestors for the first dawn of knowledge which sprang up in the East' and that India had nothing to learn from the British 'with respect to science, literature or religion'. Bankim Chandra Chatterjee, who had once hailed the British as 'a more perfect type of civilisation', later turned full circle and spent much of his time proving the superiority of the Indian.

Though traditionalism had a polemical and psychological value, it was an untenable and imparactical response to British rule. Even its most uncompromising champions could not deny that their society was in a sorry state; the ease with which it had once again fallen prey to foreign rule was a stark reminder of this. The traditionalist response had made some sense and had indeed been largely developed as a strategy of survival during periods of Muslim invasions, but none at all under the qualitatively different British rule. Industrialisation disrupted the unity of castes and their characteristic occupations, created new castes, destroyed some of the existing ones, increased social and economic mobility, created new hierarchies within castes and brought those hitherto distant into close and unfamiliar patterns of relationship. The increasingly popular liberal ideas encouraged demands for equality, basic human rights and social justice and stimulated a rationalist critique of not only the prevailing institutions and practices but also of their traditional modes of legitimation. The colonial state was busy establishing new structures of powers, as the very condition of its survival and subverting the established social order, somethimes by the apparently simple devices of giving old groups new names and reclassifying them. For these and other reasons, the traditional social order was and widely seen as untenable. Since Hindu morality was based on *Varnadharma* and closely bound up with the caste system, Hindu society faced not just a socio-economic but a deep moral and religious crisis as well. It had either to be reconstituted on new principles or it must face extinction.

The vast majority of Hindu leaders freely acknowledged that the contemporary state of their society left a great deal to be desired. Though they diagnosed their predicament diffrently and highlighted different aspects of their degeneration, there was a remarkable consensus. They had, as people, become 'inert', 'degenerate' and 'lifeless', and were 'fast asleep', in 'deep slumber', 'dreaming'. The louder the pressures of the world, the more tightly they drew the blankets and smothred themselves in mindless practices and beliefs.

The lack of unity was another recurrent theme in the writings and speeches of Hindu leaders. Their countrymen were fragmented, deeply divided and incapable of concerted action. They were split up into a large number of castes, sub-castes and local communities, each a world into itself and lacking meaningful contacts with others, with the result that they were incapable of viewing themselves as Hindus let alone as Indians. While the castes and local communities had saved Hindus from atomisation, they had also bred a pervasive 'spirit of localism', mutual distrust and 'indifference to each other's fate'. That was why the East India Company had successfully played off different groups and communities against one another, and the leaders of the 1857 rebellion had failed to build on their initial successes. The 'whole history' of India, at least during the past few centuries, had been a story of collaboration with foreigners against one's own people.

Thanks to their social isolation, the Hindus had failed to develop a sense of mutual concern and social compassion and brutally exploited their weaker compatriots. As Vivekananda put it, no society 'puts its foot on the neck of the wretched so mercilessly as does that of India. The treatment of the poor, the lower castes and the untouchables was an obvious example of this. Man was defined in terms of his caste and his humanity was exhausted in his social status.

In the opinion of Hindu leaders, they had become quarrelsome, factious, envious, petty and unable to sustain cooperative enterprises. Gokhale observed, If we are deficient in one quality more than any other, it is in the instinct and habit of cooperation. The self-willed Hindu, determined to pursue his own or his family's interest, insisted on cooperating with others on his own terms and refused to subordinate his views and interests to those of others even when this was in his own long-term interest. Since no organisation could be sustained on such a basis, the Hindus failed to evolve voluntary associations based on considerations other than caste and village. Not used to the discipline of concerted action they were unable to cope with disagreement and criticism. They did not appreciate that criticism could be inspired by a genuine difference of opinion rather than jealousy and that men could disagree withiout being hostile to one another. As a result, no one freely spoke his mind, disagreements were not brought into the open and resolved, and there was in every organisation a false atmosphere of peace and harmony. Such an unnatural unanimity spawned the corrosive spirit of distrust, suspicion and cynicism, which eventually destroyed the organisation concerned.

The Hindus were not only deeply divided among themselves but also from the other communities, especially the Muslims. This question had not exercised earlier generations of leaders because they did not see its importance, were contemptuous of the Muslims with whom they thought they had historical scores to settle, or because they assumed that the Muslim masses would accept their cultural leadership. After 1857, they could ignore it no longer. Such factors as the British policy of initially favouring Hindus and then Muslims, the land settlement which benefitted the former at the expense of the latter, the lack of Muslim participation in the ongoing dialogue between the Hindus and the British rulers with the consequent Hindu tendency to equate theirs with Indian nationalism, and the uneven economic and social progress of the two communiteis opened up a deep divide between them.

Hindu leaders had no clear explanation of the causes of their degeneration and kept blaming different factors without analysing and establishing clear relations between them. For some, especially the modernists, their civilisation had been structurally flawed from the very beginning, and the causes of its subsequent degeneration lay in such factors as the oppressive inequality of the caste system, the other worldliness of their religion, the chaotic individualism of their culture and the systematic suppression of the spirit of critical inquiry by the Brahmanic champions of the dominant advaita tradition. Some others, such as Bankim Chandra Chatterjee, blamed the Indian 'exaltation of asceticism', the absence of inductive method, the pervasive ethos of inequality, a lack of interest in political power and the climate. Vivekananda thought that since the Hindus enjoyed an amazing degree of religious freedom, they could only be held together by a fairly rigid social structure which under crisis, and especially under foreign rule, became excessively rigid and oppressive.

Part of the reason why Hindu leaders did not undertake a systematic and searching analysis of the causes of their degeneration lay in the fact that most of them felt convinced that Muslim rule had played an important part in it. Some said so openly. The rest were more discreet and knew that, since they had to find ways of working with Muslims, they should avoid raking up old historical memories. The tendency to blame Muslim rule is evident in most Hindu leaders, including Ram Mohan Roy, Bankim Chandra

Chatterjee, Ishwar Chandra Gupta, Narmada Shankar, Ishwar Chandra Vidyasagara, Gokhale, Ranade, Tilak, Vivekananada and Aurobindo. For most of them, Muslim rulers, with such solitary exceptions as Akbar, had been tyrannical, oppressive, discriminatory, intolerant and contemptuous of Hindu beliefs and practices. They forcibly converted Hindus, destroyed their temples, insulted their religion, raped their women, plundered their property, and wantonly shed their blood. The terrified and terrorised Hindus 'naturally' turned inward, and became other-worldly, servile, timid, ritualistic and too frightened to speak their minds in public. They were afraid to make even the smallest changes in their social and religious life lest these should be exploited by the rulers or lead to their disintegration. Since the whole Hindu civilisation was under threat, the *Brahmins,* its traditional custodians, assumed and were allowed to assume considerable power with the rest closing ranks behind them. Its natural growth was stunted, its vitality sapped, its self-confidence shattered and its rich tradition fragmented and frozen.

The Hindu leaders' denigration of Muslim rule seems to have owed its inspiration and appeal to several interrelated factors. Many of them confused Muslim invaders with Muslim rulers and attributed to the latter, deeds committed by the former. Unlike the lower castes who had benefited from it, higher castes, especially the *Brahmins,* suffered under Muslim rule. Being the acknowledged guardians of their religion, they were sometimes mocked, harassed, deprived of their sources of revenue and denied a social and political role. Not surprisingly, many of them never reconciled themselves to Muslim rule. Since the low view of it was not confined to the *Brahmins,* it probably had deeper cultural roots. The Islamic identification of religion with the state had no parallel in their thought and puzzled the Hindus. Its austere view of religion sat ill with the Hindu love of music, rituals, symbols, images and idols. Hindus found Islamic theology intellectually uninteresting and were disappointed not to find in it gods and goddesses depicting the full range of normal human emotions. Although relations between the two communities were never as bad as presented by Hindu writers and had led in some parts of the country to a creative blend of the two religions and cultures, mutual curiosity and respect were not very common. It is striking that during the several hundred years of Muslim rule, only a handful of Hindus wrote commentaries on the *Koran*, translated it into regional languages or undertook a comparative study of the two societies. The relative Muslim lack of interest in Hindu philosophy, culture and social structure, except during a few decades of Mughal rule, is just as striking. Some of the *puranas* written in the aftermath of Islamic rule contain most unflattering references to Muslim habits, hygience, sexual practices and mode of thought and give a fairly good idea of what the Hindus thought of them at the time.

The British historians of India also played an important part in shaping the Hindu view. Sir William Jones, the earliest and one of the most eminent of them, read Indian history through the distorting prism of the Enlightenment view of European history. Determined to 'Know India better than any other European ever knew it', he concluded that ancient Hindus were the 'Athenians of Asia', just as creative and brilliant and 'splendid in arts and arms, happy in government, wise in legislation and eminent in various knowledge'. Their subsequent decline had to be explained, and Jones turned to the Muslims as the Asian equivalent of the European barbarians. The British, representing the third phase of Indian history, finally put an end to the Muslim-ruled 'dark ages', rediscovered its past and launched its Renaissance.

Hindu antipathy to Muslim rule then had a complex origin. Although the ideologically biased British historiography created a seductive intellectual framework, it would not have been so influential if deeper cultural factors had not been at work, if the history of the relations between the two communities had been less stormy, and if the leadership of the independence movement had not come from higher castes, especially the *Brahmins.*

India needed a 'new moral and social order', 'new principles of morality and social organisation, 'a new moral consensus' and a 'new national character and culture'. "The search for new principles was reflected in the countless journals, pamphlets, newspapers, books, debating societies and research organisations which sprang up all over the country containing such words as truth, light, essence, search and research in their titles and names. It would seem that, in the opinion of the Hindu leaders, India needed not only new truths but also a new mode of discovering and validating them. Not surprisingly, modern science became extemely popular and almost every leader turned to scientific research and 'scientific method' to generate 'scientific ethics' and 'scientific principles of society'. Bengal was for a while full of Comte and found in his positivism a method of discovering new truths. Ranade advocated 'Bacon's method', Gokhale thought that J.S. Mill's 'method of empiricism' alone was reliable, and Aurobindo turned to a combination of Darwin and Einstein.

The Hindu leaders were convinced that their salvation lay in creating a strong Indian state. Since such a state presupposed industrialisation, modern science and technology and a rationalist culture, they needed these as well. In other words, India's salvation lay in embracing modernity. Since Britain had successfully modernised itself and was indeed a world leader, India had a good deal to learn from it. As its good fortune would have it, Britain was already in India busy establishing modern institutions. Ram Mohan Roy offered 'thanks to the supreme disposer of the universe' for the British presence. The ebullient K.C. Sen thought that 'the contact of England with India was Providential and not a mere accident. And even the sober Naoroji could not help seeing a divine hand in such an encouter at such a ripe moment.

The bulk of Hindu leaders, including Dwarkanath Tagore, Bankim Chandra Chatterjee, Ranade, Tilak, Dadabhai Naoroji, Surendranath Banerjee, B.C. Pal, Rabindranath Tagore, Lala Lajpat Rai, Aurobindo, Narmada Shankar, Motilal Nehru and the early Gandhi thought that British rule was both a consequence of India's degenerate state and an opportunity to turn the corner." Like their rulers, they too conceptualised the colonial encounter in pedagogical terms. Indians needed to 'improve' themselves, 'sit at the feet' of their rulers and 'learn' all the skills and virtues necessary for their regeneration." Although arrogant and aloof, the British were 'wise gurus' giving them useful 'political training', and if the Indians could for a while become 'apt pupils', they would one day be 'fully qualified' for self-rule. Even the reflective Bankim Chanra Chatterjee called them 'good teachers'. In his *Anandamath*, the *Sanayasis* did not follow up their successful rebellion under the divine advice that continued foreign rule was necessary for India's 'growth'. Later, Narmada Shankar asked India to 'rejoice' that it was being prepared for political adulthood by Britain. Lokahitwadi even thought that as a 'child takes ten or twenty years to become educated', a country 'must require two or four hundred years'.

Despite such encomia, Hindu leaders were under no illusion about the limitations of the British rule. They knew it was racist, held them in contempt and had, after 1857, kept them at a respectable social distance. The agitation surrounding the Ilbert Bill brought home the intensity of the Anglo-Indian hatred for the 'native niggers' even to those busy ingratiating themselves with their masters. As the nationalist movement gained momentum, Anglo-Indian racism became rabid and the incidents of their bad manners and violence to even middle class Indians were quite rampant.

The Hindu leaders were also acutely aware that their political system was an inferior and highly distorted copy of the British original and that their rulers' practices rarely matched their rhetoric. Their form of government was autocratic and 'under the iron heel of a despot', as a leader in the *Bangalee* put it in 1900, and their demands for representative institutions were constantly thwarted. The government was intolerant of even mild criticism and had sunk to the lowest level of brutality in its treatment of not only the rebels but also innocent citizens in the aftermath of the 1857 rebellion. The rule of law was precarious and surrounded by vast areas of arbitrariness at the opposite ends of the administrative system. The judiciary was deeply biased in favour of British residents in India and there was no equality before the law between them and the Indians. The executive was not subject to legislative control and in certain crucial areas not even to judicial control. The press was subject to severe constraints and largely controlled by the Anglo-Indians.

While all this is true, it would be wrong to dismiss the Hindu leaders as collaborators, ideologically brainwashed henchmen of the Raj or as unscrupulous men willing to support whoever served their interests. Many of them were genuinely patriotic, honourable and independent-minded men who felt convinced that the Raj was in India's long-term interest. As we saw, they were deeply disturbed by the degeneration of their civilisation and knew that it preceded and facilitated colonial rule and could not be blamed upon the Raj. They were anxious to do something about it and thought that British rule had both shaken them out of their inertia and released regenerative forces. That was why almost all of them discussed it in the context of and assessed it in terms of its contribution to national revitalisation. The work of the British and Indian archaeologists and historians recreated their past for them and increased their sense of pride and shame. They realised how much they had fallen and why, and thought that they would turn the corner if they developed, for reasons discussed earlier, a strong and united state of their own. With all its limitations, British rule was taking them in that direction. It was thus a historical necessity and they could not allow their temporary personal and collective frustrations to damage their long term interests. But, at the same time, they could do nothing without the active support of the masses. And this mass-mobilization became a handy tool for both Tilak and Gandhi.

In the history of India's struggle for freedom from British rule and in the story of shaping the people's militant nationalism into a powerful instrument to that end, no two names appear more prominently than those of Tilak and Gandhi, the *Lokamanya* and the *Mahatma*. Both of them led a life of dedication not merely to achieve independence but to inculcate in the people the necessary pride in their own culture and to promote the basic qualities required for self-rule or *Swaraj*.

They were persons of very high calibre and character, known for integrity and transparent sincerity. They worked ceaselessly for the regeneration of India and the all-round development of the Indian people. Both of them believed in the 'Higher Powers', which rule the destinities of men and nations. This faith, coupled with their faith in the people of India, made them the fearless advocates of *Swarja* and democracy.

Tilak and Gandhi were the products of Indian culture which, through the ages, had thrown up from time to time, creative geniuses of those who have blazened the path of human progress. Both Tilak and Gandhi started their public life with a deep sense of mission. Though the common period of these two personalities in the political field was too short, it should be remebered that period ((1915-1920) was the most crucial one in the history of modern India from many points of view. It was a period of world crisis on account of the First World War. In India, it symbolised extraordinary awakening, alongwith a period of transition in the techniques of the struggle. Added to the scene was the interplay of the two mightly colourful persons in their approach to problems and the remedies they wanted to adopt.

It is an open secret that Tilak and Gandhi differed. But their real greatness lay in not allowing the conflict of ideas and ideals to assume the proportions of a conflict of wills which would have led to a split between them. The restraint which they exercised in this matter was the measure of their inner culture and political maturity. However, like Napoleon picking the crown with his sword, both Tilak and Gandhi assumed national leadership with their own elan and effort. It is only an academic pursuit to search for similarity and continuity between the politics of Tilak and Gandhi.

Gandhi hailed Gokhale as his political guru, but that relationship was purely "a personal matter". He claimed that Gokhale had given him the message to spiritualise the political life and political institutions of the country.[1] He remained true to his master's memory and did not gravitate towards Tilak despite his respect for him which bordered on veneration. In 1921, Gandhi denied the soft impeachment that he had taken up a cause that was dearest to Tilak's heart though he called himself Gokhale's disciple. Gandhi wrote, "I cannot claim the honour of being a follower of the late *Lokamanya*. I admire him like millions of his countrymen for his indomitable will, his vast learning, his love for country, and above all the purity of his private life and great sacrifice. Of all the men of modern times, he captivated most the imagination of his people. He breathed into us the spirit of *Swaraj*. No one perhaps realised the evil of the existing system of Government as Tilak did. And in all humility, I claim to deliver his message to the country as truly as the best of his disciples. But I am conscious that my method is not his method and that is why I have still difficulty with some of the Maharashtra leaders."[2]

Anyone who cursorily glances at the life and writings of Tilak and Gandhi would see that both were products primarily and predominantly of Indian culture. They were not only proud of it, but their very source of inspiration was the Indian culture and the spiritual basis of Indian life. Tilak was grounded in the Sanskrit learning and the scriptures from his childhood. Gandhi came to them much later, but he had his mother and the domestic religious atmosphere which initiated him into a devotional and dedicated life, and his almost instinctive love of truth helped him on, from step to step in his search for spiritual realisation.

Both Tilak and Gandhi wrote commentaries on the *Bhagavad Gita,* and interpreted its message to suit their own genious. For Tilak, the *Gita* put forth a doctrine of action that was applicable in every sphere of human activity; it urged activity and yet related that activity to traditional Hindu paths of spiritual release and freedom. In Tilak's mind, spiritual and political freedom were symbolized by the concept of *Swaraj.* Without it the Hindu individual or community was not free to follow *dharma,* and chaos and disintegration were the result; without it there would be no real industrial, educational or social progress. Thus, the Gita was an ideal text with which Hindus could identify, and in which they could base and legitimize their religious and political aspirations. Tilak used the *Gita* for those purposes, but not merely as a tool for his own ends. What he wanted to symbolise was the path of *karmayoga.*[3]

On the other hand, Gandhi put forward his own interpretation with confidence and a show of authority. He put forward the view that Gita was not a work of history; but a religions text that seized on the 'occasion' of the *Mahabharata* war in order to draw attention to "the war going on in our own bodies between the forces of Good *(Pandavas)* and the forces of Evil *(Kauravas).*"[4] The basis of Gandhi's interpretation of the authority of the *shastras* was his conviction of their historical character—that no scriptures are eternal in themselves, but they are all the limited products of a particular time. On the one side, Gandhi accepted that the *shastras* suffered from severe historical limitations, but on the other he stood by their authotity. What he tried to imply was that interpretation is not a process of establishing the literal meaning of the text, but interpretation by its very nature means 'new' interpretation, expansion of the literal meaning and application to new circumstances.[5] The recitation of the *Gita* was a regular feature of life in Gandhi's *ashram.* In fact, it was the principal religious ritual.

Unlike Tilak, Gandhi, being on the road of a "religious activist", provided a spiritual content in terms of *bhakti* and *gyana* and not specifically in the context of *karma.* However, the two interpretations are at par with one another in the sense that both were written during the time when Tilak and Gandhi were serving sentences in jails. Tilak wrote *Srimad Bhagavadgita Rahasya* in Mandalya jail in 1910-11. Gandhi translated *Gita* into Gujarati, with an introduction and commentary, which was entitled *Anasaktiyoga,* in Yeravada jail in 1929. This was later translated into English by Mahadev Desai, and published as *'The Gita according to Gandhi'.*

Tilak was a *Brahmin,* but this did not make him a slave to orthodox rigidity, rather he fought against atrophied orthodoxy and the divisiveness of casteism. But in his busy and eventful life, he concentrated on politics and went the extent of saying that social and other reforms could be taken up later. Tilak's emphasis on the principle of political realism was in sharp contradiction to Gandhi's insistence on ethical consistency. Tilak used religion as a psychological force to mobilize the masses on a common platform for the political emancipation of the country. Contrarily, Gandhi believed religion to be an integral part of politics. As he said, "No Indian who aspires to follow the way of true religion can afford to remain aloof from politics. In other words, one who aspires to a truly religious life cannot fail to undertake public service as his mission, and we are today so much caught up in the political machine that service of the people is impossible without taking part in politics."[6]

Gandhi declared that his devotion to truth had drawn him into politics, that his power in the political field was derived from his spiritual experiments with himself, and that those who say religion has nothing to do with politics do not know what religion means. Gandhi was from the first, determined to approach politics, as everything else, in a religious spirit, while he had no doubt that his own fundamental concern was with the religious life.

Gandhi disagreed that political methods hindered the religious pursuit and the highest moral and spiritual ends.

His main controversy in this regard remained with Tilak who held that politics could not be regarded solely from a religious standpoint.

In January, 1920, Tilak wrote to Gandhi: "Politics is a game of worldly people, and not of *sadhus*, and instead of the maxim *'akkhodhenajine kkhodham'* (conquer anger by non-anger) as preached by Buddha, I prefer to rely on the maxim of *Sri Krishna, 'ye gatthaa mam parapadyamthe thaamsthatthaiva bhajaamyaham"* (in whatever way men resort to me, even so do I render to them). Both methods are equally honest and righteous but the one is more suited to this world than the other." Gandhi replied: "With deference to the *Lokamanya*, I venture to say that it betrays mental laziness to think that the world is not for *sadhus*. The epitome of religions is to promote *Purushartha*, and *Purushartha* is nothing but a desperate attempt to become a *sadhu*, i.e., to become a gentleman in every sense of the term."[7]

Gandhi did not refute Tilak but merely met his assertions with counter-assertions. If they differed in their conceptions of politics, this was because they also diverged in their views of religion. Perhaps, it was the *Mahatma* concept that underlined Gandhi's efforts to combine religion and politics, to bring morality into the sphere of political mobilization. And the *Lokamanya* remained a proud individual who valued physical strength and force and did not place much emphasis on asceticism.

On another occasion, Tilak said in connection with a political campaign of Gandhi's: "A religious ideal may be a very high guide but there must be a practical ideal in our political activities. A mere high religious ideal does not prove very useful in practical politics."[8] Gandhi appreciated the difference between the ideal and the immediately practicable, but he differed from Tilak about what was immediately practicable and what should be regarded at any time as immediately practicable, which is not merely an empirical matter but ultimately a question of faith. The real point for Gandhi was his refusal to distinguish between religious and political ideals.

Though Gandhi's attitude to religion holds the key to the understanding of his life and thought, its significance still remains a mystery for both his admirers and his critics. Left-wing critics, like M.N. Roy, R.P. Dutt and E.M.S. Namboodiripad accused Gandhi of exploiting religion to rouse the masses and then deliberately curbing their political consciousness in the interest of the Indian bourgeoisie. Among Gandhi's own adherents there were not a few radicals who chafed under the moral constraints he imposed on the struggle with the British. Then there were the 'modernists' who equated all religions with irrationalism and obscurantism and resented Gandhi's saintly idiom. Finally, some later-day historians advanced the thesis that by using Hindu-symbols, Gandhi contributed to the communal polarisation which culminated in the division of India.[9]

Gandhi combined in himself the dual role of a saint and a politician. He has been called by some 'the most saintly among the politicians', and by others the most 'political saint'. However, this has only led to a dichotomy between the devotion that a saint deserves, and the expectations and achievements that a leader entails. He was equally mistrusted by both Hindus and Muslims. All the way he preached *ahimsa* or non-violence. But in the hour of crisis, this *ahimsa* was rejected, and violence voluntarily chosen. And most unfortunately, fate never permitted Gandhi the time in retrospect!

Tilak, on the other hand, brought religion into the political fold to preach the national revolution. His tactics were to agitate and to organise the masses, to voice the inchoate frustrations and discontent of the downtrodden, and to depict the scapegoat foreigner as the single simple cause of their multiple miseries. Tilak was far too practical a man voluntarily to court martyrdom or self-destruction. He rallied, his forces by devious means, and directed them in techniques other than the frontal assault.

Tilak adhered to no dogmatic revolutionary theory, and he outlined no long-range programme of action or social reorganisation. His ultimate goal was independent India. His immediate goal, to secure the reins of political power. He was neither squeamish nor doctrinaire about the methods he employed, so long as they helped further his ends.

Tilak saw no inherent contradiction in providing ethical and philosophical justification for political assassination, racial and religious antipathy, or the use of duplicity. In rallying support he did not scruple against appealing to prejudice or mass anxiety, and he did not succumb to the distraction of concerning himself with the aftermath of his tactics. He stimulated the revival of Hindu religious consciousness through the Ganapati festivals and similar movements without scant apprehension about their impact. He stirred Maharashtrian regional pride through the Shivaji festivals and his *Kesari* editorials, but did not look to the day when militant regionalism might present a challenge or prove a hindrance to the growth of national unity. However, the nationalism in Maharashtra was not dressed in a religio-mystical philosophical garb, but merely confined itself to the resuscitation of the memory of the cultural past of India, so that India could shake off her inferiority complex and reassert her personality.

Tilak's single-minded devotion to the cause of the Indian masses also knew that once the spiritual and religious springs of India's great past were revitalized, the greatness and glory of her future were assured. To him India seemed to have a character, a tradition, a personality—as distinct as the characteristics and qualities of individual men and women. What mattered to him was the preservation of those ways of living which are peculiar to India, through which alone, he said, she could rediscover her soul, her strength and attain her emancipation.

However, inference could be drawn that the vision of both Tilak's militant realism and Gandhi's spiritual idealism was communicated because it was based on India's own vision. The political movements led by Tilak and Gandhi were a result of mass-responses. Religion brought about a rare amalgamation of their public and personal lives. It culminated itself into self-realisation on the one hand, and service of the humanity on the other, although the order of preference varied for both. And all in all, both Tilak and Gandhi must attribute their thinking to the flexibility and catholicity of the Hindu civilisation, that has the power of both renewal and change.

Religion for political mobilization then was used as a means with pure and selfless intentions. It was more a part of the patriotic fervour that had engulfed the country. The interplay of religion and politics was qualitatively different. It was an idea and ideal of *sarva dharma sambhava* . One cannot deny the fact that religious attitude is a thing of permanent value to mankind, individually and collectively. There is an urgent need for a full and free exchange of our differing religious experiences, in a spirit of mutual respect, appreciation and sympathy. Religion can be for our growth and. development, as also for our downfall and decay—the authority of choice lies with us. However, the acceptance of religion in the secular context with spiritual content, is an alternative without challenges. It stands apart.

The hold of both Tilak and Gandhi on the masses in their deeply-held respect for the religion of their fore-fathers was utmost. For Tilak, all that was ancient and truly noble in the Hindu tradition was sacred to him. Indeed, his profound reverence for and knowledge of the *Vedas* were his sheet-anchor amid all the social and religious upheavals of his day, which only too easily became tempestuous storms at the slightest change in the atmosphere. However, political emancipation of the country remained Tilak's sole obsession in arousing the religious fervour of the masses in the light of Hindu traditionalism. He realised that the basic weakness of the Indian people lay in the loss of their self-respect and feeling of nationhood. Unless the people's respect for their own history, culture and religion was restored, he felt convinced all talk of political and social emancipation would prove idle and fruitless.

An American writer, William Holland, in his analysis of Asian nationalism, has observed that "religion played an important role in India where the nationalist movement was characterised by a strain of Hindu revivalism. Like all empires, the British suppressed political meetings but they observed a hands-off policy with regard to religion. This provided a loophole, which natioalists like Tilak exploited to the full for their own purposes." [10] By galvanizing the masses with a new spirit, and by organising them in a national movement, Tilak"s leadership provided politics with a democratic base. And in doing so, he did not seek the help of the princes, aristocrats and landlords to regain the lost independece of India; he wooed the masses and by doing so laid the foundations of a truly democratic state. Some of the arm-chair politicians who were frankly contemptuous of any contact with the masses, called Tilak "a leader of oilmen and betel-nut sellers", meaning the common man of India, the worker and the peasant.[11] And though Tilak was never anti-Muslim, he remained, at heart, an ardent Hindu with a rare amalgamation of both tradition and modernity.

On the contrary, with a noble heart, Gandhi in a rather over-simplified manner, developed the notion of treating all religions alike without differentiating the essential religious identities which were responsible for the latent and obvious animosities between Hindus and Muslims. In 1938, Gandhi elaborated: "My Hinduism is not sectarian. It includes all that I know to be best in Islam, Christianity, Buddhism and Zoroastrianism. I approach politics as everything else in a relgious spirit. Truth is my religion and *Ahimsa* is the only way of its realisation. I have rejected once and for all the doctrine of the sword." [12] Similarly, Gandhi emphasized that the *Gita*, the *Quran*, the *Bible*, the *Granth Sahib* and *Zend Aveste* contained the gems of wisdom.

Gandhi can be justified in interpreting secularism in his own terms, giving it a spiritualist bias. Gandhi embodied a *Vedantic* vision of a core of truth in all religions and taught not only tolerance of, but respect for all religions. Gandhi stood for secularism though he claimed to be a staunch *Sanatani* Hindu and a *Vaishnava*. His secularism found theoretical justification in his workings. Gandhi rejected the concept of coercion in the field of religion and earnestly pleaded for leaving every individual to follow the religion of their choice, without any interference from the state. He categorically stated that the state should undoubtedly be secular. Therefore, when he perceived in the national development, an underlying current of communal hatred and violence, he stressed Hindu-Muslim unity to the extent that he supported the Khilafat movement.

From Hindu traditionalism to the western connotation of secularism, one had to emphasize India's democratic and secular character even in the post-independence era, in order to counter the forces of communalism and violence. The use of the word 'secular' in the Indian context has given rise to ambiguity, because secularism is a term which is strictly Western in connotation, and it originated within the specific socio-economic milieu of the western world. In India, although the spirit of secularism has been enshrined in the constitution, the use of the word secular gives rise to several conflicting interpretations. The concept which is applicable to the West is sometimes strictly inappropriate in the Indian context, because in India, religion and politics, unlike the West, have gone together, and any attempt to separate the two would be unrealistic.

The evolution of life in India over the centuries has maintained an intimate relationship between religion, morality, spirituality and politics. Spirituality is conceived in India as the foundation of social, economic and political goals. In the West, religion may be a way of worship and may imply a separation of church from the state. However, in the Indian situation, social life is determined by religious norms. Religion is a way of life and cannot be separated from the state.

REFERENCES

1. *Collected Works of Mahatma Gandhi*, Government of India: Publications Division, Ministry of Information and Broadcasting, 1964, Vol. XIII, p. 66.
2. T.V. Parvate, *Tilak and Gandhi: Conceptions and Misconceptions*, Varinder Grover (ed.), Political Thinkers of Modern India. New Delhi: Deep and Deep Publications, Vol. 4, p. 405.
3. Robert W. Stevenson, *"Tilak and The Bhagavadgita's Doctrine of Karmayoga"*, Robert N. Minor (ed.), *Modern Indian Interpreters of the Bhagavadgita*, Albany: State University of New York Press, 1986, p. 60.
4. *Collected Works of Mahatma Gandhi, supra n.1*, Vol. XV, p. 288.
5. J.T.F. Jordens, *"Gandhi and the Bhagavadgita"*, Robert N. Minor, *supra n. 3*, pp. 91-95.

6. *Colleced Works of Mahatma Gandhi, supra n. 1,* Vol. XIV, pp. 201-2.
7. Raghavan N. Iyer, *The Moral and Political Thought of Mahatma Gandhi,* New York: Oxford University Press, 1973, pp. 50-51.
8. *Ibid.*, p. 51.
9. B.R. Nanda, *Gandhi and Religion,* Gandhi Marg, New Delhi: Gandhi Peace Foundation, April-June, 1990, Vol. XII, No. 1, p. 5.
10. D.V. Tahmankar, *Lokamanya Tilak: Father of the Indian Unrest and Maker of Modern India,* London: John Murray Publishers Ltd., 1956, pp. 61-62.
11. *Ibid.*, pp. 66-67.
12. *Harijan* (Ahmedabad), 30 April, 1938, p. 99.

CHAPTER 5

INTERACTION BETWEEN RELIGION AND SECULARISM

The oft-quoted maxim "What is ethically wrong cannot be politically right" goes aptly in the Indian situation. However, a study of history indictes that a few problems are more difficult to solve, like that of discovering a theoretically valid and workable application of religion to political life.

Religion has played an important role in all the civilizations known to man. In some situations, religion may even be said to be the key best-fitted for understanding and interpreting their ways of life. Accordingly, it is quite impossible to understand most historic civilizations without a comprehension of the role religion played in them. The significance of religion cannot easily be overlooked. Religion has held a strong sway over every aspect of Indian life. It has the capacity to rouse the entire society to its faults and shortcomings. It is that one firm and steadfast supremacist, yet gentle and yielding, that has the power to amalgamate the entire human race with the feeling of unity and equality, if understood, and adopted in its right perspective.[1]

What is the situation today? In modern times, some would question whether religion is still as vital a force in the lives of individuals and of socieities as it had been in the past. It is unsound, however, simply to generalize, as many do, and assume that religion was alive and important in the past but that in contemporary civilizations, it is unimportant or even dying. For, even in our own time, there is much evidence that people are more inclined to inquire into the nature and meaning of religion than they have been for decades. If one wished to cite statistics, in our nation a greater percentage of the population than at any time in our history sustains a membership of some religious institution. Scholars committed to study the problems of man and society, whatever their attitude towards religion may be, acknowledge the important role that religion actually plays in modern life.

Many of them would even point to what is frequently called a "return to religion" and assert that this return is characteristic not only of the so-called higher intellectual circles, but also of the man in the street. It is not necessary for us to express a judgement on the degree to which religion seems to be playing a more important role in contemporary life, but it is important to recognise that we apparently are far from dealing with a dying phenomenon. On the contrary, whether one is hostile or favourable to religion one must recognise it as a factor so significant in the past and in the present that no thoughtful person can hope to understand the world in which he lives without understanding something about religion. Yet this understanding ranges from recognising the universality and significance of religion to a widespread ignorance and inarticulateness concerning it.

Religion claims the final loyalty of man, and in the realms of personal and collective ethics seeks to disclose and develop within men the attitudes, principles and the spirit of the good life. Religion thus conceived cannot, without being false to its purpose, remain indifferent to the political and social conditions that affect each and every citizen. At an even deeper level, moreover, there are areas of belief in which religion and political theory overlap. To be specific, all the main political philosophies have certain assumptions about the nature of man. This is a legitimate and important aspect of political theory.

Religion, again, has, as one of its basic elements, certain beliefs about man-his origin, nature and destiny-and it cannot help but be concerned about whether, how, and to what extent any political sysem relates itself to these beliefs. Another specific set of problems that exists is the mutual concern of religion and political theory: freedom, equality of opportunity, and justice. Finally, there is present in every political theory, the normative as well as the descriptive element. This means that political philosophy always faces, sooner or later, the fundamental questions regarding what ought to be the relation between citizens and states, what is the goal of any state, and what is the ultimate status of justice and law. Here political thought undeniably ovelaps with ethical and religious philosophy.[2]

There has always been a very close link between religion and politics from the earliest times to the present. However, the pattern of interaction between the two has varied from time to time and it has had varied social consequences. Religion has never been able to fully extricate itself from politics nor could politics ever rid itself fully of religion. Thus, it is easy to trace signs of politicization of religion in some manifest or latent form at all stages of our history.

As the close affinity between religion and politics continued in the post-independence era, it was essential to base the polity on the principle of secularism. A plural society like India, with a multiplicity of religions, creeds and cultures, kept this principle in the limelight so that democracy could survive, nay, flourish! Dr. S. Radhakrishanan explicitly related the Hindu view of reality to the conception of a secular state. "It may appear somewhat strange", he wrote in 1955, "that our government should be a secular one while our culture is rooted in spiritual values." Secularism here does not mean irreligion or atheism or even stress on material comforts. It proclaims that it lays stress on the universality of spiritual values which may be attained by a variety of ways. Emphasizing the unity of the religious experience despite all doctrinal differences, he declared: "This is the meaning of a secular conception of the state though it is not generally understood."[3]

Unfortunately, the secular social fabric of the Indian society is currently under very great strain. Religious groups, under the garb of defence mechanism, are resorting to various types of revivalism and fundamentalism, and the very edifice of our glorious composite culture built by various communities of Indian citizens over a period of centuries is being torn. We are regressing back to our religious identities—the more and more of us are once again looking upon ourselves as 'Sikhs' or 'Muslims' or 'Hindus' rather than as Indians. One is thus distancing oneself from the other—the US from the THEM.

Every issue today appears as a 'Hindu vs. Sikh' or a 'Hindu vs. Muslim' issue. Whether a run-down building is a mosque or the birthplace of Lord Rama, whether a seventy five year old woman should get alimony or not, whether a procession should proceed along one route or another—none of these remains the specific, trivial question that it is. Each becomes a matter of honour, a trial of strength, a prelude to some eventual but great calamity or victory.[4]

Secularism is no longer everyone's favourite expression. The magnetism once enjoyed by it is missing. Yet, no word in the current Indian lexicon, or the contemporary political discourse, is more baffling and intriguing than the word secularism, and yet the ease with which it is used in the political parlance is amazing. It has become a convenient hobby-horse of the mediamen, politicians, professionals, religious leaders, ideologues and the public. There have been majoritarian and minoritarian versions of the term, as also the so-called 'genuine', 'positive' as against 'pseudo' and 'negative' categories.[5]

Violence, communal mistrust, separatism, and secessionism have grown in recent decades. Over most of this period "secularists" have ruled India. In Punjab, Kashmir and Asam separatism's fires have been stroked by prolonged neglect, denial of democracy, corruption in the limbs of the state, a perception of betrayal and unemployment, not by secularism. Even so, separatism's growth during the rule of secularists has clipped secularism's prestige.

Our constitution prescribes secularism as a norm for the state and its limbs, and our freedom struggle bequeathed secularism as a desirable attitude for the citizen. But we do not always clarify whether it is the state's or the citizen's secularism that we are speaking of. To some, secularism is a belief that all religions are essentially the same. Such a state would in fact be a religious state with the equal worth of all faiths as its religion.[6]

It appears that the adoption of the term secularism demanded from our people either total conformity to a concept nurtured and grown in an entirely different cultural environment or the disowning of the concept altogether. A more open-minded approach to this question would treat secularism, in what is called, the spirit or sentiment behind this concept in the special Indian scenerio of constitution-making when an equivalent word from Sanskrit like *Dharma-sapeksha* could have been used. However, equal treatment of all religious communities by the state, *Sarva-dharma-sambhava,* became the central idea of Indian Secularism. One cannot apply western division of state and religion, for it is unbelievable that in the Indian case the two cannot be separated. Religion affects not only social and economic lives of the citizens, it also affects their political activities.[7]

One functionary of a secular state may view Hinduism as a religion that excels and not merely equals other religions, antoher functionary may accord pride of place to Islam, a third to Sikhism, a fourth to Christianity, a fifth to Buddhism, a sixth to none and a seventh to all, yet such a state can be secular. A dictionary meaning of secular is "worldly or material, not religious or spiritual", which would make a secular state a materialistic or irreligious state. But the founders of our Republic perhaps did not have such a state in mind when they insisted that India would be seculaı. What they meant was that though India was preponderantly Hindu, it would not be a *'Hindu Rashtra'*, that Hindus and non-Hindus would have equal rights and opportunities in it.

'Sarva-dharma-samabhava (Equal respect for all religions) excellently spell out a secular state's rejection of the concept of a favoured community, but it would be perfectly legitimate for a citizen in such a state or, in his private capacity, for a functionary of such a state to believe in the superiority of his religion over others. But what a secular citizen or functionary will not do is to treat some people better and others worse because of their religion. A nation being a combinatin of state and people, that nation is secualr where, irrespective of religion, citizens enjoy equal rights from the state and grant equal respect to one another.[8]

It follows from the above that a secular state will separate religion from governance and that its limbs and institutions, be they legislatures, courts, police stations or state-run schools, will not be used to propagate any particular religion or sect. But it would be neither possible nor desirable in today's or tomorrow's India to demand the banishment of all religious symbols from the state's ceremonials, public platforms and public property.

In sum, the temple or dome of secularism rests on the pillars of equity (i.e. justice), tolerance and goodwill. We know that these pillars have been tremor-prone. Earlier separatism's growth under secular rulers had damaged secularism's prestige. When equity, tolerance and goodwill are shaky, the survival of secularism's temple comes into question. Exuding passion, many Hindus have charged that secular governments have appeased Muslims (at times appeasement of Sikhs and/or of Christians is also alleged) and thus shaken equity. Violence directed at Hindus celebrating festivals and the killing and kidnapping of Hindus in Kashmir and Punjab have hurt the goodwill and tolerance. Gross exaggerations of the undisputed and photographed fact that some Hindus died in police firing in Ayodha in October-November, 1990 have affected grassroots Hindu sentiment. The undisputed and photographed fact that Hindu volunteers climbed the domes of the Babri Masjid and waved the saffron flag from its heights has affected grassroots Muslim sentiment. In 1984 the storage by secessionists of arms in the Golden Temple had hurt goodwill towards Sikhs; the Operation Bluestar outraged the Sikhs. Linking Article 371 to Kashmir's Muslim factor, rahter than to the combination of circumstances that led to Kashmir's accession to the Indian Union, has injured Hindu-Muslim trust. Similar has been the result of propaganda that the police forces of some of our states can never be just to Muslims.

Growing number seem to regard Hinduism and nationalism as synonymous. Thus they would see a bomb blast by Khalistani separatists as an anti-Hindu as well as anti-Indian act. Given India's Hindus preponderance, such a reaction cannot be called strange. But given India's variety such a reaction cannot be called wise. Divided into castes as well as communities, into ethnic as well as sectarian groups, Indians have to understand the hazards of reacting to events as Hindus or Muslims or Sikhs rather than as Indians and human beings. For if one responds to one provocative event as a Hindu one cannot complain if another wishes to respond to a different provocative event as a tribal or a Dalit or a Muslim or a Shiva-worshipper or a Vishnu-worshipper or whatever. In our land of infinite diversity, to legitimise a sectional response is to legitimise ceaseless and widespread strife.

The practice of any religion by an individual or citizen is in a way an acknowledgement by man of the fact that he comes from God, that he is dependent on him, that he is sustained by him at every moment, that he must live and practise certain basic principles and norms which any religion teaches and prepare himself in this way to one day go to his father's kingdom where badges of Hinduism, Islam, Buddhism, et. al. will not be required to be worn at all. This is something that any man can do with the greatest of ease at all moments of his life in a true, secular democracy, and throughout his life, without any disturbance to his neighbour or without interfering with his neighbour's freedom to do likewise or not do anything of that kind. Problems arise either when a person believes that he alone has the freedom to practise his religion and is not prepared to concede it to others, or when he believes that his religion alone should be practised by everyone and not any other or wants to drive away those who claim equal freedom to practise any religion they like.

Religion is a highly emotional and psychologically motivated subject. Especially in India, religion rouses passions and emotions very easily and everyone is aware of this. It has been dragged into politics in order to achieve results which probably would have been difficult to achieve by straightforward, democratic means. Of course, a man does not cease to be a man of religion when he enters public life or politics or matters connected with the state and the government. Consciousness regarding. religion and religious beliefs and practices continues. However, it is expected not to mix one's religion with politics. Neither is one expected to make it a political ideology or to bring in religion into politics because that is an arena there are people with different religious beliefs or practising various religions who come together to work for the counry and its people, for the common good. This does not mean, however, that they have foresaken their religion. When we fail to appreciate this or fail to respect other people's views on this subject, mis-understandings are arisen and dissatisfaction sprouts. Behaviours and actions are resented, and the cumulative effect of all that is accusations and counter-accusations of being communalists, of being religious fanatics, of religious bigotry, or wanting to impose our religion on others.

All this leads to hatred and enmity among various communities. The desire to live in peace and harmony which should be the norm among the citizens disappears and what remains is bitterness, discord, riots, commotion, civil wars and misunderstandings and distrust. Keeping all this in mind and with a desire to bring about in our midst a nation where people would practise any religion they like but live in peace and harmony, where the citizens, irrespective of their religion, would work to build the nation and take it forward, where they would all engage in some creative and not destructive, activity, where the worth of an individual would be decided on the basis of his abilities and his contribution for the growth and development of the nation, the constituent Assembly produced a Constitution which would ensure that all the citizens would be equal in all respects; they would be free to pursue their own vocation or profession in life, work for the good of the country, for its progress and prosperity, and at the same time, be free to practise and propagate a religion of their choice. The choice of any religion would not make anyone more or less equal than others; it would not give anyone any special status, position, power or access to any office under the State. All citizens would be free to aspire for and attain any position, status or public office within the country and their religious beliefs or convictions would neither help them to do so nor prevent or hinder them in any way from doing whatever they like. These are highly progressive, modern concepts and ideas embodied in our secularism, and, therefore, one fails to understand how anyone with some common-sense can find fault with it. These literal concepts and ideas show the statesmanship, the magnanimity, the training, the intellectual calibre of those who drafted the constitution. That outlook on life and society enabled them also to frame the country's policies in the formative years in such a way that India could march forward as a progressive and modern nation. That is what is called secularism of the most progressive variety where man fearlessly and with absolute confidence is able to march forward. It is the blossoming of ancient India's genius. It is not the secularism which was known in the West in the past, and to which scholars, writers and religious leaders of the medieval and subsequent ages frequently refer to. In the West, secularism implied a somewhat irreligious or anti-religious society; a society where the State would not encourage any religion or help relgious leaders in any way and religious tenets would find no place in state matters. It implied a society where religion has separated almost totally from the state. But secularism "even in its western forms, is not the logical opposite of religious faith, but a theme with many variations, united by a basic rejection of intolerance, religious strife and state persecution."[9] State may not have encouraged any religion or allowed religion to be mixed with politics, but there was no attempt to turn any religion into an official religion of the State or to force anyone to embrace the majority religion.

The concept of Indian secularism is a gift to the entire world. Complete freedom has been given to every citizen of India to practise any religion one likes, and everyone has been acknowledged to be equal in all respects in the eyes of the law: and everyone is free to pursue any vocation in life and work for one's country or for oneself without anyone interfering with anybody in any manner whatsover. If, despite so much backwardness, ignorance, obscurantism, caste system and relgious bigotry, this has been accepted as a way of life and as a future goal, then every Indian must struggle to maintain it. The logical attitude of getting rid of religion altogether was too utopian for the Indian Society, when so many religious have been deeply entrenched. So the more practical answer was not opposition to religion but the removal of religion from public affairs, the separation of State from all faiths, the insistence on religion as a private matter for the individual with no bearing on civic rights and duties, and freedom for the profession of diverse forms of religious worship provided they did not come into conflict with each other. These are elements of the most practical approach. Only secularism of this type, not defined in any dictionary or in accordance with western experience, but adapted to the Indian context, can be the cornerstone of an egalitarian, forward-looking society with religious pluralism, complete civil liberties and equal opportunities. This is secularism where religion is very much a part of us. It is not discarded from our society. It is acknowledged as necessary for us and the State is made to enforce the right to religion.

The secularism embodied in the Indian political system is not devoid of or hostile to spiritual or religious values. It acknowledges the universally accepted dictum that in a democracy man must have a right to practise his religion. It is also the right embodied by the United Nations in its Universal Human Rights Declaration Statement.[10] Practise of any religion is man's right in a democracy and that practise cannot make him inferior or superior to any one. Democracy cannot but be a hypocrisy if it is not secular. If every member of the society is to enjoy equal human rights and participate without discrimination in the processes of the government, communal and religious exclusion or preferential position for communities of certain faiths is a negation of the concept of government by the people. In matters of state concern, a secular culture obligates active neutrality so that no one suffers disadvantages or enjoys greater privileges on grounds of creed, caste or sect. Effective separation between religious and temporal matters, with the state being kept out of the former, and God being kept out of the latter, is secularism.[11]

The urge for a secular society among the citizens must be given content, shape and respectability. The entire mass of citizenry must develop regard and respect for secular thought, secular institutions and secular society. The citizens are and will always be totally and unreservedly free to practice and propagate whichever religion they choose to. But religion *per se* will not be and must not be carried into politics; it must not be preached as a political ideology by any political party; it must not be used as a platform to appeal to the voters to secure their support. Voters should be asked to vote for the party and its candidates on the basis of its programme for political, econimic and social action. Its policy statements, its manifestoes, its performance, its past record should vouch for its secular credentials.

But the parties will be secualr and democratic to the extent to which the citizens also in the country are imbued with a democratic spirit and are committed to a secular ideology. The people must develop respect for secularism. They must be bathed in secularism, making it their way of life at all moments of the day and unconcerned about the private life, personal beliefs, and the practice of religion of others. This is the type of attitude towards religion which progressive societies have developed over the centuries and it is working quite satisfactorily in many of the western and developed countries in particular. These nations have not become godless. They have not given up the practice of religion. Religion is very much alive in those societies. But what those societies have learnt to do is to keep their religion to themselves when they deal with public affairs; they have learnt to make a moral, spiritual man come alive in society through his actions, through a life of honesty and uprightness. Secularism does not ask anyone to forsake his religion or his life of morality and ethical behaviour. All that it asks the citizens to do is not to mix religion with politics or ask anyone to vote for a particular candidate because he practices a particular religion. He should be elected on the basis of his achievements, his loyalty to the country and his work for the poor and the downtrodden.

India cannot claim to be a civilised nation and pursue policies which are directly a negation of all that it implies. It cannot be a progressive nation and yet be a slave to obscurantist, backward-looking, hatred-ridden social policies. The nation that our freedom fighters, our Founding Fathers conceived was a progressive, modern, strong, united one where the least among its citizens would enjoy a modicum of decent life and comfort, a life free from tensions, fights, riots, wars and destruction of life and property.

It is the younger generation that must now take to the centrestage. They must take the initiative and act. They must develop a new vision of India—and india free from turmoil and commotion, an India free from communal hatred and discord; an India determined to go forward, to march shoulder to shoulder with other progressive, modern nations; an India where they and their offspring will have enough to live on, to clothe and shelter themselves, where they will have something to look forward to, and not a life based on herd mentality, or communal hatred. It is the youth that must take this task upon itself or else they will continue to live in the same morass, in the lifeless decadence in which their forefathers lived for thousands of years. The communal-minded politicians do not seem to even care to give a second thought to the consequences of their actions. The average citizen of India, the man who is struggling to eke out a living for himself and his family is unconcerned about the religion of his neighbour or his colleague or fellow-worker. He wants to see whether he has enough to exist, whether his family has enough to keep the pot boiling in the evening, whether his children can be sent to a school the next day to learn to read and write, to acquire a trade or a profession, and whether they will find a job to make a living for themselves when they grow up. They want to know when the freedom that their forefathers had fought for and won 53 years ago is going to be a reality to them in the form of a happy, contended, peaceful life, or whether it is going to be a hell on earth all their life.

The country cannot make progress unless there is peace and harmony. The older generation of politicians whose entire thought-process begins and ends with religious bigotry, who cannot think of anything without bringing the religion of the other person into play, who cannot think of winning an election in any way except by asking for votes on the basis of religion, cannot be expected to help the country to make progress. The country will make progress when it leaves each person to practise whichever religion he likes but in public life, in politics, in social and economic activities gets every citizen to work with determination to succeed and take the country forward. In this effort it is the youth, the rising generation that must catch the bull by the horns and act. They must refuse to accept the old slavish mentality when it was thought that whatever the elders asked them to do was Gospel truth which had to be obeyed and carried out in letter and in spirit. Today's youth must realise that they have a whole future before them, and that future has to be worked out and shaped largely by themselves. It cannot be done if they are at daggers drawn with the followers of other religions. It cannot be done if they look at every second person as their enemy just because that person practises a different religion. They should learn to work with anyone whatever his private life, beliefs and convictions. They should elect those candidates in an election who are enlightened, competent, capable, educated and ready to work for India and not for any particular community. In a democracy alone it is possible for the whole mass of people to act—to see who is working for them and who is not; whose policies can help the country to make progress and whose policies will retard its progress. Elections are meant not to meekly submit to those who want to dupe them and secure their votes, but to assert themselves and correct the policies, reverse the trends, reject the chauvinists. India can become a great world power. It is in the hands of people to make it happen. They must refuse to yield to obscurantists, communalists and selfish politicians.

It cannot be overlooked also that the people themselves have come to realise much of this. Many of them know that they cannot be silent spectators of this sordid, communal drama which has been unfolding itself for the last several years. The only result of it is bloodshed, bitterness and hatred all around. One can go on making every imaginable claim to the disputed site by citing concocted history as evidence; one can also advance the argument that the problem is one of faith, and that no argument, no evidence, no Court can decide such matters. It must be appreciated, therefore, that precisely because it is a delicate issue of belief and faith it deserves to be dealth with differently. Politicians, Government and even the Judiciary should be left to attend to the problems they are expected to attend to and solve.

God is the Supreme Being, the beginning and end of all things. The Supreme Being cannot be predicated. It cannot be confined to a particular place, to a certain day, or to a particular point in time. If the Hindus really believe that Ram is that Supreme Being, then they can neither claim that he was born at Ayodhya nor can he be allotted a tiny spot on earth as his. Everything and everypart of the universe should be his and, therefore, it is a contradiction in terms to want to confine him to a remote corner in India. God has no beginning and no end. God is everywhere. God is to be worshipped in spirit which is possible for man to do anywhere, anytime. Much less can anyone claim to worship the Supreme Being and do his will if it is done by destroying and existing place of worship because all places of worship are His, built in His honour. He is the Supreme Being who has created all human beings, who loves, cares and sustains all of them, whatever may be the religion that they claim to belong to or practise. It is only when we appreciate the real significance of religion that we will recognise that religion must make us love one another, work for one another, and treat everyone with reverence and respect, because they are all children of the same Maker.

REFERENCES

1. Jyoti Trehan, *Veer Savarkar: Thought and Action of Vinayak Damodar Savarkar,* New Delhi: Deep and Deep Publications, 1991, p. 141.
2. George G. Hackman, Charles W. Kegley, Viljo K. Nikander, *Religion in Modrn Life,* New York: The MacMillan Company, 1958, pp. 1428-29.
3. S. Radhakrishnan, "Foreword", in S. Abid Hussain, *The National Culture of India,* Bombay: Jaico Publishing House, 1956, pp. vii-viii.
4. Arun Shourie, *Religion in Politics,* New Delhi: Roli Books International, 1987, p. 287.
5. M.M. Sankhdher, "Understanding Secularism"., in M.M. Sankhdher (ed.), *Secularism in India:* Dilemmas and Challenges, New Delhi, Deep and Deep Publications, 1992, p. 1.
6. Rajmohan Gandhi, *"Secularism Vs. Pseudo-Secularism"* Hindustan Times (New Delhi), 15 December, 1991.
7. M.M. Sankahdher, *Understanding Secularism,* in M.M. Sankhdher (ed.), *supra n. 5,* pp. 3-4.
8. Rajmohan Gandhi, *supra n. 6.*
9. Sumit Sarkar, *Roots of Secularism: Not an Elitist Concept,* The Times of India, 26 March, 1993.
10. Sarto Esteves, *Nationalism, Securalism and Communalism,* New Delhi: South Asia Publications, 1996, pp. 94-95.
11. *Ibid.,* pp. 96.

APPENDIX-1

BRAHMANIC SYSTEM

The root of the relationship between religious diversity and continuity in India can be found first in the Indian value system (particularly the Brahmanic value system) and its structural manifestation, the caste system, and second in the structure of the centres of Indian civilization.

The core of Indian traditional identity was the Brahmanic system of beliefs and values. This had its roots in two earlier streams of religious thought. One was the religion of the early Aryans, a group of pastoral tribes that conquered northern India in a series of invasions in the second millennium B.C. The heart of their religion was found in the *Rig Veda,* a great collection of hymns originally used at the sacrifices of the aristocratic Aryan cult and still, in theory, thought to be the most sacred of the numerous Hindu texts. The chief objects of worship were the *devas* or male deities connected chiefly with the sky. To the *Rig Veda* were later added three more *Vedas (Sama, Yajur and Atharva)* and an extensive set of appendics known as the *Brahmanas* with instructions on the ritual use of the *Vedas.* Later the *Aranyakas* and *Upanishads* were added to explicate them philosophically. Together these complete the literature generally known as *Vedic.*

The second steam of religious thought was the *Deshya* or indigenous tradition. This centered around the worship of household fire and of fertility, the use of magic in dealing with problems of every day life, and the belief in metempsychosis according to which the souls of the dead enter animals, plants, or natural objects before being reborn in a human body.

The centre of Aryan ritual was sacrifice, which formed the core of complex rites whose chief purpose was the gratification of the gods in order to obtain boons from them. The priests alone knew the mysteries of the sacrifice that summoned the gods. In the synthesis, sacrifice took on a magical cast. Priests by their sacred chants *(mantras)* could possess that mysterious power or entity called *Brahman* and thereby become *Brahmana*. By repeating the primeval sacrifice from which the universe itself arose, they renewed it. Ultimately it was not the gods but the *Brahmans,* who compelled the gods by magic, who maintained cosmic order. They were more powerful than any god or earthly king, for without their services the world, and with it human society, would collapse.

This priestly dominance was the basis for the Brahmanic social system. Implicit in it was a concept of hierarchy based on the concept of ritual purity. The core of Indian identity was this conception of parallelism between cosmic and social purity and pollution, and of the symbolic expression of this parallelism in the ritual and social spheres. The locus of Indian identity lay neither in an organized, homogeneous, unified cultural centre nor in a centralized political state. It was to be found in the priestly caste and in the many networks and ritual subcenters of which they were a part.

The Brahmanic system of values was reinforced by the religious idelogy that emerged in the synthesis. Belief in metempsychosis had developed by the sixth century B.C. into the doctrines of *samsara* or transmigration, and *karma* (literally 'deed'), the law that one's next life is determined by the deeds of one's past and present lives. These linked all forms of life into a single system in which animals, insects, plants, earth, and even the gods themselves are subject to *karma* and *samsara*. The universe and its parallel, human society, were seen as organic wholes in which each *jat* (on the cosmic scene a form of life, on the social scene a caste) has a specific task *(dharma)* to perform. Only in the faithful dispassionate performance of this duty can an individual acquire merit and a higher station in the next life. Brahmanic cosmology provided the rational for heterogeneity, hierarchy, and specialization within a single body.

The social order that emerged out of this system of values and ideology was the caste system. In Brahmanic ideology this was seen as a single organic society in which the many different functions and occupations were served by different castes on the basis of their socio-ritual status. At the top were the priestly castes, followed by the rulers and warriors *(Kshatriyas)*, the merchants and traders *(Vaishyas)*, and, finally, the artisans and manual workers *(Shudras)*.

In reality, this *varna* model of the caste system broke down into a great many local caste hierarchies influenced by such factors as the dominance of the *Brahmans* in the region, the caste and strength of the local rulers, the size and economic fortunes of the various castes, and the fortunes of their striving for higher ranks. There were in fact a multiplicity of legitimate channels of social mobility and access to higher positions. This flexibility allowed the upwardly mobile to pursue their aspirations while reinforcing the fundamental structure of the system itself.

The second explanation for the continuity of the core of Indian civilization amidst diversity has to do with its centres of cultural identity. Unlike centres in the other great civilizations, those in India were not tied to any given political framework. To be sure, a great many states and imperial capitals, large and small, arose throughout the course of Indian history, but the centres of Brahmanic tradition were to be course of Indian history, but the centres of Brahmanic tradition were to be found in the many temples, *mutts*, and other ritual centres and in the networks of relationships that bound the Brahman priests together. The political centres that did emerge were relatively weak in terms of the major religio-cultural values of the region and the commitments they could command thereby. Consequently, the fortunes of the socio-cultural system were not tied to the stability of any particular political state.

Brahmanic centres were, of course, not completely independent of political influence, even though in theory priests ranked higher than kings. In practice rulers often defined the relative ritual standing of various caste groups and at times ignored the *Brahmans* altogether. But the former only reinforced the caste system itself, and the latter rarely had more than temporary regional effects.

Despite a measure of flexibililty in the Brahmanic system, the apparent futility of an unending series of rebirths and the constraints of a caste system that denied spiritual attainments to all but the priests led to a religious revolt. By the time of the *Upanishads* asceticism had emerged as an alternative path to the ritual sacrifice. Some ascetics dwelt alone in the depths of the forest, and others suffered self-inflicted tortures of hunger, thirst, heat, cold, and rain, but most lived on the outskirts of towns and villages, alone or in groups, meditating on explanations of the cosmic mystery. But asceticism only provided the dissatisfied with a way to drop out of society and the ritual order, and thereby bled off some of the frustrations that developed within the system. It did not provide a viable alternative model for society as a whole.

The Brahmanic synthesis laid the basis for continuity of the indian identity based upon heterogeneity and hierarchy. But dissociating the core of the culture from the political centers and relating it to the priestly castes with their multiplicity of centers and networks, and by rooting social structure in the cosmic order, it made heterogeneity and flexibility the basis for an adaptive response to change. New ideas and peoples could be assimilated without undermining the basic structures of religion and society.

The Brahmanic synthesis on the supremacy of the priestly castes was challenged by the *Kshatriyas* or royal castes and by the heterodox religions to which they gave their support, namely Buddhism and Jainism. The first of these was founded by Siddhartha, a *Kshatriya* prince who, when confronted by the evils of old age, sickness, and death, realized that all human pleasures are vanity, and orthodox sacrifices to no avail. Renouncing his throne, he set out to find enlightement by the paths of religious asceticism. Finding these also wanting, he turned to meditation and achieved enlightenment.

The sect spread rapidly with the support of the kings, to whom it gave primacy over the priests. Under royal patronage, missionaries were sent throughout India, to Ceylon, and to Southeast Asia. Their success is testified to by the fact that between 200 B.C. and 200 A.D. the number of Buddhist archaeological remains in India outnumbered those of Brahmanism and Jainism combined.

The new religion held that all life is plagued by sorrow and sufferings and that these can be eliminated only by giving up ambition, desire, and selfishness. This can be achieved not by the pursuit of pleasures or by the pursuit of pain and hardship, both of which lead to rebirths, but by following the Middle Way of right views, right resolve, right conduct, right livelihood, right effort, right recollection, and right meditation. In short, self-indulgence and extreme asceticism were rejected in favour of a moral, well-ordered life.

Buddhism accepted transmigration but denied the ultimate existence of a personal or universal soul. Even *Brahman,* the World Soul, was held to be an illusion. The only stable entity was *nirvana,* a state of bliss that was neither being nor annihilation.

Buddhism split into two parts after Buddha's death: the strictly orthodox *Hinayan* or Lesser Vehicle and the more popular *Mahayana* or Greater Vehicle. In the latter Buddha came to be worshipped with circumambulations, prostrations, offerings of flowers, incense, and waving lamps, and with deep devotion just as a Hindu god.

The new religion remained the dominant religion in Ceylon, but its decline and eventual extinction in India was due to a number of factors. Anti-Buddhist persecutions by Hindu kings during the sixth and seventh centuries A.D. were not uncommon. More significant was the revival and reform of Hinduism, which spread northwards from the south in the ninth century, coupled with the absorption of Buddha into Hinduism as the ninth of Vishnu's ten incarnations. The final blow came as the invading Muslims destroyed the great monasteries which were the heart of Buddhism.

The origins of Jainism have come to be identified with Mahavira, who, like Siddhartha, was born a prince in northern India and renounced his throne in pursuit of truth. Like the Buddha he found enlightenment through meditation.

Jainism accepted the concept of transmigration of all things, including stones, water, and objects but sought release from rebirth by dispelling the *karma* from previous lives that adheres to the soul like atomic dust. Liberation was to be accomplished by penance and by disciplined conduct including fasting, meditation, and the renunciation of killing, stealing, sexual activity, and ownership of property-in short, through mendicancy.

Jainism flourished through the twelfth century, under the patronage of many kings, but died out as Shaivism and Vaishinavism grew. Today there are only about three million Jains in India, most of them prosperous merchants.

Both Jainism and Buddhism appealed to the ruling classes and challenged the supremacy of the *Brahman* priest. Both stressed agnostic materialism and ethical behavior as well as sensory control for attaining liberation. In retaining their heterodoxy and confrontation with Brahmanism, they were able for a long time to remain distinct from it, despite its inclusivism.

The final triumph of reformed Brahmanism in the form of Hinduism was due to a number of factors. First, as has been noted, the centres of Indian civilization were not the political centres of power but the many autonomous religious centres scattered across the land. Although Buddhism and Jainism frequently gained the backing of the state, they were unable to destroy the many centres of Brahmanism that provided the core cultural identity for the largely rural populace. Second, the heterogeneity inherent in Brahmanism, and the tolerance for variety it fostered, enabled Hinduism to encompass the heterodox movements and to incorporate them as sects and castes within the society. Finally, the door to religious salvation was opened to more than the *Brahmans* by the introduction of the concept of *bhakti,* which offered liberation from the endless cycle of rebirths to all on the basis of personal devotion to a theistic God.

The *bhakti* movement began in the ninth century with the teaching of Shankara, a Shaivite Brahman, and Ramanuja, a Vaishnavite brahman, both of whom wrote commentaries reinterpreting the *Gita,* the great devotional poem that was the epitomy of the Brahmanic synthesis. Ramanuja stressed a personal god, full of love for his creation, who overrides the power of *karma* for those who approach him in devotion. The end for such devotees was not a loss of identity and abosorption into *Brahman,* but to dwell with God in heaven.

If the basis rite of Brahmanism had been the sacrifice, in Hinduism it became worship. Gods of an almost infinite number and variety of forms were enshrined as icons in temples. They were awakened with music, bells, and conches; bathed, dried, and dressed; fed rice and fruit; offered flowers, incense, and swinging lamps; and taken to their bedrooms at night to join their wives. Annually they were married, and on special occasions given tours of the village in a chariot pulled by their devotees. But although there were significant changes in religious beliefs and practices with the emergence of Hinduism, the core values and structures of Brahmanism remained unchanged. Heterogeneity, and hierarchy based upon concepts of socio-religious purity and pollution, remained central to everyday life. The path of release through *bhakti* was assimilated into theology as one of many paths to *moksha;* and their many religious sub-centres remained the centre of Indian civilization. Brahmanism survived change by adaptation and assimilation.

Less than a century after the death of the prophet Mohammed, the Muslims arrived in India. The first of them were Arab traders who moved along the intercontinental and maritime trade routes, establishing colonies that contained all the dynamic forces and institutions of a young and vigorous Islam. They often took local wives and adopted local dress and language.

The traders were followed by the Sufis or mystics, who went about the countryside as missionaries. The message they brought was that of the unity and transcedence of God, a passionate rejection of polytheism and idolatry, and the brotherhood of men. The Muslim or 'follower of God' was one who submitted himself completely to Allah, who had revealed Himself through Mohammed in the sacred word, the *Quran,* and the sacred law of Shari'a. This theological simplicity and the economic benefits of converting to the new faith account, in part, for the rapid spread of Islam.

The emphasis on the brotherhood of men stood in stark contrast to the ritual hierarchy and social caste system of Hinduism. This undoubtedly appealed to the low-caste people and accounts for their widespread conversion to Islam. But belief in equality was tempered by the social realities of castelike divisions which appeared within the Muslim community between Arab immigrants and local converts and between converts from different social ranks.

The traders and missionaries were followed by soldiers. As early as 711 A.D. Muhammed Bin Quasim raided Sind, in the northwest. In the eleventh century Mahmud Ghazni began a conquest that, by the sixteenth century, led to Muslim rule over most of India, a rule that was finally replaced by the British in the eighteenth century.

Islam faced several problems in India. The first was the relationship between religion and government. Wherever it had spread, Islam had taken over political control. Islamic values and beliefs were centralized in religio-political institutions. There was no separation of mosque and state. Moreover, there was implicit in Islam the concept of a universal Islamic state in which all citizens were Muslims. Now it was forced to face the reality that it was a minority ruling over Hindus who were not even 'people of a book'.

In its confrontation with Islam, the strength of Hinduism lay in the diffuse nature of its centres. While Islam was closely identified with the seats of political power, the core of Hinduism lay in the many ritual centres scattered around the countryside and in the socio-religious structures of the villages and towns. The whole complex of castes, villages and the various networks of cultural communication were to a high degree autonomous and self-regulating in terms of their own cultural and society identity, and had only limited recourse to major political centres. Consequently, although the Muslims gained political control over much of India, they failed to undermine either Hinduism or the caste system to which it was integrally related. Beyond the immediate circles of the imperial capitals, the Hindu temples and village social structures continued largely unchanged. Where Muslim communities did arise in rural areas, they were assimilated as castes, and they themselves developed internal castelike segments.

The second problem Islam faced in India was its relationship to Indian culture and the values underlying it. In time there developed an Indian-Islamic tradition in the arts and architecture. But the issue of cultural synthesis went deeper than the expressive arts. Islam was based on revelational absolutes and was dogmatic, exclusive, and missionary. By contrast, Hinduism, which was based on pluralism, stressed relativism, inclusivism, and tolerance. On the social level the Muslim values stressed equality and a strong sense of community, which stood in sharp contrast to the stratified diversity of Hindu society. These fundamental differences between the two led to frequent conflicts over such things as idols and visual representations of gods as human, the killing of cows, and the playing of music near mosques.

Despite the strength of Hinduism in its dissociation with political centres and its association with social structures, Islam did have a significant impact on the countryside, particularly in northern India. Many Hindus converted to Islam through force, for economic gains, and by personal choice. Moreover, Muslims gained control of many of the petty kingdoms that covered the land and challenged the authority of the Brahmans on the local level. In the face of this threat, Hindu revitalization came through two types of movements: *bhakti* movements, that were born in the south, and syncretistic movements in the north that sought to make Hinduism more compatible to Islam.

Between the thirteenth and sixteenth centuries, *bhakti* movements using the vernacular languages arose within each of the linguistic regions of India. The leaders were saints who came from all walks of life and all levels of the social order. There were artisans, farmers, and servants; priests, officials, and untouchables; men and women; and even a princess. They wrote and spoke the language of the people, and their teachings were spread to every village by bards and saints by means of song, drama, dance, and narrative.

The dominant theme of *bhakti* movements was the spiritual equality of all people. They raised the *Shudras* to a position of spiritual power and social importance almost equal to that of the *Brahmans*, and they blurred caste distinctions. They subordinated rituals, pilgrimages, fasts, and meditation to the higher excellence of worship by means of love and faith. But while these ideals counter the egalitarian ideals of Islam, they were expressed chiefly in the spiritual realm in the form of personal worship. They did not bring about changes in the caste system or the dominance of the *Brahmans*. There was no social instrument to institute the change. Neither Hindu nor Muslim states interfered in the internal operations of the castes, guilds and religious denominations. Temples and monasteries were managed by autonomous bodies, generally in the hands of *Brahmans*, that raised funds through private and state gifts. They were regulated by the *Dharma Shastras* or treatises on religious law, which were reinterpreted to accommodate changes in the society. Each new prophet went to the centres of learning, to challenge the entrenched theologians in contests of debate called *Digvijayas* (conquests in all directions) before learned boards of referees, and often in the presence of a king. In many cases the court and the people converted to the teachings of the victor. But in the end these religious conversions did not undermine the caste system itself.

The best known of the syncretistic movements was Sikhism. Nanak, a follower of Kabir, tried to find a common bond between Hinduism and Islam. He taught that there is no Muslim or Hindu, and that humans will be saved not on the basis of their tribe or sect but on the basis of what they have done. He preached his message in mosques and temples alike, gathering Sikhs or disciple. Most of these came from the farmer castes. In the Hindu tradition he appointed one of his disciples to succeed him as a guru.

The Sikh creed stressed castelessness, but social practices rarely lived up to the level of faith. Sikh villages today have endogamous occupational groups ranked like castes along a social hierarchy. Moreover, there has been little marriage between converts from different castes, even though there is no caste discrimination in the rites and temples.

Although Sikhism gained a wide following in northern India, it was unable to reform orthodox Hinduism. Its strength lay in its powerful socio-political organization that enabled it to mobilize its members for political ends. In the twentieth century a number of Sikh sects joined together and formed the SGPC, an elected committee that acts as a Sikh government within the state and central governments. It looks after the welfare of the Sikhs and their temples, which until that time were being badly run. Through this organization the Sikhs exerted the political pressures that led to the division of the state of Punjab in 1966 into Punjab Subah, in which Sikhs constitute the majority, and Haryana.

The fourth period in the development of Hinduism as we know it today began with the colonization of India and the rise of Christian missions. Under the Muslim hegemony, castes, guilds, and religious orders were left largely alone. The British, however, instituted a centralized state which took the initiative in codifying personal and community law and in bringing these under government control. Moreover, their concept of the ideal government rested on the principles of equal individual rights and representation and of government responsibility for the welfare of the people. In the nineteenth century they began to extend the court system into rural areas and to initiate state control of hospitals and education, including the teaching of Sanskrit, which was so essential to orthodox Hinduism. A major step towards the formulation of a uniform civil code for all Indians was taken with the passage of the Hindu Code in 1954-1955, after Indian Independence.

Reactions to the spread of the British policy of establishing political authority as the foundation of society and of extending its control over areas of life traditionally the domains of religion took the form of military uprisings that appealed to religious loyalties. However, these failed due to a lack of large-scale organization, discipline, and the ability to subordinate personal interests to a common purpose. With no tradition of political centralization and nothing in their ideological systems to hold them back in the face of temptations of personal power, Hindu leaders, both political and religious, broke up into rival factions, unable to unite to halt a common foe. As they could not defeat the British by force, many of the princes and orthodox religious leaders withdrew from confrontation with Western ideas into their petty kingdoms and temples and sought refuge in an unquestioning reliance on their textual authorities.

The second challenge to Hinduism brought by the Europeans was Christianity. Catholic missionaries appeared soon after the Portuguese gained control of Goa in 1510 A.D. The Protestants arrived two centuries. later. The missionaries established schools, hospitals, presses, and churches. The initial response was conversion. Some of the earlier students in Calcutta turned to rationalism and utilitarianism. Others, chiefly Brahmans, turned to Christianity. But the movement was retarded by a strong conservative reaction on the part of Hindu religious leaders.

Nevertheless, English education and Christianity had made an impact. By the mid-nineteenth century educated high-caste Hindu across the country were concerned with social reform: first with the emancipation of women and later with reforms of Hindu rituals, untouchability, and religiously sanctioned prostitution. Judged by Christian ideals, many of the widely practiced popular Hindu customs such as *sati* (the immolation of widows on the funeral pyres of their husbands), the refusal by orthodox high-caste Hindus to allow widows to remarry, the worship of idols, and the caste system itself appeared rude or barbaric. But to many of the Hindu-educated elite exposed to Western thought, Hinduism still had a core of truth that needed to be revived, and they turned back to the *Vedas* in order to discover the beauty and rigor of their neglected Hindu heritage. The result was a number of movements that aimed at religious reform and revitalization, and, later, some that sought political reform and independence.

Reform movements such as the *Brahmo Samaj* (Fellowship of Believers of the One True God) and the *Prarthana Samaj* (Fellowship of Prayer) sought to modify Hinduism by creating a synthesis of its best teachings with those of Islam and Christianity. They called for a radical transformation of Hinduism by submitting Hindu scriptures and teachings to the tests of rationality. The result was a synthesis of Vedic idealism, Islamic monotheism, and Christian ethics. Most of the members were upper-caste, reform-minded Hindus, and their chief activities were in the area of social reform such as the abolition of *sati* and polygamy, the establishment of minimum age for marriage, and women's rights. As religious movements, they failed to produce a viable synthesis that could atttract the orthodox religious leaders.

Revitalization movements such as the *Arya Samaj* and the *Rama Krishna Mission* tried to eliminate the undesirable customs by treating them as later and degenerate accretions to the pure Vedic forms. They opposed idolatry, untouchability, and the inequality of women, and simplified Hindu rites in worship and family ceremonies. Their largest gains were in the upper-caste Hindus. Their weakness lay in their dogmatic appeal to authority and their inability to face up to the spread of science and rationalism.

The reform and revival movements were essentially *Brahman* movements aimed at consolidating the position of *Brahman* leaders in the area of religion. But Western ideas of egalitarianism sparked anti-*Brahman* movements among the lower castes, who were seeking a higher social status. Some such movements permitted non-*Brahmans* to perform rites heretofore reserved for *Brahmans*. Others, such as Ambedkar's neo-Buddhist movement, sought to offer untouchables social and religious equality by converting them to some other religion.

If ideological values and socio-religious reform were the two main arenas of intellectual and practical endeavor for educated Indians during the nineteenth century, in the first half of the twentieth it became political reform and nationalism. The Congress party, started in 1885 as a debating society in search of political reform along the Western lines, at first attracted only a few individuals, but it soon became the national and cultural arena within which were fought the religious and ideological battles of the new Hindu India. True to the core Indian value of heterogeneity within a single structure, the Congress party reflected a wide range of differing and often conflicting points of view. There were followers of Gandhi's new HInduism with its slogan 'Back to the Village', of Nehru's secularism and Western democracy, of Patel's militant Hinduism, and of Rajagopalachari's brahmanized liberalism. The only ones to be excluded were the orthodox extremists, who rejected the West, and the Communists, who rejected India's Hindu roots.

Gandhi combined the attributes of a Hindu saint (devotion, poverty, and asceticism) and the intellect of a Western-trained lawyer. In being so he sought to bridge the gap between the simple and the urbane, the conservative and the radical. He took the old Hindu principle of *ahimsa* or non-violation of life, reinterpreted it within the Christian ethic of modern social concern, and forged it into the revolutionary method of passive resistance. Moreover, he and Patel extended Congress control beyond the new middle class that had been its backbone and included the peasants by stressing the traditional values of asceticism and renunciation. The new capitalists were won in the name of economic nationalism. Only industrial labourers were lost to the Communists.

'Congress' was more than a political movement for freedom. It gave its blessings to a wide variety of cultural and social movements. The uplift of untouchables begun by Christian missionaries was 'baptized as it were into Hinduism and confirmed into the Congress fold'. The same was true for women's rights and the reform of personal law. Congress came to stand for modern Hindu social reform.

After Gandhi's death, the Congress party had to decide whether it would follow Nehru's secular democracy or Patel's militant Hinduism. For six years Nehru fought the orthodox Hindus in his own party, and in the end Congress passed Hindu personal laws that ran counter to the ancient Hindu laws pescribed by Manu. Polygamy was outlawed, divorce was recognized, and women were given equal rights with men. The rights of all religions were reaffirmed. India was becoming a secular state, and the leaders of Hindu orthodoxy began to fear the effects of secularism and politicization on their authority.

What impact did British rule have on Indian religion and culture? The first impression one receives from historical and anthropological studies is one of overwhelming continuity, if not identity, between the core of traditional and modern Indian cultures. To be sure, there have been changes in the relative standing of different caste groups, and the introduction of new avenues for social advancement. New technologies and economic systems as well as new political institutions were introduced that opened up new legitimate channels of access to positions or symbols of higher standing. But Indian society had always had a great multiplicity of different reference orientations of structural channels for advancement; and the response of Indian civilization to change had already been one of adaptation. Members of traditional groups had shown a great readiness to undertake new tasks, to participate in new groups that emerged through the internal differentiation of roles and tasks, and to incorporate these new roles into the society. They had also shown a willingness to tolerate new systems of beliefs and values.

However, this impression of continuity between traditional and modern Indian societies overlooks several fundamental changes that began to take place with the introduction of British rule. One of these was the great expansion in the nature and scope of social and symbolic participation by local groups and communities beyond their given locality or region. In several instances in traditional India, wider societal frameworks did develop. But after the introduction of British rule, the scope became India-wide, not only in an ethnic or ritual sense but also in a territorial sense. The 'participation of various caste, territorial or kinship groups in the broad cultural, 'national' community became more and more direct and less and less mediated by traditional, ideological and structural links, and based on a new type of organization'. Groups increasingly became part of countrywide organizations. The result was the growth of territoriality as a major autonomous basis of social organization and a concomitant weakening of traditional links of kinship, caste, and ritual. The whole conception of the caste order changed from a sacred to a sectarian or associational view. The sacral mode which was predominant in traditional Indian settings became at most one variant in an array of modes for organizing society.

A second fundamental change introduced by British rule was the creation of a new centralized polity with a specifically modern ideology of political participation. The result on the one hand was to bring the dispersed religious and cultural centres under political control, thereby removing the autonomy that had enabled them to survive earlier political conquests. On the other hand it was to begin the redefinition of India's collective identity not only in cultural or ritual-cosmic terms but also in terms of a common political centre and order.

In short, British rule attacked both the core Indian values of heterogeneity and ritual hierarchy, the caste system to which these gave rise, and the decentralized autonomy of Indian religio-cultural centre. In doing so the British initiated changes not only in the position of groups in the society but also in the fundamental structures of Indian religion and society. The outcome of these changes will be examined later.

The coming of the British caused an even more major readjustment among the Indian Muslims. They lost their political power. They also lost out in the social and economic spheres to the rising Hindu middle class made up largely of the professional, clerical and commercial groups that had gained most of the positions within the colonial government.

Under the leadership of Sir Sayid Ahmad Khan, Iqbal, and later Jinnah, the Muslims developed a political consciousness in opposition to that of the Hindus. When it became apparent that British rule was coming to an end and that Hindus would dominate the new government, the Muslims pressed for, and finally got, the Islamic state of Pakistan. But in the division of India into two nations on the basis of religion, half a million people lost their lives in bitter reprisals and twelve million more fled for their lives.

The Muslims in Pakistan and Bangladesh have been able to realize their ideal of creating Muslim states. Those in India face the problems of a powerless minority having a theology of political dominance. Economically backward and largely illiterate, they have fears, whether real or imagined, of oppression by the Hindus. They see democracy and secular laws such as the Uniform Civil Code as conspiracies against their religious and cultural identity, yet they lack the leadership necessary to unite them in concerted action, for most of the elite moved to Pakistan at partition.

Muslims in India also face serious ideological questions. Should they accept a secular, democratic, and pluralistic society, and what are the implications for Islamic law and ethics if they do so? Will this not restrict God's sovereignty to a few areas of life? Can they recognize the equal humanity and spirituality of non-Muslims?

Finally, the Muslims in India face the question of caste. Over the centuries they have adjusted to and been absorbed by the Indian social order, and in the process they have developed castelike divisions and concepts of untouchability. True, Muslims of all castes generally interdine, worship in the same mosque, and participate in the same ceremonies. Moreover, hypergamy is more common and social mobility is easier. Nevertheless the divisions persist in the face of an ideology that preaches the equality of all Muslims.

Several Muslim political parties have been formed to deal with these problems. On the one hand the Jamait Islamis are seeking to adapt Islam to modern India, and on the other the Tablighit Jamaitis, drawn largely from rural Muslims, are seeking to find an answer in rigid orthodoxy. The Muslim League, concentrated largely in the south, concerns itself only with Muslim political interests. In an attempt to coordinate these many diverse factions and to face the threat of communal riots, the Majlis-e-Mushawarat, a congregation of all-Muslim organizations and parties, was founded in 1963.

Christianity has had a long history in India, beginning with the founding of the Thomas church sometime before the third century A.D., but its greatest impact was felt after the beginning of the Catholic missions in the sixteenth century and of Protestant missions in the eighteenth century. At first the growth of Christianity was slow, but in the nineteenth and twentieth centuries a massive influx into the churches occurred. The growth was due to several factors. First, the East India Company ended its restrictions on the entry of missionaries, and a great many entered the country. Most of them became involved in a wide range of programmes for social welfare: hospitals, orphanages, homes for widows, schools, and colleges. Although the number of conversions through these institutions was never large, they did train many of India's leaders, most of whom retained an appreciation for Christian values.

Second, mission associations decided not to compete in the same geographic areas. They divided the land between them. The result was that villagers were confronted by a single Christian voice. This was to bear fruit in the twentieth century when many Indian Christians, with few ties to the historical roots of their denominations, moved towards cooperation and eventually to unite. This started an ecumenical movement that was to sweep across Christianity all over the world.

A third factor was the stress on equality, which attracted the untouchables. Most Protestant missionaires preached both to the high and the low castes, and the first responses were often from the higher castes. But when the untouchables joined the church in large numbers and the missionaries remained adamant that all converts join the same church, the high-caste converts drew back. The result was a church largely identified with the untouchable community.

A final factor was the success of Christianity among the tribals. For example, beginning in 1850 the Lutheran church in Chota Nagpur grew to more than 200,000 baptized members. The Roman Catholics were equally successful among the Kols. The rapid conversion of tribals in the north-west regions led to the formation of one of India's strongest churches among the Nagas and similar tribes.

The current religious scene is one of great diversity and rapid change. Forest tribesmen, modern industrial tycoons, veiled women, rural farmers, orthodox priests, and university professors–they are all part of India.

A great deal of village life centres upon religious beliefs and activities. There is no sharp distinction between religion, entertainment, social organization, and economics. There are religious rituals associated with planting and harvesting the crops, with building a house and digging a well, with curing diseases, and arranging a business deal. Village music, art, drama, and dance are essentially religious activities. Even the local geography takes on a religious dimension.

There is no village in India, however mean, that has not a rich *sthala-purana,* or legendary history, of its own. Some god or godlike hero has passed by the village–Rama might have rested under this pipal-tree, Sita might have dried her clothes, after her bath, on this yellow stone, or the *Mahatma* himself, on one of his many pilgrimages through the country, might have slept in this hut, the low one by the village gate. In this way the past mingles with the present and the gods mingle with men.

It is this weaving together of all aspects of life around religion and its concomitant caste system that makes Hinduism a way of life so powerful in the village.

Hinduism in the village is only distantly related to that discussed in modern literature and university courses, or even that taught in Hindu monasteries and orthodox publications.

Hinduism as it is practiced in the village is not the Hinduism of the classical philosophical systems of India, for it possesses neither the metaphysical heights nor the abstract content of the latter. It is a religion of fasts, feasts and festivals in which prescribed rituals cover all the major crises of life.

Religion in the village falls roughly into two overlapping domains. On the one hand are elements identified with Hinduism, and on the other are localized animistic elements not associated with any literate religious tradition. Broadly speaking, the further down one goes in the caste hierarchy the fewer Hindu and the more animistic features a person finds.

There is no single list of practices that constitutes the core of Hinduism, no centralized institutional structure, no set of orthodox beliefs. Basically Hinduism is an ethnic religion–one is born a Hindu. As long as one does not openly reject Hinduism or convert to another religion, one remains a Hindu.

The diversity found in Hinduism may be organised along a continuum ranging from 'Sanskritic Hinduism' to 'Popular Hinduism'. The former embodies the practices and values associated with the *Brahmans* and the Sanskritic scriptures. It includes acceptance of Brahmanic rites, worship of high Hindu gods, avoidance of ritual pollution, belief in the doctrines of just rewards *(karma)*, duty to the caste and task to which one is born *(dharma)*, rebirth *(samsara)*, and the goal of release from rebirths by merger back into the ultimate reality *(moksha)*.

According to Sanskritic Hinduism, society is divided into four parts *(varnas)*, each with its ideal lifestyle. The *Brahmans* or priestly castes are to be vegetarians and teetotalers. They should prohibit the remarriage of their widows, wear the sacred thread marking them as the twice-born capable of interpreting the scriptures, and eat only with others of their own subcaste. The *Kshatriyas* or rulers should conquer in war and rule in peace. They should employ *Brahman* priests to perform religious rites, build temples, patronize the arts, adopt Brahmanic festivals, maintain caste purity in their land, and rule in righteousness. As rulers they must fight and kill, and as warriors they are permitted meat and strong drink. Neverthelesss, because such practices are the duties of the *Kshatriyas,* these do not defile them. The *Vaishyas* are called to trade and industry, and they are not expected to observe the austerities of the *Brahmans.* Ideally they represent a life of wealth and sumptuous living. Finally, the *Shudras,* the lowest of the *varnas,* are to be honest, hardworking labourers who will reap their rewards in a future life.

Orthodox forms of Sanskritic Hinduism is found chiefly in the great temples, the monastic centers, and the ascetic orders of India. As one moves from these centres into the villages, Sanskritic rites tend to be mongrelized. The chief practitioners are the *Brahmans,* particularly the family and temple priests, but many of those in the village hold hereditary offices and have no formal training apart from a local apprenticeship. Consequently they are only vaguely familiar with the philosophical and ritual elaborations that characterize Sanskritic Hinduism.

Popular Hinduism is rooted not in the *Vedic* scriptures and in abstract theological discourses but in the myths of the Epics and *Puranas* and in local village histories. These myths are re-enacted in festivals, dramas, and dances; sung by mothers to their children, by women working in the fields, and by families and friends in devotional song services; and told and retold by passing bards and beggars. They are depicted in polychrome pictures hung in the homes and in the sculptures that adorn the temples. Their message is that there are many gods and that the devotee should worship the one of his choice in order to obtain divine blessings on earth and escape from hell after death.

The centres of popular Hinduism are the household shrines, and the village temples and other holy sites where Epic and Puranic gods are worshipped. Elderly members of the family make daily offerings to the family deities, and on special occasions, such as devotional services held in honour of a particular deity, the hereditary family priest *(purohita)* officiates. For the high castes the priest is usually a *Brahman,* and for the low castes and untouchables a man from one of the lower priestly castes. Of particular importance are the rites of passage marking the transitions in the life of family members: births, investitures with the sacred thread, marriages, births of first sons and deaths. On these occasions family members and, to a extent, members of the same lineage, are involved in transition and purification rites, presided over by the family priest.

Hereditary priests of another order *(pujaris)* officiate in the temple, conducting rites each morning and evening and organizing festivals marking the life cycles of the temple deities. Some festivals such as *Dasara, Devali,* and *Holi,* are celebrated throughout India, but most are regional or local festivals observed by a village as a whole or by one or two castes or religious sects within the village.

There are common symbols linking Sanskritic and popular Hinduism. The gods of both are either found in the Hindu pantheon or are thought to be one of their incarnations. They are ethical beings representings good and righteousness and warring with demons and other forces of evil. They marry, bear offspring, and establish patriarchal families.

Worship of the Hindu gods centres around temples and household shrines. A *Brahman* or other ritually clean priest performs the rites using dung, ash, mango leaves, flowers, incense, coloured, powders, coconuts, lamps and offerings of fire and vegetarian food. At festivals the gods are often bathed, clothed, and taken on procession through the village.

Hinduism by no means constitutes the whole of religious activities for villagers. A great many religious practices centre around animistic deities, most of whom are not linked to the Hindu pantheon. For the most part, these are female goddesses associated with the village; with rivers, hills, trees, and wells; or with particular diseases and disasters. Amoral in nature, they did a faithful devotee, but in a fit of jealousy they strike a negligent worshipper or village with drought, fire, plague, and barren wives.

Devathas (female godesses) are rarely housed in temples. They are found in the form of rocks in the fields, marks on a tree, or roughly carved images in small shelters or in shrines in low-caste and untouchable homes. Because they demand sacrifices of blood and liquor, *brahmans* refuse to serve them, although the *Brahmans* often send a sacrifice by the hand of a servant. *Devathas* are propitiated by low-caste and untouchable shaman.

At times the goddesses come in the form of plagues and disasters that strike a whole community. They are then propitiated by Hindus, Muslims, and Christians alike, for they are not perceived to be unique to Hindus. There is, in fact, little difference between them and the Muslim *jinns* in the minds of the villagers.

A wide variety of ghosts, demons, and other spirits also inhabit the countryside. Some look like snakes, or animals, or bright lights. Some have fangs and dishevelled hair and inhabit wells, cremation and burial grounds, or wooded areas and ravines. They attack wayfarers at night, women (particularly new mothers), and other unsuspecting persons. They do so not as a punishment for misdeeds or oversights, and consequently they cannot normally be propitiated with offerings. Rather, they are often the disembodied souls of deceased people seeking a body in which to dwell. The only protection against them is magic in the forms of charms, *mantras* (chants), black colour, iron, scorpion plants, and other powerful objects.

Possession by a ghost or spirit is qualitatively different from possession by a Hindu god. A person possessed by a ghost or spirit begins to tremble and cannot control his behaviour. Other symptoms are a fever, eyes rolled back, insensitivity to pain, inability to talk coherently, and a catatonic adherence to a particular posture. Generally the spirit will not leave by itself. A shaman must be called to divine the spirit involved. He then refers the case to an exorcist who drives out the spirit by means of *mantras*, amulets, and, occasionally, sacrifices.

After death the deceased is often feared until the funeral rites are completed. These are carefully performed to ensure that the dead will pass on unmolested by malevolent ghosts who continue to haunt the village. The latter are, for the most part, those who have died with jealously or strong desires and those who have died premature deaths. These often return to torment the living. Ghosts of barren women plague new mothers, and a neglected father troubles his sons.

In addition to spirits, there are impersonal supernatural forces. Many old women and men know how to use simple magic to cure minor illnesses and to protect family members from ordinary dangers. But it takes shamans trained in the use of powerful forms of magic to end plagues or prevent disasters—or to curse an enemy with slow or sudden death.

The handling of powerful magic is a difficult art. A shaman must receive extensive training at the hand of a guru and then undergo a secret initiation rite. To keep his power he must observe numerous taboos. He must never treat a pregnant woman, for the unborn foetus will draw away his power. He must avoid certain foods, and if he sees a snake, a rope, a corpse, a scorpion, or any of a long list of bad omens, he must leave his meal unfinished. Not many take up the art, for even a slight mistake in ritual can result in the death of the practitioner.

A milder form of evil power is the 'evil eye'. Certain people are born with it, and when they look with covetousness or greed upon a person, animal, or object, it is harmed. Children and newly married couples are particularly susceptible and fall sick. Animals bloat or cease to give milk, and objects break. Cooked food becomes indigestible when seen by an evil eye.

Most people having an evil eye are not aware of it, and those who are may try to remove it with magic. To counter its harm, mothers blacken the eyes of their children or tie charms to their wrists. Those who have lost several sons may raise a boy as a girl for several years until he has strength enough to counter the evil eye and jealous spirits that plague particular families. Brides and grooms wear elaborate headdresses to ward off the evil eye, and beautiful women put false blemishes on their skin to distract from their beauty. Craftsmen put flaws in their products to distract from their desirability, and farmers put pots covered with spots on poles in fields to distract the gaze of those inflicted with the evil.

The distinction between Hindu and animistic practices in the village is sometimes unclear. Village goddesses are occasionally seen as remote incarnations of Hindu goddesses, and blood sacrifices are practiced in the worship of a few Hindu deities, such as Durga. Nevertheless, it is useful to treat the two as distinct domains of religious activity, for each offers solutions to certain types of problems and serves different functions within the village.

Broadly speaking, Hinduism provides solutions to problems of an ultimate nature. It answers questions of ultimate order and meaning by dealing with issues of the origins, purpose, and destiny of the universe and its inhabitants. In Hinduism, order rests upon a tension between polar forms: between good and evil, and between the forces of degeneration and regeneration. Resolution lies not in the conquest of one by the other but in the merger of both back into the one source of their being. In sexuality there is maleness and femaleness that merge in union. In relationships with the gods, humans are caught between the extremes of asceticism and eroticism, both of which threaten to destroy the social order. The resolution is in marriage and the four stages of life that control the unbridled drives of sex. In life there is tension between birth and death resolved by rebirth and ultimately by the merger of both into the absolute.

This cosmic order serves as a model and as a rationale for the caste system. It is reflected in the order of the Hindu temples and their rituals. The latter generally follow the orderly sequence of the seasons and of the cycles of life.

Family rites such as those at birth, marriage, and death reinforce the traditional kin and caste structures. Public festivals celebrating the births and marriages of the gods and the seasons of the sun and moon reaffirm the social and cosmic order. Ideally these rituals are performed by Brahman priests using traditional Hindu symbols in accord with the Vedic formulas, with other castes performing their hereditary duties.

In contrast to the ordered Hindu cosmos, the village goddesses belong to the earth with its immediacy and disorder. They are local being whose powers extend no more than a dozen miles from their abodes. The same goddess is often enshrined in many villages within a region and in various fields and homes of the same village; but in each she is thought to have her own personality. Goddesses are capricious and amoral, blessing those who satisfy their whims and cursing those who neglect them. Although female in nature, they are essentially asexual in character, neither marrying nor bearing offspiring. They demand blood sacrifices which are offered by low-caste shaman. Their images are rocks and rude images placed under trees and rock shelters and in homes.

Rituals associated with the goddesses are generally crisis rites performed to prevent death and destruction caused by drought, disease, fire and flood. In the face of such plagues, villagers untie in village ceremonies to propitiate an angry goddess by offering a goat or water buffalo at the village navel stone or at its ritual boundaries. Caste and religious distinctions break down as all segments of the community unite to ward off a common enemy. Occasionally goddesses pass through the land and must be ritually passed on to the next village. The ultimate concern here is not the triumph of good over evil but of order over chaos.

For the villagers these two domains plus those of medicine, such as *ayurveda* and *unani,* provide alternative solutions to life's problems. For most people the ordinary religius routine of fairs, festivals, and family rituals is broken only when the gods, spirits, and supernatural forces make their presence felt by imposing troubles on the people such as poor crops, dry cows, financial losses, mysterious disappearance of belongings, faithless spouses, sterility, and, above all, disease or death to people and animals. Some respond by making special offerings or vows to a god or by going on a pilgrimage to a distant shrine. Others turn to local experts: herbal doctors who specialize in local medicines, ayurvedic and *unani* doctors trained in homeopathic medicines, allopathic doctors trained in modern medicines, witch doctors who treat witchcraft, and astrologers who handle planetary forces.

Failure to gain relief calls for divination at the hands of a shaman, often a man or woman from a low caste. Some shamen go into a trance in which they are possessed by a spirit that identifies the god, goddess, spirit, ghost, or human that has caused the trouble. In such states they are impervious to pain such as that caused by touching red-hot metal. Others gaze into drops of tree sap or into candles to see past actions. Still others use oracle birds or roll millstones to divine some mystery. Having diagnosed the causes of a problem, shamen often refer the person to an appropriate specialist for treatment, although some prescribe remedial actions such as the offering of sacrifices to the gods or goddesses, the exorcism of a malevolent spirit, or the countering of a spell by the use of more powerful magic.

The strength of Hindu tradition lay, to a considerable extent, in the multiplicity and autonomy of its religious centres. Many of the great temples with their religious specialists, elaborate rituals, and debates on orthodoxy were found in urban centres and patronized by kings. Yet they manifested a very high degree of autonomy and self-regulation in terms of their own religious and institutional identity. Their ties to political centres of power were limited.

Today that cultural leadership and autonomy are threatened by the forces of modernism. Contemporary systems of communication have expanded the very scope of the field of socio-cultural participation. True, in the past the Brahmanic ideology and system of worship was in a sense India-wide, but the religious institutions that gave these expression were local and regional in their operations. Today new, wider societal frameworks with more encompassing religious centres and communities are emerging. At the same time the rise of nationalism and the politicization of the society make these new frameworks more vulnerable to political control. Added to this are the secularizing forces of modern science and education.

What effects have these forces had on the religious patterns of modern cities? Singer has found a shift away from ritual observances and sacred learning to popular religious and cultural performances communicated through the mass media. This had led to a weakening of Brahmanic traditions. Fewer *Brahmans* are studying Sanskrit and the *Vedas* to enter the priesthood, and more are turning to professions, politics and industry. This is due in part to the fact that the government has taken over the Sanskrit schools and opened them to students of all castes, thereby destroying the concepts of a Brahmanic order, purity, and supremacy, and with them Hindu orthodoxy. The result has been a decline in the performance of the elaborate Vedic rituals.

On the other hand, there has been an increase in different expressions of popular Hinduism, particularly those that focus on *bhakti* or personal devtion to God. New temples are being constructed and old ones renovated as popular pilgrim centres. There has been a revival of classical and popular dance, devotional song associations *(bhajans)*, dramas of various sorts, and bardic performances–all recounting the Puranic and Epic mythologies. To this have been added modern films, cultural performances, radio programmes, and public speeches that reach many thousands. There are, indeed, secularizing tendencies in these modern media, particularly as they replace the priest with the stage performer, but they have not yet cut off urban culture from a religious matrix. What has happened is that that matrix has shifted from a Brahmanic to a Puranic frame of reference and that the leadership and organization of religious institutions are shifting from hereditary structues based on caste and concepts of hierarhy and purity to those based on voluntary association.

Secularism is beginning to make inroads into areas of life formerly dealt with by magic and animistic practices, but mainly among the upper, more educated classes. Many of the low-caste and low-class people are crowded into *bustis* or small urban communities that act in many ways like encapsulated villages. Migrants frequently being along their village goddesses to guard themselves against the thievery, verbal abuse by others, strange ghosts, and dread of death in a strange place that characterizes the city. For the most part they follow parallel solutions to the problems of disease and misfortune. They turn to magic and village medicines for cure from non-incapacitating troubles such as stomach-aches, worms, asthma, rheumatism; from conditions characterized by drawn-out suffering and debilitiation; and from diseases such as smallpox that are traditional scourges of the village. But they turn to 'doctor' medicines for such violent problems where village remedies have been ineffective–for acute appendicitis, severe burns, hernias, pneumonia, and boils, and for the strange and frightening maladies of the city. Witchcraft persists in the village, primarily as an answer to problems of relationships not answered by magic or medicine-problems of tensions in extended families, of conflicts in inter-personal relationships, and of the low esteem of women. For problems of the soul, people still go to the temple or to a distant pilgrim site. The fact that these problem-solving systems appear to the outsider to be mutually contradictory is irrelevant. The point is to recover from trouble, not to construct a systematic world view.

While magic, astrology and witchcraft persist in urban areas, they have not been unaffected by modern technology. Natural charms and amulets such as bones, seeds, and shells are giving way to printed drawings, diagrams, and other manufactured talismen. These are durable and accessible, and their power lies not in their material or manufacture but in their endowment of a spiritual force by a shaman. Similarly, in the city, there is less use of blood and more of coloured powders, stings, and objects.

The greatest impact of urbanization on relgious practices is probably in the modern industrial estates. Here individual families are housed in large apartment buildings without regard for kin and caste ties. Moreover, the construction of temples and shrines is forbidden within many estates. The result is that often the people are left alone and without religious ties.

Often overlooked in the analysis of South Asian religious structures are the regional networks that link individuals and villages over large areas. Bards and drama troupes have traditionally moved around their hereditary circuits of villages, which often extend into more than one linguistic region. Castes establish hostels at sacred shrines to serve their members. Transient priests bring their gods, and wandering fortune tellers and palm readers sell their skills.

Three important types of regional networks are saints, religious fairs and pilgirmages. Saints or gurus serve as spiritual advisors to people. Some are hereditary mentors to specific castes, making the rounds of their villages and cities, expounding the scriputres of that caste to their clients, and settling local intracaste disputes that often deal with matters of orthodoxy. Others are personal spiritual counsellors. Most are local saints with small followings, but some, such as Sri Sai Baba of Shirdi, Sri Sati Godavari Mataji of Maharashtra, Sri Narayan Guru of Kerala, and Sri Sathya Sai Baba, have national followings and their movements have become religious sects.

The movements centred around saints and their personal followers have a number of things in common. First, they generally preach *bhakti* or intense inner devotion to God as the way to salvation. This message cuts through the elaborate theologies and rituals of the formal religious orders and allows the individual, irrespective of caste, education, or wealth, to find spiritual salvation. Second, these movements stress equality rather than hierarchy among followers. Caste and even religious distinctions are minimized or consciously ignored. It is not uncommon for Hindus to follow a Muslim saint or for Muslims to seek a Hindu guru. Finally, such movements lie outside the constraints of local caste structures and constitute an area of life in which a person can exercise a great deal of individual initiative. Much of ordinary life is minutely prescribed by caste and family norms, leaving the individual with little choice. But one may defy family and caste in choosing a guru, for this is recognized to be part of an intesely personal quest for salvation. The guru-disciple relationship provides people restive in their faith and restless in their social order with an escape from roles for which they do not feel suited, and it satisfies the personal needs of the gifted, the deviant, and the discontented for fellowship, council and hope.

Religious fairs and pilgrimages also provide individuals with a measure of freedom from the constraints of social life. The former attract anywhere from a few hundered local worshippers to more than half a million from all parts of India. At larger ones, vendors set up temporary shelters from which they ply their foods and wares, and entertainers set up their wooden ferris wheels and merry-go-rounds. Days are spent visiting relatives and friends from other villages, and in private worship. Nights are times for dramas, dances, processions of the gods on temple chariots, and other public rites and entertainment. Fairs are organized to commemorate the birth or marriage of a god, to placate a local goddess, or to honour a saint.

Pilgrimage too, offers an escape from the confines of village and urban life. Many of the major temples have become centers of pilgrimage. In the past pilgrims often travelled long distances by foot or cart to some distant or inaccessible shrine. Today, private travel agencies organize bus tours that take in half a dozen or more religious centers, and special trains are run to accommodate the crowds going to temples such as Tirupati and Kasi. At these shrines pilgrims are received into the presence of the presiding deity *(darshan)* and thereby receive merit.

These networks of cultural communication have contributed much to a common countrywide caste and religious consciousness. In theory, caste categories were defined for the whole region. In reality, however, there were not central social or religious institutions that could bring about a unified, countrywide caste system and religious orthodoxy. There existed thousands of caste organizations and temples organized locally, in villages, regions, and principalities. But beneath them lay a common Brahmanic ideology and system of worship that served as their foundation and these were disseminated along the networks that criss-crossed the land.

The core of Indian tradition has shown a great resiliency or continuity in the face of foreign intrusions and rapid cultural change. This is due in part to the fact that India's response to new ideas has been one of adaptation and assimilation rather than of violent rejection and conflict. The caste system has incorporated new groups so long as they operate within its framework; and members of traditional groups have shown a great readiness to undertake new tasks and to participate in new groups through the process of role differentiation and ideological diversification. Brahmanism provided individuals and groups with a sense of identity within the framework of the caste system that was based upon the Hindu values of purity, hierarchy, and religious dominance.

While Indian civilization has incorporated a great deal of change in the past without losing its core values and structures, the question arises whether the extent, pace, and nature of change today are of a different order. In fact, are the foundations of traditional culture changing in the face of the forces of modernism? At root this is a question of identity, for definitions of self, community and nation are being forged out of situations where tradition and modernity make conflicting appeals, producing a rebirth of pride in one's heritage along with the determination to benefit by opportunities unknown in the past. This problem of personal and corporate identity, arising in a variety of forms as religious and social structures encounter, stimulate, and resist forces of change, is one of the single most recurring features of the modern Indian scene. And the question of identity is more a religious than an ethnic, social, or political issue.

A people's identity consists in part of the personal and corporate goals for which they strive, in other words the kinds of people they try to become.

Within the Brahmanic framework, the ideals were defined by religion and the caste systems to which these gave rise. Social mobility was directed primarily towards the emulation of the Brahmanic societal elite in a process called Sanskritization.

The primary goal of Sanskritization is the emulation of *Brahmans.* Castes seeking to rise in the social order often become vegetarians and teetotalers, prohibit the remarriage of their widows, try to get *Brahman* priests to perform their family rituals, and adopt Brahmanic gods, rites, and ideals. By this process the Brahmanic way of life has tended to seep down through the caste system.

Sanskritization has been present throughout Indian history, but today it has become more common as the traditional power of the Brahmans, and other high castes, to keep the lower castes from adopting their symbols has declined, and as social mobility and stress on reform have increased. With the rapid spread of communications, tribal and marginal populations are being absorbed into Hinduism by the process. Moreover, some low-caste and even untouchable groups are adopting Brahmanic ways in their attempts to rise in the social order, and with some measure of success.

But the Brahmanic model of society offered more than one set of identities for individuals and groups. In addition to the *Brahman* priests, the caste system recognized the superiority of *Kshatriyas* or rulers and *Vaishya* or merchants. The former offered prestige based on power rather than purity, and the latter on wealth and luxury. Both have been emulated by various groups in various parts of the country.

In the past the royal model, sometimes referred to as 'Rajputization', was commonly used by tribal chiefs and leaders of invading hordes to assimilate into Indian society and gain legitimacy. They invited *Brahmans* to their courts, adopted Brahmanic festivals and rites, and claimed *Kshatriya* descent by means of myths created by court historians. In time they were able to inter-marry with other kingly families and join the royal elite. The rulers themselves were often not orthodox in their religious practices. It was sufficient that they had *Brahman* priests performing the necessary rituals. Nevertheless, they gained legitimacy by adopting Brahmanic Hinduism and used it to compete with other kings in the performance of rituals. With the end of the feudal kingdoms, castes rising to power (often based on land and agriculture) have begun to turn to the political arena and the *Kshatriya* model to gain legitimacy. Their leaders are often too busy to observe the time-consuming orthodox rites, but they are able to hire priests to perform the rituals for them.

The *Vaishya* or merchant role model provided a second Sanskritic alternative to the *Brahman* elite. Modern Indian businessmen and industrialists often choose this as their ideal, for it permits them to forego the demands of austerity and to interact freely with people of all castes in the modern business world, even as they maintain their orthodoxy by contributing to temple funds and hiring priests to perform rites in their homes.

Contact with the western world introduced new technologies, institutions, and alternatives to social identity and mobility. In many instances the underlying goals were no longer religious but economic or political. Modern industry, communication, and transportation opened up new vocations and fostered geographic mobility. Western-style education and parliamentary democracy introduced values that threatened the Sanskritic concepts of specialization and hierarchy *(varna),* social responsibility *(dharma),* privilege before the law, and the sacralization of all areas of life. Many individuals and groups have chosen to emulate the western elite in a process called westernization.

The interaction between Sanskritization and Westernization has been a complex one; although the two concepts are not antithetical. In some ways Westernization is in conflict with Sanskritization. The introduction of advanced Western-style education that calls into question the traditional beliefs and practices of orthodox Hinduism has attracted the best students into the sciences, humanities, law, engineering, medicine, and social work. Many of them come from the highest castes. The greatest changes between the occupations of fathers and their sons occur among the *Brahmans.* The result is an erosion of the priestly authority that lies at the heart of traditional Indian culture and the rise of a new leadership of a westernized elite that often seeks to strip Hinduism of its sacrifices, beliefs, and practices.

On the other hand, many Indians accommodated both modern science and traditional faith into their thinking and lifestyles. *Brahmans* who have studied abroad and become lawyers, engineers, doctors and politicians continue to regard themselves as good Hindus. They may not have time for all the traditional ritual observances and Sanskritic training, but they are often among the chief contributors to Hindu temples and monastic orders.

Confronted by western values, organizational forms, and religious beliefs, the modern Hinduism of the urban and rural social elite has itself undergone a radical transformation. Hindu reformers, such as Swami

Vivekananda, Sri Aurobindo, Swami Sivananda, and Dayanand have simplified the traditional Hindu world view and reduced religious teachings in large measure to moral exhortations. They preach devotion to God, equality, monotheism, love, and social service. They reject ritual, caste differences, polytheism, the worship of idols, and withdrawal from the world. Although they appeal to the *Vedas* and retain some of the Sanskritic symbols such as those of purity and pollution, their eclecticism undermines the orthodox Hindu teachings of *dharma,* and social hierarcy, polytheism, and ritual obligations as well as Hinduism's claim to be the true religion. The religious communities founded by these reformers are based on principles of association rather than kinship, and organizationally they are more like denominations than castes.

The introduction of modern technology has also had its effects-at times undermining Hindu beliefs and practices and at times reinforcing and changing them. The use of tables, chairs, stainless steel plates, buses, trains, and modern restaurants undermines the *brahmanic* concepts of purity, but printing has been a major force in the revival of Hindu mythology, and neon lights, loudspeakers, and modern transportation play an important part in contemporary temple services. The mass media has not secularized but democratized religion. The stories of the *Puranas* and Epics are told in textbooks, comic books, children's magazines, and films, and devotional songs are broadcast on All India Radio. Nevertheless, the mass media has tended to vulgarize the religious stories and introduce into them the universal themes of sex, dance and song.

The rapid and demanding pace of modern life has also taken its toll, particularly in the cities with their factory and business hours. *Brahmans* have less time to spend on daily rituals, and the traditional life-cycle rites that often ran for a number of days have been telescoped or abandoned altogether.

In many cases people from the upper castes have turned to modern professions that require higher education as symbols of higher status, even as members of the lower castes, particularly those in the villages where rigid caste restrictions who move into the cities and take modern jobs in modern factories and offices that require little literacy generally use their new wealth to make their rites more orthodox.

A second factor in the crisis of identity in India has been the attempt to redefine the nature of India's collective identity not only in cultural or ritual-cosmic but also in the political terms of a common political centre and order. As Panikkar points out, 'Clearly, our new democratic egalitarian and secular state is not built upon the foundations of ancient India, or of Hindu thought'. The ideal of a modern secular state was incorporated into the Indian Constitution, which affirms the freedom of religion, institutional separation of church and state, and equal citizenship. It is constitutional law that has been the West's single most important instrument of change in modern times.

The result of this redefinition of the identity of Indian civilization has been a conflict between the new relatively autonomous political-ideological order and centre and the old social-ritual ones. The central issue has not been one of religious freedom, for tolerance of religious differences has been a hall-mark of Hindu thought, which holds that all religions eventually lead to God. Although at times the freedom to propagate one's religion and to proselytize has been raised, the constitution specifically guarantees its citizens these rights. Moreover, despite considerable opposition on the part of some Hindu sects, and careful scrutiny of some cases of mass conversions, the government has by and large upheld the right to proselytize so long as this does not disturb the public order.

The primary question has been whether religion or secular constitutional law would serve as the ultimate foundation of Indian society. The answer, so far, has been that the new legal-ideological order is not only defining the rights of Indian citizens and of castes but also delineating the rights and limits of religion. Although in principle recognizing the separation of church and state, the government has intervened where it feels religious freedom violates the basic rights of its citizens. In so doing, it holds that an Indian's primarily identity is that of citizen rather than religious identity.

One area of religous activity in which the government has intervened is the operation of Hindu temples. According to Hindu scriptures and tradition, Harijans are not permitted to worship inside a temple. However, with the growing acceptance of equality and individual rights, there was increasing political pressure to admit them without discrimination. A major break with tradition occurred when the Maharaja of Travancore, a native state, opened the temples of his kingdom to untouchables. Later the Constitution of India was to guarantee the rights of Hindus of all castes to enter Hindu religious institutions. This was challenged, but in 1958 the Supreme Court reaffirmed the constitutional position. Laws were also passed to abolish the customs of having dancing girls in the temples and the sacrificing of animals and birds.

Of equal significance has been the government's attempts to reform the administration of religious institutions. In 1951 the State of Madras established a department of Hindu religious and charitable endowments that has had the task of supervising temples and monastic orders. When this was challenged, the courts did restore the authority of the abbots to administer their monastic organizations but upheld the rights of the state to regulate public temples. In 1962 the Hindu Religious Endowments Commission recommended that the central government regulate temple administration, establish training centres for temple priests, set qualifications and pay for religious functionaries, and appoint temple teachers to deliver discourses to the Hindu public. Although not all of these have been implemented, the states are involved in regulating temple affairs, and under state pressures many of the public temples have begun to use their incomes for establishing orphanages, homes for widows, colleges, and other programmes of social welfare.

The concept that offerings should be used for the service of humankind is itself a basic shift from traditional Hindu concepts of giving. The sacred texts affirmed that giving a gift to the gods or to *Brahmans* in itself earns merit. Consequently, the giver is unconcerned with what happens to the gift after it has been given. It is the modern Indian intelligentsia, influenced by Western concepts, that believes religious endowments should exist for the spiritual and social benefits to the worshippers.

In addition to the public temples, there are a great many privately owned and endowed temples and trusts. So far the Indian legislatures have not attempted to introduce reforms in their administration. But it appears that the development and reform of public temples and the misuse of power in the private ones is leading to the decline of the latter, and there is little government encouragement that they should be maintained.

Attempts at regulating the wandering mendicants *(sadhus)* have been less successful, but government pressures led indirectly to the fomation of the Bharat Sadhu Samaj. Although this is a non-governmental association, it has begun to organize and regulate the *sadhus* in an attempt to restore the dignity of the ascetic orders.

Another area in which government policies are affecting religious institutions of that of education. Most of the traditional schools in India were private or religious institutions. Under the British policy of strict neutrality in religious matters, a parallel set of government schools was established. Nevertheless, the government continued to provide grants-in-aid to private schools for much of their secular instruction.

Following independence, the Indian States continued to give grants to private religious schools. The incompatibility of this policy with the government's declared secular stance has been most acutely felt when private schools have compulsory religious instruction. Most states have made their grants contingent upon the school's dropping such requirements and making religious instruction optional. In some states the governments have begn to regulate the hiring of teachers in state-aided schools, undermining further the distinctive religious purposes for which these schools were founded.

On the broader scene, modern nationalism in India has shown as strong interest in recovering and reinterpreting traditional Indian arts, and with independence this has received official sanction. Classical music, dance, drama and cultural performances have become symbols of modern Indian identity alongside the national emblem, Five-Year Plans and atomic installations.

Although the politicization of the nation has had a profound effect on religious institutions, the influence has not been only one way. Religious and caste loyalties remain strong in the minds of the people, and interest groups based on them exert a greater influence in the Indian political arena than pressure groups based on class or occupation. Caste and religious solidarity make for bloc-voting, and political competition has given rise to caste associations and led to the formation of religion based political parties such as the Hindu Mahasabha, the Jan Sangh, the Muslim League, and the Buddhist Republican party. In southern India, reaction to the dominance of the *Brahmans* has led to anti-*Brahman* parties such as the Dravida Munnetra Kazhagam.

Communal politics has not been particularly successful in the central government, although religiously based political parties are often outspoken on particular issues. But they have been important factors in many state governments. Sikh agitations led to the establishment of the predominantly Sikh state of Punjab. And the political histories of Kerala and Madras cannot be understood without the communal parties.

A third feature of India's search for identity is the increasing rejection by those who have been politically disenfranchised and economically impotent of a permanently debased status. An example of this is the movement among the Mahars and other untouchables of Maharashtra led by Ambedkar. Others have rejected the caste system, but as Gokhale points out, it was Ambedkar who was the first of the untouchables to articulate the tradegy and hopes of his people in terms of modern thought and to fight for their equality on the basis of modern forms of political and social action. He believed that the Indian religious system could not reform itself and provide the untouchables a place of equality in society. Although Ambedkar's move to lead the Mahars into neo-Buddhism in order to find equality may be more dramatic than most movements for equal rights in India, it by no means stands alone. Increasingly, other untouchables and low castes such as the Izhava of Kerala see religious identity as intrinsic to their social debasement and are seeking equality on the basis of their political identity as citizens of India.

The mainstream of government and political activity has accepted the ideal of full equality in human terms and rejected the degraded status of untouchability. As we have seen, untouchables were admitted to Hindu temples, and untouchability was forbidden by the Constitution. While castes are recognized as corporate bodies with the rights to promulgate and enforce their own religious doctrines, ritual and leadership, and can do so by excommunication if need be, the government is moving to treat them as denominations based on voluntary affiliation rather than on ascription. In so doing it has undermined the ultimate legitimation of the caste system in terms of a cosmic ritual hierarcy and replaced it with a view of society based on voluntary association. In many instances the traditional local castes are being replaced on the regional and national level by caste associations in which numbers of castes are merged on the basis of common self-interest. The shift, has been from a sacred view of caste to a sectarian one.

The government has not only attacked discrimination but also undertaken programmes of positive assistance in order to raise the socio-economic standards of the untouchables and depressed tribes. It has done so by allocating them reserved seats in state and national legislatures and village councils, by providing them with job quotas in government service, and by giving them special educational and economic aid. In most cases, however, these privileges have been given only to those untouchables and tribals who have remained Hindu.

A second move by the government to establish equality has been to introduce a uniform code of personal law. Communal differences are deeply rooted in Indian life, and governments traditionally have recognized the rights of castes and religious groups to administer their own personal and community laws. This was in accord with the Hindu concept of an ordered society which recognized differences in the rights and duties of the different castes. Modern India is committed by its Constitution to the elimination of these differences and to work for a uniform civil code. In 1955 and 1956, after more than a decade of discussion, four imporatnt bills were passed: the Hindu Marriage Bill, the Hindu Succession Bill, the Hindu Minority and Guardianship Bill, and Hindu Adoption and Maintenance Bill.

The first of these contained three provisions which were radical departures from the principles of traditional Hindu law, namely, inter-caste marriages were legalized, bigamous marriages were prohibited, and the grounds for divorce were liberalized. The second bill granted to daughters the right to be simultaneous heirs along with sons and widows. Under traditional Hindu law daughters did not inherit any part of the father's estate. The third bill permitted the adoption of daughters as well as sons. This, too, stood in sharp contrast to the Hindu custom allowing for the adoption of a son who could carry out the required funeral rites of the parents, but not for the adoption of daughters.

The Hindu bills are the first step towards a uniform code of personal law for all Indians. So far the government has moved more cautiously on the explosive issue of changing Muslim personal laws to fit a uniform code. Indian Muslims have tended to regard any alteration of their personal law as a grave violation of their freedom of religion.

One important feature arising from hopes generated through legal and political actions aimed at equality is the revolution of rising expectations. But the time lag between promises of social and economic justice and the actual achievement of significant gains is potentially disastrous. Expectations left unfulfilled too long give way to disillusionment, falling expectations, and a sense of hopelessness, or as in Sri Lanka, to insurgency and revolution.

How has religion affected development in India? Max Weber, seeking to explain different rates of economic growth in Europe and the great civilizations of the East, found that all showed manifestations of 'capitalism and capitalistic enterprises', but only in Europe did there develop a 'sober bourgeois capitalism with its rational organization of free labour'. This he assumed to be the basis of the industrial revolution. The reason for the difference, he argued, was to be found in fundamental differences in religious beliefs. While Reformation Protestantism fostered economic development, the effects of Hinduism were essentially negative. Moreover, the core of the obstruction was not to be found in specific religious institutions and rituals which 'every one of the great religious systems in its ways has placed, or has seemed to place in the way of modern economy' but in the 'spirit' of the whole system. 'A ritual law in which every change of occupation, every change in work technique, may result in ritual degradation is certainly not capable of giving birth to economic and technical revolutions from within itself or even of facilitating the first germination of capitalism in its minds. The 'spirit' Weber found in the Hindu concepts of *samsara* (the cycles of rebirth), *karma* (the belief that actions in this life determine one's fortunes and status in the next), *dharma* (the prescription that one should fulfill the specific role set for him by his caste), and *moksha* (salvation by renouncing the world and desire). The social expression of these beliefs, he argued, was a rigid caste system.

Weber was seeking an answer to the broad historical question whether Hinduism prevented in India the independent creation of modern capitalism, but his thesis raised serious doubts about the ability of South Asia even to be a successful follower of imported development programmes. Political Scientists like Myrdal, Kapp and Eisenstadt. Many scholars have argued that Indians are motivated by religious incentives and that they reject as materialistic the economic incentives and rationalizations that are the basis of economic development. Consequently a fundamental change must take place in the Indian world view before development is possible.

Others have pointed out several weaknesses in Weber's model. Weber drew his analysis of the Indian world view essentially from the scriptural texts and assumed that there is a uniform orthodox Hinduism in which most people believe. Using a psychological approach in which he sought to predict the behaviour of Hindus by trying to think as they think, he came to the conclusion that Indians lack the achievement motivation to innovate or take risks. In the analysis Weber overlooked the fact that Hinduism is highly diverse and has no uniform, orthodox creed; that Hinduism in fact provides for various models such as a kingly and a merchant model; that a great many Indians are not highly religious; that there is no single Indian psychology; and that people vary greatly in the ways they interpret and apply text to specific human contexts.

In conclusion, to what extent do modern changes affect the very core of Indian tradition? This, lies in the highly autonomous organization-ritual subcentres with their Brahmanic ideology and systems to which they gave legitimation. True, with modernization has come new agrarian structures, educational frameworks, channels of occupational mobility, and cultural orientations. But Indian civilization has undergone similar changes in the past and yet retained a continuity of identity and values. This has been due to India's ability to incorporate a great heterogeneity, both in ideology and in structure, in single cultural system. Today modern economic, professional, and political activities have introduced new patterns of mobility and structural change alongside the traditional ones.

But modernization is introducing seeds of change that are beginning to alter the core of Indian traditions. Modern communications are broadening the scope of symbolic and social participation not only within India but also between India and the rest of the world. As a result, religious centres and networks have become weakened as economic, secular, cultural and political centres are emerging. Moreover, although the emergence of regional and national caste associations have given greater power to their members, the basis upon which they are formed is not that of the traditional caste system. Together with political parties, trade unions, and other forms of associations, they threaten to provide India with a basis for social organization that is an alternative to the caste system.

The greatest source of change has been the creation of a new, centralized polity that has sought to replace the socioritual ideology of Brahmanism and the caste system with a modern ideology of political participation as the basis for India's collective identity. Not only have the new political centres introduced far-reaching changes in the caste order which found its legitimation in a cosmic ritual hierarchy, but they have also circumscribed the scope of public religious activities themselves.

As a result of these changes, the relationship between the religious and secular orders has begun to reverse. Traditionally, success in achieving secular goals provided people and groups with avenues to participate in the ritual sphere, which provided them with their ultimate status and identity. Today, secular goals in political and economic frameworks have become legitimate goals in themselves, and the basis for a new and modern identity.

APPENDIX-2

PAKISTAN—NOTIONS AND FACTS

The Growing feeling of mutual distrust and suspicion between the Hindus and Muslims, partly nurtured consciously or unconsciously by a section of alien bureaucracy and British policies towards India, led a group of Muslim intelligentsia to make a move for a separate homeland for the Muslims. As a result, a number of schemes were proposed either for separate zones for the Muslims within India or for separate independent sovereign Muslim state or states.

The scattered ideas of the demand for a separate homeland for Muslims can be traced back to the 19th century. John Bright, a British radical statesman, probably seems to be the first person to have suggested the idea of division of the sub-continent in 1877. He recommended the formation of five semi-independent Indian presidencies with capitals at Agra, Bombay, Calcutta, Lahore and Madras. They were to be largely independent and wholly separate from one another but controlled by Britain. However, the division was not based on religious differences between the major communities of India.

The famous Pan Islamist Afghani, on the idea for establishment of an Indian Muslim state, stated thus:

"...the Muslim majority areas of the North-West India, Afghanistan and the states of Turkistan should be consolidated in a single state."

An English writer, Wilfred Scawen Blunt, who came to India during the Ripon administration made a suggestion of dividing India into a Northern Indian Muslim state and a Southern Indian Muslim state, both largely self governing within the British Indian Empire. He believed that the scheme would provide the solution to India's problem of racial and cultural heterogeneity.

Abdul Halim Sharar, novelist and editor of Urdu weekly *Muhazzib* was perhaps the first Indian Muslim to suggest the idea of separate homeland for the Muslims in 1890. He observed:

"If both Hindus and Muslims cannot live together in peace and mutual respect, then it is better for them to divide India into Hindu and Muslim provinces and exchange their population".

It appears that Stalin, in 1912, foresaw the redistribution of the geographical borders of Indian provinces on the basis of nationalities as he was reported to have expressed:

"In the case of India, too, it will probably be found that innumerable nationalities, till then lying dormant, would come into life with the further course of Bourgeois development."

In 1913, Maulana Mohammed Ali while discussing the solution of Hindu. Muslim problem suggested that North India may be assigned to the Muslims and rest to the Hindus. An identical idea of the division of India into Hindu and Muslim provinces was advanced by Abdul Jabbar and Abdul Sattar, at the International Socialist Conference at Stockholm in 1917. Later, a Pathan chief, Mohammad Gulkhan, suggested the establishment of a separate homeland for the Muslims in the North-West extending as far as Agra.

Some writers have found in Lajpat Rai's suggestion of the division of the Punjab into two provinces an affirmation of the concept of Pakistan. He wrote in 1924:

> "Punjab should be partitioned into two provinces, the Western Punjab with a large Muslim majority, to be a Muslim governed province; and the Eastern Punjab, with a large Hindu-Sikh majority, to be a non-Muslim governed province."

The recommendation, however, did not uphold the two-nation theory. Nor did it involve the creation of a separate independent state ruled either by Muslim or by Hindu majority. It only recognised the genuine aspirations of the three communities. His object was to remove all impediments to communal unity in the Punjab that followed the marginal majority of the Muslims and the claims of the Hindu and the Sikh minorities.

Dr. Iqbal was probably the first important Muslim political leader to put forth the idea of a separate homeland for the Muslims on the basis of two-nation theory from the official platform of the League. In his Presidential Address at the All-India Muslim League, Allahabad Session in 1930, he observed that the Hindus and the Muslims had differences based on culture, caste and religion and as such the two communities could not live in harmony. According to him, the principle of European Democracy did not suit India as it was the homeland of heterogeneous people with different languages, religions, cultures and castes. He advocated due representation for the various communal groups. He pleaded:

> "If the principle that the Indian Muslim is entitled to full and free development on the lines of his own culture and tradition in his own Indian homeland, is recognised

as the basis of a permanent communal settlement, he will be ready to stake his all for the freedom of India.

He proposed the amalgamation of the Muslim dominated provinces comprising the Punjab, North West Frontier Province, Sind and Baluchistan into a single self-governing autonomous Muslim state under a central Indian authority, which would have such limited powers as given to it by the federating units. He tried to philosophise and spiritualise the Muslim politics. His aim was to create Muslim majority areas within Indian where Islamic culture could flourish. As yet, Iqbal was not advocating a separate sovereign state for the Muslims, having no political or administrative connection with India.

But some writers have maintained that Iqbal stood for the creation of a separate Muslim state. In support of their contention, they quoted the letter that Iqbal wrote to Jinnah on May 28, 1937 in which he had argued:

"... But the enforcement and development of the Shariat of Islam is impossible in this country without a free Muslim state or states. This has been my honest conviction for many years and I still believe this to be the only way... It is necessary to redistribute the country and to provide one or more Muslim states with absolute majorities. Do not you think that the time for such a demand has already arrived?"

Again on June 21, 1937, Iqbal wrote to Jinnah:

"...In this connection it is obvious that the only way to peaceful India is a distribution of the country on the lines of racial, religious and linguistic affinities."

He condemned the idea of a single India Federation and criticised the Government of India Act 1935. He said:

"A separate federation of Muslim provinces reformed on the lines I have suggested above is the only course by which we can secure a peaceful India and save Muslims from the domination of non-Muslims. Why should not the Muslims of North-West India and Bengal be considered as nations entitled to self-determination just as other nations in India and outside India are?..."

However, these letters do not conclusively prove that the Muslim homeland of Iqbal's conception was sovereign and independent as his ideas could be well accommodated in several plans that were put forth by Indian leaders and British statesmen as alternatives to Pakistan in the decade preceding the partition of India. According to Moin Shakir, he undoubtedly provided the Muslim with an ideological weapon which was used by the Muslim leadership as the basis for a separate Muslim homeland. Even Jinnah gave credit to Iqbal for initiating the move for an independent sovereign Muslim state in the Indian subcontinent.

The word 'Pakistan' was mentioned for the first time in a leaflet 'Now or Never' issued by a party of young Muslim students studying at Cambridge. Chaudhry Rahmat Ali coined this word which comprised the first letters of the provinces which were at that time claimed as the land of Indian Muslims i.e., Punjab, Afghanistan, Kashmir, Sind and Baluchistan (Tan stands for Baluchistan). Explaining the composition of Pakistan, he wrote later:

"Pakistan is both a Persian and an Urdu word. It is composed of letters taken from the names of all our homelands—'Indian' and 'Asian' That is, Punjab, Afghania (North West Frontier Province), Kashmir, Iran, Sindh (including Kachch and Kathiawar), Tukharistan, Afghanistan and Balochistan. It means the lands of the Paks...the spiritually pure and clean. It symbolizes the religious beliefs and the ethnical stocks of our people; and it stands for all the territorial constituents of our original Fatherland. It has no other origin and no other meaning; and it does not admit of any other interpretation."

He issued a circular on July 8, 1935 pleading the necessity of Pakistan:

"The very basis and content of our national life is founded on fundamentals essentially different from those on which Hinduism lives and prospers. Our age-long social system and ancient national tradition have given us a civilization with a philosophy, a culture, a language, literature and an art basically and fundamentally different from that of Hindustan. This is not all, we do not interdine, we do not intermarry. Our national customs and calendars, even our diet and dress are different."

Rahmat Ali stood for a separate sovereign and independent Muslim state. But at that time he did not include Bengal in his Pakistan. Later in his scheme of 1940, contained in the pamphlet 'The Millat of Islam and the Menace of Indianism', he spoke of a federation of three Muslim-majority states viz. Pakistan (Punjab, Afghanistan, Kashmir, Sind and Baluchistan), Bang-i-Islam (Bengal and Assam), and Usmanistan (Hyderabad and Deccan). He proposed that the three states should have an alliance in order to link the national domains to one another. To quote him:

"For this alone would set the final seal at our separation from India, inspire the Millat and impress the world as nothing else would."

However, these ideas attracted little attention when the pamphlet was published. The Muslim leaders at the Joint Select Committe in 1933, are reported to have said in reply to a question by Sir R. Craddock that they had considered the scheme chimercial and impracticable. Abdullah Yusuf Ali, another member, described it as only a student scheme.

By the year 1938-39, the Pakistan idea had taken deep roots as is evident from the proposals put forward by Sayed Abdul Latif, Khaliq uz-Zaman, Skikander Hayat Khan, Professor Syed Zaful Hasan and Mohammed Afzal Hussain Qadri, a Punjabi and Sir Abdullah Haroon for the reorganisation of the country on the basis of federation, confederation or vivisection.

All such proposals involving the division of the country and readjustment of territorial boundaries on the basis of religion culminated in the All India Muslim League Lahore Resolution of 1940. The mutual distrust between the two communities and the failure of the leaders of the League and the Congress to arrive at an understanding about the share of power in the political set up of the country led to the demand for the partition of the country.

Jinnah, one time an ardent nationalist, became the protagonist of the Pakistan Plan. In his Presidential Address at the Lahore Session of the All-India Muslim League in 1940, he formally enunciated his 'two nation theory' from the League's platform. He said,

> "Notwithstanding a thousand years of close contact, these nationalities are as divergent today as ever, and they cannot at any time be expected to transform themselves into one nation merely by means of subjecting them to a democratic constitution and holding them forcibly together by the unnatural and artificial methods of British Parliamentary statutes."

He further observed that the Hindus and the Muslims were not religious communities but constituted two nations with different customs, literatures and religious philosophies. Their views on life were different. To keep these two nations together under a common government, according to him, would lead to their discontent and ultimate destruction of the country.

In this context, he argued that the Indian problem was more of an international nature rather than of a communal character. He said.

"Mussalmans are a nation according to any definition of a nation and they must have their homelands, their territory and their state."

The two-nation theory and the vivisection of the country was adopted as the creed of the All-India Muslim League in its session held at Lahore from March 22 to March 24, 1940. Moving the resolution, Fazl-ul-Huq, the Premier of Bengal said that they were not against any kind of federation. Eighty million Muslims were numerically in weak position in all the provinces. Their interests were bound to suffer in any form of constitution as was evident during the last three years of working of the provincial autonomy. Continuing, he said,

"This session of the All-India Muslim League emphatically reiterates that the scheme of federation embodied in the Government of India act, 1935 is totally unsuited to and unworkable in the peculiar conditions of this country and is altogether unacceptable to Muslim India."

He read out the Resolution:

"Resolved that it is the considered view of this session of the All-India Muslim League that no constitutional plan would be workable in this country or acceptable to the Muslims unless it is designed on the following basic principles viz. geographically contiguous units are demarcated into regions which should be so constituted with such territorial readjustments as may be necessary that the areas in which the Muslims are numerically in a majority, as in the North Western and Eastern zones of India, should be so grouped to constitute

'Independent States' in which the constituent units shall be autonoumous and sovereign."

That adequate, effective and mandatory safeguards should be specifically provided in the constitution for minorities in these units and in the regions for the protection of their religious, cultural, economic, political, administrative and other rights and interests in consultation with them and in other parts of India where the Mussalmans are in a minority adequate, effective and mandatory safeguards shall be specifically provided in the Constitution for them and other minorities for the protection of their religious, cultural, economic, political, administrative and other rights and interests in consultation with them.

This session further authorises the working Committee to frame a scheme of constitution in accordance with these basic principles providing for the assumption finally by the respective regions of all powers such as defence, external affairs, communications, customs and such other matters as may be necessary."

Khaliq-uz-Zaman, who seconded the Resolution said that the British Government considered India as one nation so that it could exploit the various communities living in the country. He accused the Congress and held it responsible for forcing the Muslims to put forth the demand of partition of the country. He added that those Muslims, who opposed the League and joined hands with other rival Muslim or Hindu organisations, aggravated the situation further.

Various Muslim leaders spoke in support of the Lahore Resolution. Maulana Zafar Ali Khan, the Editor of *Zamindar* and once a prominent Muslim leader of the Congress in the Punjab having close contacts with Gandhi said that he had been advocating Hindu-Muslim unity for a long time and had been in the Congress for a number of years. During his stay in the Congress, he had found that the Congress was not anxious to get freedom but wanted to suppress the minorities. He added that the Congress had achieved its present position because of the support of the Muslim League. Sardar Aurangzeb Khan, Leader of the Opposition in the Frontier Assembly, expressed his thanks to the Muslims living in minority provinces for supporting the Resolution which meant freedom for six crores of Muslims. Sir Abdullah Haroon, M.L.A. Central, went to the extent that if the Hindus did not treat the Muslims fairly, the latter would treat the Hindus in the same way as Hitler treated the Sudetans.

Abdul Hamid Khan, a Muslim leader of Madras, said that the League had been cooperating with the Congress to secure independence for the country with a belief that freedom of the country would mean freedom for all individuals and not for the Congress members alone. The belief of the League has been shaken by the Congress rule of two and a half years in seven out of eleven provinces. He expressed his thanks to the Congress for awakening the Muslims and for being instrumental in the consolidation of the League. Dr. Mohammed Alam, who was earlier an eminent leader of the Congress in the Punjab and an admirer of Gandhi, blamed the Congress and said that it simply aimed at establishing *Hindu Raj* within British India.

However, all the Muslim leaders did not favour this demand of the League. Various nationalist Muslim groups were generally critical of it. Begum Abdul Aziz, President Nationalist Muslim Women's Association, characterised the scheme as mischievous, impracticable and against the Islamic principles. Azad Muslim Conference comprising the representatives of various nationalist groups such as Jamiat-ul-Ulema, All India Organisation of Muslim Divines and Scholars, Majlis-i-Ahrar-i-Islam, the Independent Party of

Bihar, the Krishak Praja Party of Bengal, the All India Momin Conference, the Anjuman e-Watan of Baluchistan and the Central Standing Committee of All India Shia Conference condemned the partition plan put forward by the League and disputed the claim of the League to be the only representative body of the Muslims.

Khan Bahadur Allah Bux, Premier of Sind, presiding over the Azad Muslim Conference said that a majority of the Ninety million Indian Muslims who were descendants of the earlier inhabitants of India were in no sense other than sons of the soil. He characterised the Pakistan scheme as harmful and fantastic and opined that it sought to create another Palestine under British mandate. He exhorted the Muslims to live like brothers in a joint family. Maulana Azad was equally forceful in rejecting this demand on the ground of historic unity of India. He described the scheme as "meaningless and absurd. Maulvi Abdul Majid, presiding over U.P. Azad Muslim Political Conferecne on July 28, 1940, emphatically repudiated the demand for Pakistan and appealed to Indian Muslims to shun the minority complex. He said,

> "No power on earth can deprive the Muslims of their religion, culture and other rights if they themselves are determined to stand on their own legs".

Sir Sikander Hayat Khan, Premier of Punjab, also did not like the idea of dividing India into two independent sovereign states having no common links. Clarifying his position, he said—

"If Pakistan means *Muslim Raj*, I will have nothing to do with it. I drafted the Lahore Resolution of the Muslim League, but now it cannot be called my resolution because the last part which related to a coordinating central authority was deleted."

Khan Abdul Qaiyum, who later became Jinnah's lieutenant, declared: "The Frontier Province will resist the partition of India with its blood. Sir Habibur Rahman. President All-Bengal Krishak Praja Party, remarked that all the Muslim majority provinces of India namely the Punjab, the Frontier, Sind, and Bengal etc., had now openly turned down the Pakistan scheme of Jinnah. He further observed that the proposal was not only absurd, chimerical and visionary, but also would remain for ever a castle in the air.

Jim Masselos, who has made a study of the growth of Indian nationalism also observed that the Muslim League Resolution was not widely accepted seriously even by Muslim intellectuals and leaders, much less by middle class and masses.

The Hindus and the Sikhs were shocked by the League's Resolution. Savarkar, President All-India Hindu Mahasabha, during the course of a speech at Madras on March 26, 1940, said that the Hindu Mahasabha would oppose the division of India into two zones.

Speaking at the Tilak anniversary, Jayakar referred to the Pakistan movement and said,

> "Its technique is very skilful and astute, and is primarily intended to create panic amongst the Hindu community in the hope that in the panicky condition, the Hindus would surrender more and more rights in order to avoid the advent of Pakistan..."

On another occasion, he said in a public meeting:

> "The remedy for India was not vivisection, but was greater fraternisation and mutual understanding."

Nehru in a speech at Allahabad said,

> "We will have nothing to do with this mad scheme. The whole problem has taken a new complexion and there is no question of settlement or negotiations."

He appreciated the stand taken by the League Leader in as much as it cleared all misunderstanding that might have prevailed in some minds and showed the League leaders in their true colours. He further commented that the attitude of the Muslim League had simplified the issue without solving it. Rajagopalachari characterised it as a medieval conception and observed that it could not be accepted as it meant vivisection of India.

Sardar Ujjal Singh, Parliamentary Secretary to Government of Punjab, said that Khalsa would resist attempt to divide India. Master Tara Singh reacted violently to the Lahore Resolution in the U.P. Sikh Conference held at Lucknow on April 15, 1940. He warned: If the Muslim League wants to establish Pakistan; they will have to pass through an ocean of Sikh blood.

The nationalist press was equally critical of the Lahore Resolution. According to the Government reports the *Amrit Bazar Patrika* considered the Resolution as an 'absurd scheme' because the states carved out according to the proposed plan shall not be free from the majority and minority problem. The Advance observed:

> "The child, Mr. Jinnah has begotten, is already dead, still he hugs it if only he can thereby spite the Congress by proclaiming to the world the disunity between the Hindus and the Muslims in India."

The *Rozana Hind,* commented: It is a proof positive of the fact that Mr. Jinnah is an enemy of Indian freedom." The *Nagpur Times* observed that the two nation theory advanced by Jinnah was the crown and culmination of the communalistic attitude so elaborately built by the one time ambassador of Hindu-Muslim unity. The *Leader* commented:

"Mr. Jinnah's remedy is worse than the disease and that it will tend to create Sudetenland all over the country"

Bharat observed:

"There is talk of conflict but no effort for unity, there are instructions as to how slavery may be perpetuated but there is no hint as to how freedom may be achieved."

Even the *Manchester Guardian* commented: "For the moment Mr. Jinnah has re-established the reign of chaos in India.

The intelligence Reports from Bombay conveyed to the Government that Jinnah's Presidental Address at Lahore Session was severely criticised by all except three pro League Muslim papers. His scheme for partitioning India was characterised as:... impracticable and disastrous to the people of India including the Muslims themselves since it strikes at the very root of national unity of India. The Reports from U.P. commented that the separatist theory propounded by Jinnah at the League Session had attracted attention, but little support even in the Urdu Press. The Lahore Resolution created a baffling situation for Gandhi since he considered the two nation theory as an untruth and the demand for a separate homeland following from it as incongruous to his religious belief and general approach to Hindu Muslim unity.

For Gandhi, religion was search after Truth. It did not require adherence to any dogma or creed, but meant self-realisation through the service of humanity or identifying oneself with the cause of humanity. In his words:

"By religion, I do not mean formal religion or customary religion but that religion which underlies all religions which brings us face to face with our Maker."

Though Gandhi was a devout Hindu yet he held the belief:

> "It is not the Hindu religion which I certainly prize above all other religions but the religion which transcends Hinduism, which changes one's very nature, which binds one indissolubly to the truth within and which ever purifies. It is the permanent element in human nature which counts no cost too great in order to find full expression and which leaves the soul utterly restless until it has found itself, known its Maker and appreciated the true correspondence between the Maker and itself."

True religion, according to Gandhi, was the universal belief in the one and only God and the belief in God was the corner stone of all religions. He said,

> "We are children of the same father whom the Hindu, the Mussalmans and the Christians know by different names. The *Allah* of Islam is the same as the God of Christians and *Ishwar* of Hindus.

Living faith in God implied the acceptance of the brotherhood of man and respect for all religions. He discovered the same fundamental unity in all the religions which is found in nature with the help of the master key of Truth and Non-violence. He observed:

> "When I unlock the chest of religion with this master key, I do not find it difficult to discover its likenness with other religions. When you look at these religions as so many leaves of a tree, they seem so different, but at the trunk they are one".

He found a great similarity in men and could not believe that there could be any quarrel on the question of religion. He said,

"Why should we blaspheme God by fighting one another because we see Him through different media—the *Quran*, the *Bible*..., the *Gita*? The same sun beats on the

Himalayas as on the plains. Should the men of plains quarrel with the men of the snows because of the different feel of the sun?"

He suggested that the problem could be solved if everyone followed the best in his own religion and had equal regards for other religions and their followers. This approach makes tolerance as an essential attribute of all religions. He observed:

> "Tolerance gives us spiritual insight which is as far from fanaticism as the North Pole from the South. True knowledge of religion breaks down the barriers between faith and faith."

It was his long cherished dream that India should have perfect toleration for all religions. He said,

> "I do not expect the India of my dreams to develop one religion that is to be wholly Hindu or wholly Christian or wholly Mussalman but I want it to be wholly tolerant with its religions working side by side with one another."

Thus Gandhi believed and professed that religion did not create the consciousness of separate nationalism necessitating the demand for a separate homeland. All religions were looked upon as different roads converging on the same point and so it did not matter which road one might take because all roads must ultimately reach the same destination, that is universal brotherhood. He said,

> "Live and let live or mutual forebearance and toleration is the law of life. That is the lesson I have learnt from the *Quran,* the *Bible,* the *Zend Avesta* and the *Gita.*"

Thus religion, for Gandhi, could not be a dividing factor, rather it was a cohesive element which could produce solidarity among communities. Gandhi wanted India to be a magnificent temple for the worship of one God by different communities and different individuals in their own way.

Exposing the false premise of the two-nation theory, he said,

> "The vast majority of Muslims are converts to Islam or are the descendants of converts. They did not become a separate nation as soon as they become converts."

Haroon also asserted:

"Ninety per cent of the Muslims are sons of the soil; they or their forefathers having embraced Islam from conviction."

He cited the example of Jinnah who hailed from a Bhatia family and Sikander who belonged to Rajpur community. He confessed that he himself hailed from a Lohana family. Questioning their claim for a separate nation, Gandhi asked:

> "Are Muslims all the world over a separate nation? Or are the Muslims of India only to be a separate nation distinct from others? Is India to be vivisected into two parts, one Muslim and the other non-Muslim? And what is to happen to the handful of Muslims living in the numerous villages where the population is predominantly Hindu and conversely to the Hindus where, as in the Frontier Province or Sind, they are a handful?"

Expressing his views on the Lahore Resolution, Gandhi said:

"...I know no non-violent method of compelling the obedience of eight crores of Muslims to the will of the rest of India, however powerful a majority the rest may represent. The Muslims must have the same right of self-determination that the rest of India has. We are at present a joint family. Any member may claim a division...But I do not believe that Muslims, when it comes to a matter of actual decision, will ever want vivisection. Their good sense will prevent them. Their self-interest will deter them. Their religion will forbid the obvious suicide which the partition would mean."

Explaining his position in reply to Liaquat Ali Khan's criticism, he said that being a man of non-violence, he could not forcibly resist the proposed partition if the Muslims really insisted upon it. But he asserted:

"I can never be a willing party to the vivisection. I would employ every non-violent means to prevent it. For it means the undoing of centuries of work done by numberless Hindus and Muslims to live together as one nation. Partition means a patent untruth. My whole soul rebels against the idea that Hinduism and Islam represent two antagonistic cultures and doctrines. To assent to such a doctrine is for me denial of God...I must rebel against the idea that millions of Indians who were Hindus the other day changed their nationality on adopting Islam as their religion.

But it was not Gandhi's way to force his opinions on others. So he said:

> "But that is my belief. I cannot thrust it down the throats of the Muslims who think that they are a different nation...Their mind can only be known by a referendum. Naturally on an issue such as this there can be no arbitration. It is purely and simply a matter of self determination. I know of no other conclusive method of ascertaining the mind of the eight crores of Muslims."

Gandhi put the blame on the British for accentuating the difference between the two communities. This is evidenced by the fact that the Muslim position as represented by Jinnah at that time was unhelpful and static to a dangerous degree and unlikely to be one which could hope to hold for very long and asked him and Fazl-ul-Huq to put a constructive scheme for presenting the Muslim case. The main thrust of their policy in India during the war was to humour the League since they needed its help in the war efforts. In pursuance of their policy, Linlithgow, the Viceroy communicated to Zetland, the Secretary of State,

> "My first reaction is, I confess, that silly as the Muslim scheme for partition is, it would be a pity to throw too much cold water on it at the moment, though clearly, one cannot accept it or associate ourselves with it."

He reaffirmed it in a subsequent telegram to the Secretary of State:

"It remains as important as ever that the fullest weight should be given to the Muslim position when their assistance and support is so essential to us both from the military point of view (as they provided at the moment sixty per cent of the army) and because of possible reaction in other Muslim countries."

The Viceroy, however, felt that the scheme was more a bargaining counter. He communicate to the Secretary of State:

"Jinnah has put forward the scheme in order to show that the Muslims have a constructive scheme of their own; to offset the extreme Congress claims to independence and the contention that the Congress is the mouthpiece of India; and that a constituent assembly on the basis of adult suffrage is the only machinery for deciding future progress."

The British bureaucracy though admitted that it was an admirable rallying cry yet it had its own doubts regarding the practicability of the scheme. This is evidenced by a telegram from the Secretary of State to Viceroy:

> "...I wonder whether Jinnah has ever contemplated how the resources of their North-West unit would find the revenue for an army that could hold the frontier against Afghanistan, let alone Russia, and how does he contemplate North-West India and Bengal working

together. Pakistan would mean the beginning of endless civil war in India..."

Undoubtedly, the Muslim League Lahore Resolution was vague in certain aspects as it did not outline the procedure for the division of the country into two separate states i.e., whether the issue would be decided by plebiscite or by vote of the provincial legislative assemblies or by any alternative method.

Secondly, the protagonists of Pakistan did not clarify the status of the independent states. The Resolution simply mentioned:

> "...should be so grouped to constitute independent states in which the constituent units shall be autonomous and sovereign."

According to any definition of state, the sovereign units cannot be a part of an independent state. Such units, however, could be autonomous. The Rosolution did not clearly indicate as to whether it envisaged one sovereign state (federal or unitary) or two sovereign states one in the east and other in the North-West.

Further, the boundaries of the contemplated independent states were not defined and the population figures of the majority and minority communities inhabiting such territories were not worked out. Even the term 'area' was left undefined and it was not possible to judge whether it meant a province, a district or a group of villages. When the lacuna was pointed out to Jinnah, he refused to submit a concrete proposal perhaps either because he was not clear regarding his demand or he did not want to limit his ambitions. When Gandhi asked Jinnah to discuss the details of his contemplated independent Muslim state, the latter refused to do so and side-tracked the issue by saying that more important was the acceptance of the principle of Pakistan.

The Lahore Resolution sought for the provision of adequate, effective and mandatory safeguards in the constitution for the minorities in these units and in the regions for the protection of their religious, cultural, economic, political, administrative and other rights and interests in consultation with them and in other parts of India where the Mussalmans were in minority. The provision of safeguards even after carving out an independent Muslim state was a positive indication of the fact that the vivisection of the country did not provide a solution to the communal problem. Moreover, when such safe-guards could ensure the protection rights of 32 per cent and 48 per cent of non-Muslim minority in the North-West zone and eastern zone respectively, why could they not do so for 24 per cent of the Muslim population in the whole of India.

The Resolution was silent in so far as the authority to uphold and implement the safeguards was concerned. The sub-clause is contradictory to the stand earlier taken by the Muslim League when the Congress made a provision for the complete autonomy in the constitution for the protection of the rights and interests of all important minorities. The Muslim League did not attach importance to those guarantees on the plea that an assurance could as easily be broken as it was given. How could they now expect that the non-Muslim minorities in the Muslim dominated states would have faith in the provisions of such safeguards? The provision and implementation of the safeguards, it seems, had been entirely left to mutual trust and goodwill, which unfortunately did not exist. Either of the independent states could refuse to provide or implement the safeguards. These safeguards could as well be altered, more so, when there was no check on the independent states.

The Lahore Resolution marked a watershed in the history of Hindu-Muslim relations. It revealed that the Muslims were no longer interested in safeguards and protection of their rights and interests within the constitutional framework of one government based on the concept of one nation. They not only wanted a separate identity but also a separate homeland of their own.

BIBLIOGRAPHY

PRIMARY SOURCES

Collected Works of Mahatma Gandhi, Government of India: Publications Division, Ministry of Information and Broadcasting, 1964.

Eliade, Mircea (ed.), *The Encyclopaedia of Religion,* New York: MacMillan Publishing Company, 1987.

Gandhi, M.K., *An Autobiography or The Story of My Experiments with Truth,* Ahmedabad: Navajivan Publishing House, 1927.

—, *Hind Swaraj or Indian Hume Rule,* Madras: G.A. Natesan and Co., 1908.

—, *In Search of the Supreme,* Ahmedabad: Navajivan Publishing House, 1961, Vol. II.

—, *India of My Dreams,* Ahmedabad: Navajivan Publishing House, 1959.

—, *My Religion,* Ahmedabad: Navajivan Publishing House, 1958.

—, *The Essence of Hinduism:* Navajivan Publishing House, 1987.

Savarkar, V.D., *Hindu Rashtra Darshan,* Bombay: Veer Savarkar Prakashan, 1984.

Tilak, B.G., *Gita Rahasya: Karmayoga Sastra,* Poona: Tilak Bros., 1980.

Tilak, B.G., *The Arctic Home in the Vedas,* Poona: Tilak Bros., 1971.

—, *Writings and Speeches,* Madras: Ganesh and Co., n.d.

SECONDARY SOURCES

(A) General Works

Appadorai, A., *Documents on Political Thought in Modern India,* Delhi: Oxford University Press, 1981, Vol. I.

Brown, D. Mackenzie, *The White Umbrella: Indian Political Thought from Manu to Gandhi,* Berkeley : University of California Press, 1953.

Caldarola, Carlo (ed.), *Religions and Societies:* Asia and the Middle East, Berlin: Mouton Publishers, 1987.

Chandra, Bipan, *Communalism in Modern India,* New Delhi: Vani Educational Books, 1984.

Derrett, J.D.M., *Religion, Law and the State in India,* London: Faber and Faber Ltd., 1968.

Desai, A.R., *Social Background of Indian Nationalism,* Bombay: Popular Prakashan, 1984.

Esteves, Sarto, *Nationalism, Secularism and Communalism,* New Delhi: South Asia Publication, 1996.

French, H.W. and Sharma, Arvind, *Religious Ferment in Modern India,* New Delhi: Heritage Publishers, 1981.

Gaede, Erwin H., *Politics and Ethics: Machiavelli to Niebuhr,* New York: University Press of America, 1983.

Hackman, G., Kegley, C.W., Nikander, V.K. (ed.), *Religion in Modern Life,* New York: The MacMillan Company, 1958.

Hopkins, E.W., *Origin and Evolution of Religion,* Delhi: Bharatiya Vidya Prakashan, n.d.

Hussain, S.A., *The National Culture of India,* Bombay, Jaico Publishing House, 1956.

Jain, Girilal, *The Hindu Phenomenon,* New Delhi: UBS Publishers, 1994.

Jauhari, Manorama, *Politics and Ethics in Ancient India,* Varanasi: Bharatiya Vidya Prakashan, 1968.

Jayaswal, K.P., *Hindu Polity,* Bangalore: Bangalore Press, 1978.

Karunakaran, K.P., *Religion and Political Awakening in India,* Delhi: Meenakshi Prakashan, 1965.

Kothari, Rajni, *Politics in India,* New Delhi: Orient Longman Ltd., 1972.

Lasswell, H.D., and Cleveland, H. (ed.), *The Ethic of Power: The Interplay of Religion, Philosophy and Politics,* New York: Harper and Brothers, 1962.

Markandan, K.C. (ed.), *Concern of Politics: The Indian Context,* Jalandhar: ABS Publications, 1989.

Minor, Robert N. (ed.), *Modern Indian Interpreters of the Bhagavad gita,* Albany: State University of New York Press, 1986.

Mukherji, D.P., *Modern Indian Culture: A Sociological Study,* Bombay: Hind Kitabs Ltd., 1948.

Nandy, Ashis, *At the Edge of Psychology: Essays in Politics and Culture,* Delhi: Oxford University Press, 1980.

Nettl, J.P., *Political Mobilization: A Sociological Analysis of Methods and Concepts,* London: Faber and Faber Ltd., 1967.

Panikkar, K.M., *Asia and the Western Dominance,* London: Allen and Unwin Ltd., 1959, Part VI.

Pankaj, N.Q., *State and Religion in Ancient India,* Allahabad: Chugh Publications, 1983.

Prasad, Bisheshwar (ed., *Ideas in History,* London: Asia Publishing House, 1968.

Radhakrishnan, S., *Indian Philosophy,* London: George Allen and Unwin Ltd., 1929, Vol. I.

Sankhdher, M.M. (ed.), *Secularism in India: Dilemmas and Challenges,* New Delhi: Deep and Deep Publications, 1992.

Sharma, D.S., *Studies in the Renaissance of Hinduism in the Nineteenth and Twentieth Centuries,* Benares: Benares Hindu University, 1944.

Seshadri, K., *Studies in Indian Polity,* New Delhi: Uppal Publishing House, 1986.

Shakir, Moin (ed.), *Religion, State and Politics in India,* Delhi: Ajanta Publications, 1989.

Sharma, Ram Avtar and Yadav, Sushma (ed.), *Political Culture in Post-Independent India,* New Delhi: Printlok, 1989.

Sharma, S.R., *The Religious Policy of the Mughal Emperors,* Calcutta: Oxford University Press, 1940.

Shourie, Arun, *Religion in Politics,* New Delhi: Roli Books International, 1987.

Smith, Bardwell L. (ed.), *Religion and the Legitimation of Power in South Asia,* Netherland: E.J. Brill, 1978.

Smith, D.E., *India As a Secular State,* New Jersey: Princeton University Press, 1963.

—(ed.), *South Asian Politics and Religion.* New Jersey: Princeton University Press, 1966.

Suda, Jyoti Prasad, *Main Currents of Social and Political Thought in Modern India,* Meerut: Jai Prakash Nath and Co., 1964, Vol. II.

Trehan, Jyoti, *Veer Savarkar: Thought and Action of Vinayak Damodar Savarkar*, New Delhi: Deep and Deep Publications, 1991.

Varma, V.P., *Modern Indian Political Thought*, Agra: Lakshmi Narain Agarwal, 1986.

— *Studies in Hindu Political Thought and its Metaphysical Foundations*, Delhi: Motilal Banarsidass, 1974.

Verma, S.L, *Towards Theory of Positive Secularism*, Jaipur: Rawat Publications, 1986.

Veer, Peter Van Der, *Religious Nationalism*, New Delhi: Oxford University Press, 1994.

(B) Tilakana

Argov, Daniel, *Moderates and Extemists in Indian National Movement*, Bombay: Asia Publishing House, 1967.

Bhat, V.G., *Lokamanyat Tilak*, Poona: Prakash Publication, 1956.

Cashman, Richard I., *The Myth of the Lokamanya: Tilak and Mass Politics in Maharashtra*, Berkeley: University of California Press, 1975.

Grover, Verinder (ed.), *Political Thinkers of Modern India*, New Delhi: Deep and Deep Publications, 1990, Vol. 4.

Inamdar, N.R. (ed.), *Political Thought and Leadership of Lokamanya Tilak*, New Delhi: Concept Publishing Company, 1983.

Jog, N.G., *Builders of Modern India: Lokamanya Bal Gangadhar Tilak*, Government of India: Publications Division, Ministry of Information and Broadcasting, 1962

Kanetkar, M.J., *Tilak and Gandhi: A Comparative Character Sketch*, Nagpur: M.J. Kanetkar, 1935.

Karmarkar, D.P., *Bal Gangadhar Tilak: A Study,* Bombay: Popular Book Depot, 1956.

Kulkarni, B.R., *Lokamanya Tilak's Metaphysics of Morals,* Lokamanya Tilak Memorial Lectures, Poona University of Poona, 1973.

Parvate, T.V., *B.G. Tilak,* Ahmedabad: Navajivan Publishing House, 1958.

Pradhan, G.P. and Bhagwat, A.K., *Lokamanya Tilak: A Biography,* Bombay: Jaico Publishing House, 1959.

Reisner, I.M. and Goldberg, N.M. (ed.), *Tilak and the Struggle for Indian Freedom,* New Delhi: People's Publishing House, 1966.

Shay, T.L., *The Legacy of the Lokamanya,* Bombay: Oxford Univesity Press, 1956.

Singh, Nihar Nandan, *Lokamanya Bal Gangadhar Tilak,* New Delhi: Congress Centenary (1985) Celeberation Committee, 1985.

Tehmankar, D.V., *Lokamanya Tilak; Father of Indian Unrest and Maker of Modern India,* London: John Murray Publishers Ltd., 1956.

Varma, V.P., *The Life and Philosophy of Lokamanya Tilak,* Agra: Lakshmi Narain Agarwal, 1978.

Vidwans, M.D. (ed.), *Letters of Lokamanya Tilak,* Poona: Kesari Prakashan, 1966.

Wolpert, Stanley A., *Tilak and Gokhale: Revolution and Reform in the Making of Modern India,* Delhi: Surjeet Publications, 1982.

(C) Gandhiana

Chatterjee, Margaret, *Gandhi's Religious Thought,* London: The MacMilan Press Ltd., 1983.

Chaudhary, Sandhya, *Gandhi and the Partition of India,* New Delhi: Sterling Publishers, 1984.

Grover, Verinder (ed.), *Gandhi and Politics in India*, New Delhi: Deep and Deep Publications, 1987.

—, *Political Thinkers of Modern India*, New Delhi: Deep and Deep Publications, 1990, Vol. 7.

Iyer, Raghavan N., *The Moral and Political Thought of Mahatma Gandhi*, New York: Oxford University Press, 1973.

Keer, Dhananjay, *Mahatma Gandhi: Political Saint and Unarmed Prophet*, Bombay: Popular Prakashan, 1973.

Khan, Mohammad Afaque, *Gandhian Approach to Communal Harmony*, Delhi; Ajanta Publications, 1986.

Khanna, Suman, *Gandhi and the Good Life*, New Delhi: Gandhi Peace Foundation, 1985.

Parekh, Bhikhu, *Colonialism, Tradition and Reform; An Analysis of Gandhian Political Discourse*, New Delhi: Sage Publications, 1989.

Power, Paul F. (ed.), *The Meanings of Gandhi*, USA: The University Press of Hawaii, 1971.

Ray, Sibnarayan (ed.), *Gandhi – India and the World*, Bombay: Nachiketa Publications Ltd., 1970.

Rolland, Romain, *Mahatma Gandhi: The Man Who became One With The Universal Being*, New York: The Century Company, 1924.

Sankhdher, M.M., *Gandhi, Gandhism and the Partition of India*, New Delhi: Deep and Deep Publications, 1982.

Sodhi, Satpal Kaur, *Mahatma Gandhi: A Psycho-Dynamic Critique*, New Delhi: Commonwealth Publishers, 1988.

Tiwari, K.N., *World Religions and Gandhi*, New Delhi: Classical Publishing Company, 1988.

Wadhwa, Madhuri, *Gandhi Between Tradition and Modernity*, New Delhi: Deep and Deep Publications, 1991.

Newspapers and Views-Papers

Economic and Political Weekly (Bombay).

Gandhi Marg (New Delhi).

Harijan (Ahmedabad).

Hindustan Times (New Delhi).

Kesari (Poona).

INDEX

A

Abhaya, 179

Action of liberated/
unliberated soul, 87

Ahmedabad Labour
Satyagraha, 144-45

Ahimsa, 180, 220, 260

Allotment of Seats in
Council, 97

All India Muslim League
Session-Lahore, 304
Resolution, 304-306

Amvika Charan Mazumdar, 92

Ambedkar's movement among
Mahars, 290

Ambition (scope for)
under British, 42

Ancient India, 18

Annie Besant, 28, 96, 99
internment orders, 102
Congress Presidentship, 102-103

Anglo Indian
Press and Tilak, 105
hatred, 213

Animistic Practices, 273

Anasaktiyoga by
Gandhi, 218

Anandmath, 212

Ansari Dr., 96

Anti-Cow Killing
Society, 104

Arab and Turks, 159

Artha, 7, 19

Arthasastra, 183

Arctic Theory of
Aryans (Tilak), 80

Arrest of Gandhi,
151-52, 156

Aryan
rituals, 246
civilization (Tilak), 80

Aryas, 20

Arya Samaj, 27
programme, 28

Arnold Mathew
on religion, 4

Aspirations
under British, 43

Asceticism, 248

Asian nationalism, 223

*Asvada - Asteya -
Aparigraha*, 174

Atman, 174

Azad Muslim Conference, 306

B

Babri Masjid, 233

Badruddin Tyabji, 44

Banerjee, W.C., 44

Bankim Chandra Chatterjee,
205, 208, 212

Bannerjee, S.N., 51, 99
Banned books - 1910, 151
Bhakti, 29
Bardoli Satyagraha, 141, 145
Beni Prasad (historian)
  claims of, 17
Benaras Congress, 49
Bengal
  invasion by Mahrattas, 116
    and Maharashtra (alliance), 116
Bhakti movement, 252, 255
Bhagavadgita (Tilak), 82
Bihar
  role of Gandhi in, 144
Bismarck,
  ideals (Germany), 121-22
Bombay Presidency, 100
Bombay Provincial
  Conference, 68
Boundaries
  definition on
    partition, 316
Brahman, 87, 245, 247, 256, 267
  movements, 259-60
Brahmin (priest), 17
Brahmacharya, 179
Brahmanic system of
  beliefs, 245-48, 282
    basis, 252
Brahmo Samaj, 25, 27, 259
British
  attitude to partition,
    192, 194
  Committee of the
    Congress (London), 46
  definition of Hindus, 202
  historians distortion of
    Indian history
  model of political
    change, 41
  political philosophy,
    37, 257-58
  Rule, 22, 42, 261
Buddhism/Jainism, 249-51

C

Caste System, 21, 247, 268,
  273, 282
Caste
  and religion, 180
Cawnpore Meeting Address, 101
Change
  source of, 295
Changes under British rule, 263
Challenges to Hinduism, 257-58
Chiplunkar
  partnership with Tilak, 74
Champaran
  oppression, 141-43, 148
    Agrarian Act, 142
Chauri Chaura Violence, 155
Christianity
  rise of in India, 257-58
    Factors for growth of, 265-66
Christians and Gandhi, 173
Christ/Krishna
  as per Raychand, 175
Chirol, Sir Valentine, 111, 115
  case, 136
Church as organized
  religion, 2
Civilizations and religions, 218
Class System, 17
Commentaries on
  Bhagavad Gita (Tilak/Gandhi)
    216-17

Communal Politics, 290

Colonial Rule, 203
responses to,
modernists/
traditionalists, 203-204

Condemnation of
partition by Muslims
section, 306-308

Congressmen
first generation,
founding fathers, 41-42

Congress
on slaught (launch), 44
control by moderates, 91
leaders, 96
continuity, 48-49
clash with British, 193
ideals, 261

Constitutional Agitation
in India, 57

Continuity
modern/traditional
societies, 262

Conquest of India
views on, 55

Council's Act, 1892, 56

Cosmic Order (Hindus),
273-74

Crisis rites, 274

Critical modernism/
traditionalism, 31

D

Dadabhai Naoroji, 39, 47, 49, 57

Dayanand Saraswati, 27

Deccan Education, Society and
Tilak, 76

Democratic Awakening, 36

Deshya (indigenous tradition), 245

Devathas, 270

Development and religion, 293

Dewey John, on religion, 5

Dharma, 6-7, 16, 180

Dharmasastra, 7, 76

Dharmarajya, 18

Dickinson on politics
in religion, 9

Disobedience
by Gandhi, 140

Discrimination, 291

Dufferin, Lord
on achievements, 43
on attitude towards
Congress, 45
Successors attitude, 45

Durga Das
on Gandhi, 146

Dutt Romesh, 51

E

Economic
conflicts-approaches
to, 143
aspirations of Muslims, 189

Educational intervention, 284
and aided schools, 284

Electoral arrangements
(Tilak's), 97

Esoteric Christian Union, 172

Ethical Formula (Tilak), 73

Evil power (spirits/ghosts/demons),
271-72

Extremists
leaders, 53
view of moderates, 54
and moderates, 61-62

F

Famine and Plague (work), 117

Fasting (Gandhi's) 178

Federation of Muslim Majority
States, 302

Force
use of (Gandhi's view), 182

G

Gandhi-Tilak-Gokhale, 134

Gandhi's
assassination, 197
attributes, 260
formula of division, 196-97
biography-*Avantika* (Gokhale),
139
Campaign, 139, 152
hold over Congress, 195
victories of Satyagraha, 134

Gandhi's views, 15, 90, 133
on Tilak, 128
on Hindu Religion, 311
on truth and
non-violence, 311
on toleration of all
religions, 312
on blame on
British, 314
on Gokhale, 215

Ganapati Festival
revival by Tilak,
107-109

Ghazni attacks, 21

Gita, 174
principles embodied
in, 85-86
interpretations of by
Tilak, 85-86

Gita Rahasya (Tilak), 83-84
and philosophical
systems, 84-85

God-(reality of), 242

Godbole, K.V.,
on Tilak's opposition
to social reforms, 120

Gokhale, Gopal Krishna, 40, 47, 57
address in Benares Congress, 49
prophecy, 52
death, 53
Gandhi's views on, 215

Gymnastic Societies (Tilak), 138

H

Hardie Kein (Labour Party), 67
visit to India, 67-68

Hinduism, 4
as per Gandhi, 163
and nationalism, 233
practices/diversity, 267

Hindu Bills, 292

Hindu leadership (nature), 213

Hindu philosophy and Indian
political thought, 15

Hindu-Muslim
gulf, 105
unity, 160, 185
relations, 186
riots-1893, 109

Hindu temples
and government
intervention, 287

Hindu Religious Endowments
Commission, 288

Hindu
deficiency/degeneration,
206-208
response to colonial
rule, 205-206

Höffding Harold
on religion, 5

Home Rule
League - Tilak, 91, 97, 101
propaganda, 100

Hostility (Anglo-Indian), 46-47

Hume, A.O., 38, 42, 44, 47
  contribution, 42, 54
  advise to Congress, 54-55

I

Ideals of Tilak, 121, 123

Identity of Indian, 286, 290

Illbert Bill Agitation, 38, 213

India
  and religion, 4, 6

Indian Renaissance, 23, 36
  repercussions, 37

Indian National Congress, 38
  movement, 38, 42
  programme, 39
  meeting, 18, 85, 42

Indian hopes (under British), 43

Indian Civil Service
  (Indians in), 51

Indian traditional
  art revivalism
  (arts/music/dance), 289

Indian Unrest by
  Valentine Chirol,
  104, 136-37, 139

Independent Labour Party, 67

Interest in Hindu/
  Muslim philosophies
    lack of, 210

Interpretations of Shastras
  Gandhi's, 217
  Tilak's, 217

Islam
  advent of, 21
  conversions to, 255
  difficulties of, 253-54

Iqbal Dr.
  on Muslim homeland
    demands, 299
      letter to Jinnah, 300-301

J

Jain doctrine
  and Gandhi (176-77)

Japan
  Socio-political revolution, 122

Jehads, 22

Jinnah, 189-90
  Congress league scheme, 93
  representative of Muslims, 95
  two nation theory, 189, 192
    303-304
  negotiations with, 191
  victory in 1945-46, 193
  direct action, 194
  steadfastness, 195

K

Kama, 7

Kaira Satyagraha, 141, 145

Karma doctrine, 17, 246, 267

Kanhera (murder by), 138

Kautilya treatises, 18, 20

Keshab Chandra Sen,
  26-27, 36

Kesari (newspaper)
  article in, 98, 123
  contents, 76, 123, 138
  launch, 75-76

Kshatriya model, 283

Kurukshetra battlefield, 171

Khilafat
  Day, 161
  issue, 158, 187
  movement, 160-61

L

Lahore Resolution,
317-18
as per Gandhi, 313
criticisms by press, 309

Lajpat Rai's suggestion of
Punjab division, 299

League of Nations, 149

Liberal Party, 50

Liberals in India, 51

Literature available on
political ideas and
thoughts, 16-17

Linlithgow (Viceroy)
letter on partition
scheme, 315

Lokmanya Tilak, 128, 214

London India Society, 49

Lord Lytton (letter by), 63

Lord Curzon
on Britishers
in employment, 63

Lucknow
Pact, 96, 187
Session (Tilak), 93-94, 99

M

Macaulay's aspirations, 37

Machiavellian diplomacy, 15-16

Mac Iver
on politics and
dharma, 9

Madan Mohan
Malaviya, 95, 99

Madras Presidency, 100

Magic/astrology/witchcraft, 278

Maitland Edward
Correspondence with
Gandhi, 172-73

Mahabharata
view of Gandhian, 171

Mahatma Gandhi by
Romain Rolland, 134

Mahratta dread in
Bengal, 116

Mahratta (newspaper)
launch, 76
contents, 76, 82

Marx, Karl, 130

Marxists
contentions, 185

Maulvi Ahmed Sait
boycott of English
goods, 160

Max Muller, 105
on importance of Vedas, 77

Mazumdar, A.C., 92, 96

Mazzim (Italy)
movement/regime
of, 122

Mehta Pherozeshah,
53, 55, 56

Militant nationalism, 53

Mobilization (forms of), 11-12

Moderates
dream of Congress, 50
era-end, 53
era in Indian politics, 40
faith in British, 62
leadership in India, 51-52
view on British empire, 51
weakening, 53
non-cooperation with
Swadeshi boycott, 57

Modern technology
effect of, 285

Moksha, 83, 87, 174, 252

Montago's declaration, 52

Muslim
empire (establishment), 22

invaders, 21
in Pakistan/Bangladesh/India, 264
attitude towards, 96
coming of, 252-53
help of by Tilak, 104
leaders, 263
league, 264
League
victory/election, 193
adulation of Gandhi, 187
rule-denegration of leaders, by Hindu 208-209
political parties, 264
origin in India, 252
participation—
absence of in National Movement, 186

N

Nanak (Sikhism), 256

Natal Advertiser, 172

Nasik Meeting
address (Tilak), 101

Nationalists (Indian), 36

National Consciousness
rise of, 52

Negotiations with
Jinnah (Gandhi), 194

New Party
opposition by Moderates, 68-69

Nehru's ideals, 261

Non-violent skirmishes
with British Government (Gandhi), 135

O

Offering to God concept, 288

Oneness of
God, 185
life, 183

P

Pakistan
idea of establishing, 297

Panikkar (views on
Indian revival, 24

Partition aftermath, 195

Partition of Bengal
views of Congress, 50

Partition negotiations by
Congress, 191-92

Philosophical systems
and *Gita Rahasya*, 84-85

Pilgrimages, 279-80

Politics
and *Dharma*, 9
and religion, 29
definition, 10-11

Political
ideology of Tilak, 106
speculations, 18
science, 9
society, 10
mobilization, 11-13, 201
texts, 183

Politicizing the masses, 111

Popular Hinduism, 269
Vs Sanskritic Hinduism, 276
Prarthana Samaj, 27, 259

Pratt, James, B.,
on religion, 5-6

Priestly dominance, 246, 249
challenge, 249

Prohibited Literature
distribution (Gandhi), 151

Proposals involving division, 303

Punjab division, 299

Punjab Issue
meeting on Gandhi, 156

Q

Qualities lacking
Hindu/Muslims, 42

Queen Victoria's Proclamation, 64

R

Radhakrishnan, S.,
on secular state, 229

Rajadharma, 18

Raja Siva Prashad, 44

Rajachandra Rajivbhai, 173-75

Raja Ram Mohan Roy, 25, 36
202, 204
outlook of, 25-26

Rama Krishna Mission, 259

Ramakrishna Paramhansa, 28

Ramrajya (Gandhi), 198

Ranade, Justice Mahadev
Govind, 27. 40, 42, 90, 120, 211

Rand-Ayerst-Jackson
murders, 138

Recruiting Campaign by
Tilak/Gandhi, 135

Reform Movements, 259

Reformism/revivalism, 23

Regional Networks, 278

Religion
and political order, 14
and politics relationship, 1-3, 31,
182, 220-22
and *dharma* in political
mobilization, 23
and politics interrelation
studies, 16, 229
based political parties, 290
origin of, 1
importance of, 228

Religious
beliefs/traditions used by
political leaders, 13
fairs and pilgrimages, 280
instinct in man (reasons), 3
issues, 188

Religio-reform movement, 36

Renaissance
characteristics, 25
movement, 23-25, 75

Revivalism, 24

Resurgent movement, 24

Rig Veda, 18

Rowlatt Committee
Act protest by Gandhi, 134
Report, 111

Rowlatt
Satyagraha (Gandhi), 148, 157-58
legislation (attitude), 154

S

Saints
movements, 279

Sanyas
doctrine of, 87

Samsara doctrine, 246-47

Sanskritic Hinduism, 268

Sanskrit Schools, 276

Sanskritization/Westernization
interaction, 284

Sarvadharma Samabhava,
180, 232

Satyagraha, 134
launch by Gandhi, 145
effectiveness, 148, 154

Satyagrahi
publishing/distribution, 151

Satyagraha Sabha, 157
Scientific ethics to
  Society, 211
Schleiermacher Friedrich
  on religion, 4-5
Secular goals, 296
Secularism/secular
  States, 230-33, 237, 277
Secularism according to Gandhi, 224
Sedition against Tilak, 117
Sedition Committe Report, 110, 116
Self government, 49, 95
Self definition of Hindus, 202
Self Control exercise by
  Gandhi, 176
Shastras
  authority (Gandhi), 165-67
Shivaji
  as per Tilak, 112-13
  tomb-Poona, 113
  Festival, 114
Sikhism, 256-57
Simla Conference, 194
Sir Syed Ahmed Khan, 44, 47
Social Reforms, 37, 258
  Tilaks opposition to, 120
Sociology, 11
Social mobilization, 11-12
South Asia
  religion in, 1
South Africa phase (Gandhi),
  165, 172, 176
Special Train to
  Lucknow for
  Home Rule
  propaganda, 93
Srimad Bhagavadgita
  Rahasya (Tilak), 218
Sudras, 181
Surendranath Banerjee, 39
Stalin's vision of Indian
  division, 298
Strachey's views, 46
Swaraj, 54, 65, 93
  for Muslims, 160
  demand for, 93, 97
Swadeshi
  boycott, 57
  movement, 61, 66
  meaning (Tilak), 65
  cooperative stores, 66
  spread of, 67

T

Tagore Debendranath
  outlook of, 26, 36
Temples
  intervention, 287
  public/private, 288
Testament of Tilak, 124
Theosophy
  introduction/awareness 28, 105
The Orion by Tilak,
  77-78, 80-81
  and Vedic literature, 77
  reviews, 78
The Arctic Home in the Vedas by Tilak,
  79-81
  theme, 79
Tilak/Gandhi-differences
  and similarities, 215-16
Tilak's
  as Vedantist, 72
  and Lokmanya myth, 70
  articles by, 58-59
  entry into Congress, 53
  entry into politics, 82
  election to Bombay
    Council, 56
  Causes of success, 119
  childhood, 73-74, 83

campaign, 65-66
death, 118, 127
slogan, 54
status of in history, 71-72
tours, 100
views on Vedas, 77
views on contitutional methods, 58-59
views on extremist role, 60-61

Trevelyan's testimony, 40-41

Traditionalists response to colonial rule, 204-205

Truth and non-violence, 178

Truth as advocated by Gandhi, 177-78

Turkish empire (division of), 160

Two nation theory and Gandhi, 189-90, 313

U

Uniform Code of Law, 292

Unity
in diversity, 190
lack of, 206

Universal Human Rights Declaration Statement, 238

Untouchables movements, 290
assistance to by government, 291

Upanishads, 17

Urdu-Hindi
Clash, issue, 44

V

Vaishya, 283

Value Systems
in religion, 1

Varnas, 268

Vedic and post-Vedic literature, 17

Vedas, 174, 245
authority of, 27
language, 169

Vedang Jyotish by Tilak, 81

Vedanta philosophy, 72

Vivekananda, 29, 105
formula of, 181
views on
Indian society, 206

Village Scene
and religious beliefs, 266
practice of Hinduism in, 267

Vows made by Gandhi, 179

W

Weber Max
analysis of Indian world view, 294
on religion, 4, 10, 293-94

Western governance, 15

Western ideas
impact of, 23, 39

Westernization, 284

World War I
and Home Rule, 99

World War II
and partition, 192

Writings (religious), 16-17

Y

Young India/Navjivan
acquisition of, 154

Z

Zamindari System, 142

Zendavesta, 79, 224, 312

Zetland (Secretary of State)
on doubts of partition scheme, 315